Engaging the *Ineffable*

Toward Mindfulness and Meaning

Advance Praise for *Engaging the Ineffable*

"What a wonderful confluence of events: 'ineffable' is one of my favorite words, and Dave Krueger is one of my favorite writers."
—John David Mann, co-author of the bestselling classic *The Go-Giver*

"Dr. Krueger offers a whole host of well-written, engaging and creative ways to explore the powerful internal self and important issue of resistance to change."
—Regina Pally, M.D., Psychiatrist, Psychoanalyst, Founder and Co-Director of the Center for Reflective Communities, author of *The Reflective Parent*

"I was fortunate enough to work with Dave Krueger when my husband and I lost our life savings. His insight, wisdom, and utterly positive focus on what I could do now (rather than what I lost) helped me emerge from an initial period of fear and helplessness to one of remarkable resilience and strength. Now, in *Engaging the Ineffable,* he offers that same considerable intelligence into a day-to-day compendium of wisdom that is available to us all."
—Geneen Roth, author of the #1 *New York Times* bestseller *Women Food and God* and *This Messy Magnificent Life*

"Lively essays amounting to a livable philosophy."
—Roy A. Blount Jr., Panelist on NPR's *Wait, Wait . . . Don't Tell Me;* Ex-President of the Authors Guild; author of 24 books

Engaging the Ineffable

Toward Mindfulness and Meaning

David Krueger, M.D.

PARAGON HOUSE

First Edition 2019

Published in the United States by
Paragon House
St. Paul, MN
www.ParagonHouse.com

Cover image: https://pxhere.com/en/photo/1258740

Library of Congress Cataloging-in-Publication Data

Names: Krueger, David W., author.
Title: Engaging the ineffable : toward mindfulness and meaning / David
   Krueger, M.D.
Description: First edition. | St. Paul, MN : Paragon House, [2019]
Identifiers: LCCN 2018052356 | ISBN 9781557789372 (pbk. : alk. paper)
Subjects: LCSH: Meaning (Psychology) | Choice (Psychology) | Conduct of life.
Classification: LCC BF778 .K78 2019 | DDC 153.8/3--dc23 LC record available
at https://lccn.loc.gov/2018052356

The paper used in this publication meets the minimum requirements of American National Standard for Information Sciences—Permanence of Paper for Printed Library Materials, ANSIZ39.48-1984.

Manufactured in the United States of America
10 9 8 7 6 5 4 3 2 1

Dedication

To alchemists who believe in transformative possibility:
who consider chance to be unworthy of determining their fate,
who mindfully self-reflect in order to examine,
who talk or write in order to see what they have to say,
who engage in dialogue to learn rather than convince,
who believe the best is yet to be written or invented,
who approach each new task with a beginner's mind,
who balance continuity with creativity.

Contents

Introduction

AUGUSTINE OF HIPPO, 5th Century theologian, stated that he knew well what time is—until someone asked. Then he was at a loss for words. So it is with each of the concepts in this book. Descriptions originating in reason and logic seem dry and inadequate; depiction from experiences and emotion seem susceptible and impressionable. Yet each of these ideas enters into our daily experience in distinct ways.

Much like the unspoken attribution of meaning for a given culture, the conventions and assumptions we impart to the concepts in this book—consciously and unconsciously—constitute a silent language. And, like time, differing perceptions of meaning can lead to misunderstandings between people.

Each notion may provide a window for further understanding; yet as you draw closer to the glass, each becomes a mirror reflecting an aspect of yourself. And the secret language speaks self-statements.

The issues of this book are ones I visited daily, hourly, working intensely with patients in psychoanalysis and psychotherapy, and more recently with clients in Executive Mentor Coaching.

Like Augustine of Hippo, we may assume we know how to define and engage any of the issues I'm addressing here. Each passes through our own filter of life experiences and distinctly developed mind software to travel through the highways and villages of our unique brains.

The question of understanding highlights the further distinction of *whose* understanding it is. We record the world, not as it is, but as we experience it, transforming it through the prism of our stories, collected and created.

Although our life stories may seem predesigned by destiny or ghost-written from the past, each of us writes our personal story moment by moment and choice by choice. Core organizing assumptions, many unconscious, create themes of hope, self, mastery, and nostalgia. We generate personal storylines using default models of time, memory, feelings, and empathy. Desire, beliefs, secrets, and serendipities camouflage the invisible decisions of each moment.

In practicing and teaching psychiatry and psychoanalysis for twenty-five years, then for the last decade Mentor Coaching executives and professionals, as well as training more than 2,000 professional coaches, I have re-examined these ideas in the light of helping others co-creating successful new stories of life, money, career, relationships, and wellness.

Psychoanalytic literature tends to focus on the pathological aspects of the subjects of these chapters—on scary fantasies, cold mothers, dead people, and bad dreams—at the expense of happiness, creativity, hope, humor, inspiration, joy, and other positive transformations. Resolving conflict does not generate success; mitigating deprivation does not introduce joy. Solving problems does not create possibilities; coming to the end of an old story does not create a new one.

My intent is to catalyze reflections for you, the reader, to examine aspects of your own life story—the shadow story of beliefs and default patterns ghostwriting the surface story. Whatever we think, feel, and experience is what we create each moment. Or what we agree to.

Most of these notions are ineffable, in part, because there is no single place in the brain you can point to and say, "This is the location of memory, hope, nostalgia, mastery, desire, or serendipity." Nor are these functions, including mirroring, consciousness, and empathy, even located in a single hemisphere.

There are very specific brain locations for certain intangibles such as the sense of self, pleasure, and pain, as well as for such actions as spending, paying bills, or registering disgust. The explorations of these centers, their functions and links, have proven to be immensely useful in understanding both how we *think* we make decisions and how we *really* decide.

Desire

The Elusive Life Storyline

The best part of the best drug in the world ain't the high. It's the moment just before you take it. The dice are dancing on the table. Between now and the time they stop, that's the greatest high in the world.
—Al Pacino, *Two For The Money*

Excess Desire

SEVERAL YEARS AGO I was talking with a woman who had recently acquired a great deal of wealth. We were discussing restaurants, and she mentioned having dined the previous evening at the most fashionable and esteemed one in town, known for both "the poetry of French food" and its sumptuous dessert cart with two dozen world-class choices. She said she had ordered one of everything on the cart.

Wow!, I said. *How was that experience?*

She said simply, *I was disappointed. I was surprised at how quickly I lost my desire.*

I told her about someone else who had made that discovery some time ago. The novelist Thomas Mann described how his father taught him about desire when he was a young boy. His father assured him that once in his life, he could eat as many cream puffs as he wanted. He finally led Thomas to a pastry shop to let his dream come true. Mann recognized how quickly, as he put it, *I reached the limit of desire, which I had believed to be infinite.*

If we want too much of something, we're afraid of losing it and possibly never having it again. So we believe we have to consume or hoard in order to ensure that it will not go away or run out. We become greedy when what we get is what we think we want. When what we get fails to satisfy, we realize it is not really the answer. If one dessert doesn't do the trick, maybe the entire cart will. If $1 million isn't enough, then maybe $10 million will be. We become greedy out of the recognition that neither the dessert nor the dollar will truly satiate—at least not well enough for long enough.

Our desires may be unrealistic for a reason. We continue to desire by having goals just out of reach, or by never quite reaching them. If someone feels that losing a final ten pounds will bring happiness, then those ten pounds must never be fully lost, as the illusion of this supposed container of happiness will have to be confronted as unrealistic. Or at least that happiness doesn't reside in that loss of ten pounds.

The Contagion of Desire

Caitlin, my granddaughter who was four years old at the time, was playing with a stuffed bear in her pre-kindergarten class. Sarah, her little buddy, suddenly decided that she wanted to play with the bear as well. There were many other toys around, but Sarah was no longer satisfied until she had Caitlin's stuffed bear.

Caitlin's mother, my daughter Lauren, a clinical psychologist, was rendered as helpless as Caitlin's absent granddad in orchestrating her mastery to maintain possession of the coveted bear, or to work out a compromise for all-or-nothing four-year-old possession-oriented minds.

Caitlin will later learn how her own desires will be influenced by neuromarketing techniques based on celebrity induction, social valuation, and popular trending stuffed bears. But for now she has only impromptu strategies to wrest her bear from Sarah's immediate, induced desire.

Both girls were in the grip of the scarcity principle: When something becomes rare or scarce, it becomes more valuable, enhancing desire. When increasing scarcity interferes with our access to something, we react by wanting to possess it even more. Later in their lives, Caitlin and

Sarah will contend with marketing messages that are adult versions of the bear story: *Limited number! Only two left! One day remaining! We're not making any more!*

Mimetic desire—one person's desire mimicking that of another—is not limited to children but plays a significant role in product adoption of best-selling goods. Our neuronal system contributes to this contagion of desire. The more valued the person, the more attention we pay to that mirroring process.

The social valuation system also helps us ascribe valence to a given item. Mirror neurons and value attribution come together as both these functions become activated in the brain, based on another person's action with an object.

Desires are especially conscious when unrequited. Resulting exaggerations include a fear of not being listened to, an assumption that you are easily forgotten, the belief that you can't find a place in another's mind, the notion that you have to do something extreme to hold someone's attention, exaggerated behavior in order to register on someone's radar screen, or extreme accomplishment in order to capture someone's imagination.

Desire Is Better than Having

We know from neuroscience research, as well as from our own cumulative experiences, that the anticipation of buying creates temporary excitement, often more than the actual purchase. The *expectation* of acquisition enhances dopamine release by the pleasure center of the brain, but the associated positive emotions are short-lived, lasting only until the actual purchase. This accounts for the paradoxical reaction of less than expected pleasure at the purchase of a long-anticipated item, even of buyer's remorse. Ownership is less satisfying than desire, proving that retail therapy—shopping our way out of a bad mood—doesn't work very well or for very long.

Desire is inexplicably linked with imagined satisfaction. The fantasy and form of satisfaction, then, provide a respite from the demands of desire. Imagining satisfaction is, paradoxically, a way to *not think* about desire, to *not want*. It's as though wanting itself is uncomfortable, or even unbearable.

Fantasy can become an end in itself. Some fantasies are so elaborately constructed that they could never be fulfilled. And some are designed to *not* be fulfilled. We use fantasies as trial actions, to posit potential scenarios to consider options.

Greed

> *You're a wealthy man. One must learn to be rich. To be poor, anyone can manage.*
> —Gustavo Fring, *Breaking Bad*

Greed (actually defined as the rapacious desire for more) creates an insatiable hunger for the acquisition of things, pleasures, and experiences. Greed ensures that we do not have to fear making the wrong choice, or even make choices at all. The fantasy of incredible wealth imagines unlimited choices. If you have everything, then you don't need to choose. If you order everything on the dessert cart, no choice has to be made. So you can never be wrong, or feel that you've made an unwise choice. If my newly rich friend had chosen only one dessert, it meant not only that she would have had to mourn the unknown pleasures, but she might have also been wrong in her choice. Yet, paradoxically, she became wrong in another way—actually, more than two dozen other ways.

Greed, a state of mind of wanting to have everything, unlimited, at any time, defends against the fear of dissatisfaction, all the while attempting to self-cure feelings of helplessness. Identifiable emblems of this process of insatiable desire include food, sex, and money.

Although we usually want more than we have, instead of acknowledging that our desires may be unrealistic, we're more inclined to think that the world (or others) have let us down. Or we keep hoping. And the impossible is addictive.

Where do wishes and fantasies stop? They both omit the cost and exclude the consequences. Excess is contagious. Human beings are the only animals who have excessive appetites for things, the only animals that eat more than they need.

We can become greedy because what we are getting is not quite what we *want*, not satisfying in some way. So we believe that more would be better. If one dessert doesn't do the trick, two might, though in fact dessert isn't really the answer, or at least three would have been enough.

Greed may be a form of despair, to continue searching when what we really *need* seems inaccessible. Much like worry, greed simply holds onto things, as a form of storage.

In our fantasies, we can have things exactly as we want. Anna Freud once observed, *In our dreams, we can have our eggs cooked exactly like we want them, but we can't eat them.* Our fantasies can become a refuge, a retreat, but one that defies occupation. Probably that's the point. Our fantasies formulate our desires, sometimes in disguised form, and make them reassuringly impossible to realize. In our fantasies we can have things exactly as we want, yet our imagination is often limited to our own system.

While we always want more than we could have, we likely blame others for letting us down. Rarely do we notice that our desires are unrealistic. We are greedy only when there is some frustration we are unaware of. The more we have to control ourselves, the more difficulty we have identifying exactly what we need. The more frightened we are of frustration, the more we focus on excessive behavior. Yet each of us grows into excess in our own ways. More food, more money, more alcohol, more sex.

Why in the world would we create greed? To ensure frustration? Perhaps when we want more, we never give up. The person who ignites our envy is often the person who appears to be having more pleasure than we are, or at least has more pleasurable objects than we have.

In our fantasy life, excess and its imagined satisfaction are immensely appealing.

As we know from some psychological disorders, however, behaviors of excess show a distorted relationship with one's self. Excess consumption of food, alcohol, or other substances reveals an underlying antithesis of excess: the perception that something is lacking or missing. Excessive appetite is a symptom, often leading to violations of boundaries.

Children and adolescents who engage in excessive behavior are often unconsciously trying to find a strong, containing parent. One of the most frightening things for a child is when the parent fails to contain the child's excess. In this way, greed may be a need for containment, an unconscious desire for authority, internal or external.

We become greedy when we don't quite get what we want, when we fail to be satisfied for any reason. If something or someone fails to satisfy us, the natural conclusion is that we simply need more of it—that more would provide a better approximation of satisfaction. When we compare our inside to someone else's outside, we're inevitably dissatisfied. Yet we may fail to recognize that it's never an apples-to-apples comparison, as we only see the surface of results in another, compared to our own experience of the process of work and struggle to get results.

If we desire or love something, we certainly don't want less of it, and most certainly not too little of it. Both excesses as well as deprivations of appetite serve as self-cures for helplessness. To attempt this control is to make the locus of perceived power internal, in order to not want, as in the anorexic, or to have some desired excess, as in the bulimic.

Excess, then, is usually linked to some kind of deprivation. When we wait too long to eat, we are excessively hungry. We deplore and try to contain excessive behavior in others because it reminds us both of our own desire and that we're deprived of full satisfaction ourselves. Obvious extremes of behavior simply hold a mirror to our unlived desire.

As adults, we always have a need to balance excessive appetite and excessive refusal of appetite. Otherwise, we would spend too much now and not save for the future. And current desire alone would dictate current behavior.

How can we be fully aware of satisfaction unless we are truly frustrated? Because, after all, we conceal from ourselves what we are most desirous of, by an excess of appetite.

In Kafka's *A Hunger Artist*, the protagonist performance-fasts for a living. When asked why he devoted himself to starving in public, he indicated that he could not help doing it . . . *because I couldn't find the food*

I liked. If had found it, believe me, I should have made no fuss and stuffed myself like you and everyone else.

Obstacles

The way to solve the problem you see in life
is to live in a way that makes the problem disappear.
—Ludwig Wittgenstein, *Culture and Value*

Some time ago I saw a cartoon of a dog straining at its leash, barking ferociously at a cat, as if to say, *Just lemme at 'em.* The cat wasn't too shabby—actually looked mean—and was at least as big as the dog. All of a sudden in the middle of a ferocious bark, the leash snapped so the dog was free to go after the cat. He looked astonished. Scared to death. He quickly grabbed the leash, ran back, and tied a triple knot. Then, he could again safely strain at the leash and bark his fiery *Just lemme at 'em.*

Every story of an obstacle has a shadow story of desire.

In psychoanalysis as well as in Mentor Coaching, the professional listens for the muted voice of the client in order to understand why an obstacle is needed, and what desire it hosts.

The obstacle packs up and conceals the desire. What we seek is camouflaged in what we fear. Show me an obstacle, and I'll show you a desire. We construct an obstacle, unconsciously, to then have its icon become a conscious focus.

The surface story and the shadow story are two related entities, as they often go in opposite directions with equal force. What keeps the desire and the obstacle apart also links them. In fact, what keeps them apart may be the only connection between them.

For example, dual stories often involve a relationship with money. The surface story may be, *I want to generate significant income and create wealth.* Yet the shadow story can be, *I don't believe that I really have what it takes to do that.* The interface between the two simultaneously links and separates inner and outer reality. Money becomes the transitional object of desire and obstacle combined, the hope and impediment to whatever one's brain is wired to construct as a meaning for money (security, freedom, pleasure, etc.).

There's a secret hiding in the open here. An obstacle is the unconscious mnemonic of desire—it reminds us of what we want, but makes it safe to want if we're afraid. Someone constructs an obstacle only when the desire cannot exist alone. The obstacle offers toleration of the desire, and engages it to create continuity.

When viewing a film, if you don't want to see a scene, you cover your face with your hands as if to say, *No, I don't want to look.* But then the desire creeps in and you peek through your fingers at what you're drawn to see. The obstacle makes looking acceptable.

The desire does not reveal the obstacle, the obstacle reveals the desire. So the kind of obstacles that someone constructs tells immediately the vocabulary of impediments. So, pay attention to the obstacles that you construct.

Sometimes we need an obstacle to free a desire. When the obstacle is revealed, the forbidden desire also emerges.

So rather than strategizing to overcome, avoid, or defeat an obstacle, simply consider not creating it. It's there when you create it; consider using your energy to generate something else instead, such as what you really want. When you find yourself focusing on an obstacle (*I can't find time to exercise* or *I can't put away any savings*), reflect on the underlying desire.

When you're ready to consider that you create the obstacle, you're also ready to consider the possibility of *not* creating it.

Imagine what it would be like to not create your obstacles.

Edwin Barnes had a desire to work *with* Thomas A. Edison, not *for* him. When he initially had this desire, he was in no position to act on it. Two obstacles stood in his way. He didn't know Mr. Edison, and he didn't have enough money to pay his railroad fare to Orange, New Jersey.

When Barnes finally presented himself to Mr. Edison at his laboratory, he announced that he had come to go into business with the inventor.

Years later when Edison recalled their first meeting, Edison said, *He stood there before me, looking like an ordinary tramp, but there was something in the expression of his face which conveyed the impression that he was determined to get what he had come after. I had learned, from years of experience with men, that when a man really desires a thing so deeply that he is willing to stake his entire future on a single turn of the wheel in order to get it, he is sure to win. I gave him the opportunity he asked for, because I saw that he had made up his mind to stand by until he succeeded. Subsequent events proved that no mistake was made.*

Barnes had a clear statement of desire, and a clear plan of action. He spoke with clarity and confidence, which was evident to Edison despite his appearance and lack of history of success.

When the opportunity came to work with Edison, it appeared in a different form and from a different direction than Barnes had expected. Like some opportunities, it can slip in the back door, disguised in form. He partnered with Edison to sell and install the original dictating machine that brought Barnes $3 million in 1927 money.

He had no money to begin with, little education, and no influence, but he had initiative, faith, and belief in himself as intangible forces. And as Picasso said, *Action is the foundational key to all success.*

Perfection

After a breakup, sometimes we do something that's called a euphoric recall—to remember all the best parts of something. But you never play the tape through to the end. The remedy: watch the whole movie rather than just the good parts. And know that when one door closes, another opens.
—Dr. Dani Santino, *Unnecessary Roughness*

The desire for perfection stems from the desire for total self-sufficiency.

Psychoanalysts from Freud to Adam Phillips have examined failed perfection just as others have explored the failed God—Goethe's Mephistopheles and Milton's Satan. What we call psychological pathologies are attempted remedies for failed perfection—attempts to create effectiveness given the context in which one exists and must adapt.

Pathologies are self-cures for our frustrations and faults, a valiant attempt at resourcefulness and adaptation.

The anorexic feels that the only effectiveness she has in her entire world, certainly in her controlling family where she is viewed as an extension of her parents, is to determine what will (or won't) enter her body. She alone determines saying *no* to her desire for food. At the same time, her *no* is a declaration that *I am not an extension of you and your body or desire; this is where you end and I begin—my body is mine and mine alone.*

Perfectionists know where they want to go, even if they devote themselves to not getting there. They organize their behavior to see clearly to the end of the desire, yet to avoid fully arriving. It is better to travel hopefully than to arrive, for upon arrival the illusion of perfection is unmasked.

Symptoms have the universal dynamic and appeal of turning the passive into the active. They make someone feel as if the problem has been taken into his or her own hands.

Frustration

> *No child ever recovers from not having cured his parents.*
> —Adam Phillips, *Missing Out*

We often assume that we know more about experiences we have not had than about those that we have had and we speak with both frustration and passion about we have missed out on. A couple can speak with that same passion and frustration about how their lives would be different if only their partners were to respond in a particular way.

How can you know about an experience you haven't had? Those who speak with immense conviction about what is missing in their lives seem to have great authority as to what their lives would be like were they to have those experiences. Some of the most authoritative and informed accounts of how difficult and inconvenient children are come from those who have no children.

This authority of inexperience, along with its attendant frustration, can at times play a major role in our lives.

We often spend more time inside the experiences we *don't* have than the ones we *do* have. Most of us remember how as children, it seemed to us that the quintessential experience we had not yet had—of being adult—would be the answer to so many of the problems we perceived, so much of what we looked forward to. Conviction about the myriad as yet unrealized experiences about what the future held gave both promise and frustration.

We look at future possibility as a guiding light, an anchoring motivation to proceed hopefully. This kind of knowing the as-yet unknown seems to provide essential information. Wanting can assume more valence than proof. This, of course, ensures deprivation to override the present moment by inhabiting the elusive.

If frustration describes the experience of not having what we want, a curious natural transformation occurs with the movement into adulthood. As adults, we often work hard to keep the future like the past. That is, to avoid change. So while the child desires to transcend childhood, the adult desires to transcend change. Even in adulthood, we curiously live as though we know more about the experiences we have not had than the ones we do have.

We guard our inherent sense of identity by doing what Graham Greene describes as wanting *to find in books merely a confirmation of what is already in our minds*, to have things that we know and believe reflected back to us in what we read. This is, of course, a significant motivation for people to read books: to either find or validate themselves, or to escape some aspect of themselves. If that unwanted aspect can be deposited in a character or, better yet, in another person in real life, all responsibility forecloses.

At times we get out of something before we know exactly what we are avoiding. And usually the getting-out precedes the experience. Whenever we run away from something, we run toward something else. We often spend considerable time examining what we run toward, and very little on what we run away from. We engage in greed and excessive behavior to counter frustration. But it never works well enough for long enough, as we only temporarily forget that we were frustrated.

Fantasies originate from a compilation of prior experience, both wished for and real. The certainty of recognition is because, in a sense, we have known it through expectation rather than experience. Falling in love at first sight may be an example, feeling as though we have known someone forever, yet have never met that person before.

A related enigma occurs when a frustration comes to our awareness because we found the person or passion that had been missing. The presence of someone is required to make an absence felt. A longing may have preceded the relationship, but we only feel the full source of frustration and longing in the absence after having met. Falling in love crystallizes the awareness of what was unconsciously missing. We are always trying, in some sense, to find what is absent.

We understand satisfaction, at least in part, by understanding frustration. And because we are prone to try to obscure our frustrations, we may in that same effort deny our full satisfaction.

Frustration is an essential precondition for our satisfaction. In fact, satisfaction gives the free-floating, sometimes unconscious frustration a place to light, a way to make it make sense, as if we were aware all along. We are more likely to see an outcome as inevitable once it has occurred than we were before it took place.

A Case of Frustration

The mind is author of internal assumptions, producer of the individual life drama, and casting director of significant others.
—David Krueger, *Integrating Body Self and Psychological Self*

A woman I'll call Vivien consulted me to discuss Mentor Coaching after having several therapies and one psychoanalysis, all of which, by her account, ended unsatisfactorily. Her call was prompted by a crisis in a new romance that began within days of her move to a major eastern U.S. city. Vivien wanted to see if coaching could provide what therapy and analysis had not—a strategic plan for a serious, dedicated relationship.

She initially wanted me to validate how unfairly she was being treated, and to verify that none of the difficulties were her fault. She described how she had moved from one attachment to another for almost two decades of her adult life, searching for someone who would love and understand her, to recognize and appreciate her worth. She had been especially disappointed and frustrated in her relationships with men, having had forty-five (specifically counted) relationships, all of which had similar endings. The initial appeal of each new man was that he, like no one previously, could understand her and finally appreciate her uniqueness. Implied in her expectation was that he would join her in a deprecation of the previous injurious man, thereby validating her victimhood. She requested this of me, seemed somewhat frustrated that I did not corroborate her mistreatment by blaming the men, and was only temporarily assuaged that I resonated with her continued frustration.

Vivien described herself as fun, eclectic, romantic, full of excitement, having many adventures. Her career as a film actress had continued to thrive despite her frustrating private life. She completely enjoyed her significant career successes, in stark contrast to her failed relationships and her yearning for a significant, serious relationship. She described the men as sharing certain qualities: jet set, successful, romantic playboys who approached her and quickly became inordinately interested in her. The relationship would begin with a swirl of romantic dinners, lavish trips, and an idealized hope of continued exhilaration into the future. After a few weeks into each totally absorbing romance, though, Vivien began to recognize disappointing flaws in the man. Their romance would often end as quickly and dramatically as it began. With devastating disappointment, she renewed the search for the perfect man who would love and understand her.

Although quite bright and much attuned to others, she had not recognized the design in each relationship of being the same man with forty-five different faces, and each ending within a few months. Each man was initially idealized with the hope that he would be The One, the perfect man who would love her totally and finally appreciate her worth and goodness. Insight into and understanding of this strikingly repetitive pattern was supplanted by Vivien's search for affirmation and consolation of their bad treatment of her.

Her hope necessarily ignored history while unconsciously being informed by it. She had not seen the congruence with her past in the repetitive patterns of inappropriate men (appropriate and perfectly cast, however, for the scenario she repeatedly produced) and the dire consequences obvious to her friends and family. She romantically gazed through rose-colored fantasies of hope, unable to see the self-deceptive falsehoods. She fell in love with the same *someday fantasies*, each with a different face and name. Her fears of abandonment and loss of love created a defensive repetition ensuring their occurrence. Remembering in this way did not allow her to forget, yet it was a repetition that kept hope alive, and hope brought time.

Vivien acknowledged that as she got to know the real person, her illusion of hope faded. Her euphoria disappeared within weeks, resulting in abbreviated relationships. As her infatuated state changed and her fantasies vaporized, she acknowledged, *The man I had imagined disappears.* Each man became indifferent, withdrew, and seemed to become self-centered and critical of her.

Instead of examining her old story—which she knew well because of her many therapies—we focused on how to construct a different present story.

In her current relationship, begun a week after starting our work, she described creating the same attachment pattern as in the past—she did things to totally please the man, so he would get to know her and love her. I observed that as she attunes herself so much to the man, she loses herself. She responded by saying that no one has really known her, that each relationship has felt insecure and superficial.

Vivien began to recognize her previously disregarded needs and ideals. We focused on recognition, ownership, and assessment of her own story.

A paradox for her was that as she successfully lived up to her ideal of being loving, giving, and sacrificing to a man, the result was disappointment and lack of growth. As she configured herself into what she perceived the man wanted, becoming an extension of his interest and desire, the beautiful, accomplished, and independent woman he was attracted to disappeared. Also paradoxically, to grow and transform herself, she would have to "fail" at living up to this ideal. This recognition of a long-outdated model meant that she would have to establish a new ideal of enhancement and growth, a fundamental change not only of her beliefs and behaviors, but of her core identity.

She yearned to know what a loving, mutual, and reciprocal relationship over the seasons and years would really feel like. A part of her remained detached because ancient hurts and shattering disappointments were currently scripting unconscious vulnerabilities and conscious sensitivities. Vivien was undaunted by impossibility, yet no pattern had previously registered on her radar screen other than a perpetual attempt to find external admiration and response.

Though quite worldly, informed, and experienced, she seemed curiously naïve, particularly of herself. She had been trapped in a genre, unable to transcend it and explore the nuances and experiences of other stories. Romantic tragedy had been the organizing theme of her life, and every experience would ultimately come to rest in the empty space of unrequited love.

Vivien had been living her life in love with hopeless quests, feeling far from being an expert about it. She was expert, however, on men, on the variations of the common theme of seduction. She was practiced at pretending, yet never got beyond the point of initial captivation. Rather than recognize that she was repeatedly writing the same storyline, she felt doomed by the fate of the psyche of men who inevitably would be enamored, yet inevitably disappoint her. She had not yet recognized that she was suffering from her own core assumption of supposed defeat, fearing that if someone were really to know all of her, he would abandon her. So as not to be devastated again, she always had to leave first. Vivien recognized not only that her style of abandoning herself ensured failure, but also that her radar and preselection criteria were specifically cued to attract men who did not want a serious committed relationship.

She focused, finally, on her own story, recognizing, owning, and accessing each of her storylines. She came to know more of her needs and ideals and to stay grounded in the present. Listening to her long-muted internal voice, she made the choice of her next best action.

Nuisance

You know how bad it is when you don't know
you're embarrassed until the next day.
—Kay McConney

For there to be change, something needs to feel like a nuisance. The change does not necessarily need to be considered progress, but it has to begin with a perturbation of the natural order of things.

A nuisance is a perturbation that you can't ignore; if you could ignore it, it obviously would not be a nuisance. The nuisance, by definition, will not leave you alone until at least you come up with some new way of ignoring it that works. This is also change.

A nuisance can be an inspiration or simply a re-description, as if one is frustrated into thinking of things in a different way or into experimenting with new possibilities. Experimentation, or at least new questions, will be catalyzed by the nuisance experience.

In *Down And Out In Paris And London*, George Orwell, in 1933, addressed the question about why beggars are nuisances, and put his reflection in the context of money:

> I believe it is for the simple reason that they fail to earn a decent living. In practice, nobody cares whether work is useful or useless, productive or parasitic; the sole thing demanded is that it shall be profitable. In all the modern talk about energy, efficiency, social service, and the rest of it, what meaning is there except "get money, get it legally, and get a lot of it?" Money has become the grand test of virtue. By this test, beggars fail, and for this they are despised . . . . a beggar looked at realistically, is simply a business

man, getting his living like any other business man, in the way that comes to hand.

Obviously, beggars make a nuisance of themselves so people will give them money to cease being a nuisance. Being a nuisance is an invitation to others to do something to stop you from being a nuisance. The act of giving stimulates the altruistic center of the brain, and for some it additionally says, *I'm in a different position from you, and this gift hereby acknowledges that.*

Since money is, in Orwell's term, the grand test of virtue, we naturally question those who don't have it, just as we may be equally suspicious, or envious, or both, of those who have a lot of it.

Orwell implies that we punish criminals and reward artists for being nuisances.

Being a nuisance is at times a very adaptive maneuver. When children return home after an absence, they need to test their home environment to rediscover its reliability. They need to misbehave, lose their temper, and push limits just to be sure that the limits are there. Once they reestablish security and reassure themselves of belonging, they settle in and no longer need to be a nuisance.

In this way, being a nuisance is a developmental necessity. After a full blast of anger, the child, parent, and bond all remain intact, and the trusted home is rediscovered.

Nuisance survived by resilience becomes security, and thereby a sign of hope. Someone who can dare to be a nuisance wants more life, a better life, an expanded existence. The person who is no trouble, just like the child who can't dare to be difficult, has channeled hope into conformity.

Being a nuisance is a considerable act of faith. The *nuisance value of the symptom,* as psychoanalyst Donald Winnicott put it, resides in the symptom being given value in the way that it is responded to. When a nuisance is seen merely as a nuisance, it is a missed opportunity. It takes courage to make a nuisance of oneself, the kind of courage involved in preparing to go create the kind of world that one can live in. The capacity to create a nuisance and the capacity to tolerate—even thrive—with a nuisance are equally vital to one's autonomy and creativity.

As a psychoanalyst I saw many patients who were either afraid of being a nuisance, or not allowed to be one in growing up. So they became too good, too constrained, too limited. Or they went the other direction and became emboldened to be a nuisance in ways and places that eclipsed good judgment.

We expect our children to be a nuisance; it is part of their human nature. It is a kind of magic to become the right amount of nuisance in your life, and to have it responded to just so.

For there to be change, whether or not it is progress, something or someone has to begin to become a nuisance. A nuisance—whether an invitation, an opportunity, or an annoyance—makes us attend to something we would otherwise not—and rather not.

Just as paranoia is the self-developed cure for insignificance, being a nuisance is a cure for the indifference of others.

Satisfaction

> *We don't have relationships to get our needs met,*
> *we have relationships to discover what our needs might be.*
> —Adam Phillips, *On Balance*

The most elusive story—the one that we don't quite know how to tell, yet propels us forward hopefully—is the story of satisfaction.

Most often the anticipation of satisfaction precedes its realization. We look forward to satisfaction before it happens, meaning we begin an experience prior to its actually happening. And, of course, this kind of looking forward to something determines what we experience. This means that we can never be more certain about anything than about what our supposed satisfactions will be. And to be satisfied is to ensure not wanting, not having unrequited desire.

Real satisfaction, then, becomes a different matter. The anticipation of an experience, such as spending money or acquiring an object, engages the anticipatory sensors in the brain mediated by the sprint system of dopamine and adrenalin. When the actual experience occurs, the mediator becomes the marathon system of norepinephrine. This shift ensures that the anticipation will be experienced quite differently from the actuality.

When we achieve satisfaction in our lives, it is often by recognizing what we want and need as well as what "good enough" is. When we are rich and can eat as much as we want, we quickly discover how much is too much. Problems of food and money are really problems of energy and self-regulation. The most balanced individuals are those who self-regulate, who have a plan and stick to it.

Time

Writing a New Story

The door to the past is a strange door. It swings open and things pass through it, but they pass in one direction only. No man can return across the threshold, though he can look down still and see the green light waver in the waterweeds.
—Loren Eiseley, *The Unexpected Universe*

MY DAD'S POCKET WATCH is encased in a wooden frame on the bedroom wall of my weekend ranch, along with two pictures: one when I am barely three, sitting in Dad's lap on the tractor seat of a Farmall model H 1947 red tractor and the other picture of us working together as I approached his height. Time is standing still. The pocket watch stopped at one of the many times I asked him the repeated question, "What time is it now?" My question was partly to create a pause in our hot summer work of chopping cotton, since he had to stop work to pull out his watch to look at it, and partly to gauge how long until we'd stop for lunch.

He'd bought the white-faced, gold, Elgin pocket watch and had his initials put on the back before he left home for World War II. He wanted to know exactly how much time remained until he could return to his two passions: family and farming. I'm told that while other men in the Army had locker pin-ups of film and magazine women, Dad had a picture of his red tractor.

As I asked him the time, Dad reached for that gold pocket watch, secured by a brown shoestring safety-pinned to his overalls. That was the only catalyst needed. As he slowly pulled out the watch, it reminded him of a story. He was an inveterate storyteller. So many of the stories were about the Army and those three years, four months, eighteen days, and

six hours that generated a lifetime of memories of camaraderie with bud-
dies, nostalgically airbrushing what I knew later as the fear of combat,
his loneliness at being in another country, the separation from family.
Time's deletions generate a gentler past, as memory's artifices ensure that
the past is never quite gone. His most repeated wartime stories were of
the family holidays he missed, when he could look at his watch, and convert to Miles, Texas (population 720) time, to know what his family was
doing at that exact moment.

As we worked together, his compass pointed to the past, mine to a
future clothed in a white physician's coat, surrounded at home by my
own family. We both lost ourselves in time, perhaps for similar reasons,
though pointed in different directions.

Time's Arrow

> *Time past and time future*
> *What might have been and what has been*
> *Point to one end, which is always present.*
> —T. S. Eliot, *The Four Quartets*

The Amondawa tribe in the Amazon has no words for time, months,
years, calendars, and no clocks. They sequence events but do not have a
distinct concept of time. Yet they perceive themselves moving through
time and spatial arrangements of events in time, though their language
does not reflect it. Nature's clocks of sun and season, of day and night, are
extremely accurate.

The question of time and related puzzles, including the concept of
past and future, are among the most engaging daily ineffables as we try to
understand our stories and write new ones.

We remember the past and anticipate the future. This psychological
time is our subjective experience of temporal duration, of time passing.
The *experience* of time, not just its *perception*, is actively created by our
minds. The way we think about the past affects how we see ourselves in
time. Time is at the heart of how we organize and experience our lives.

In psychological time—flow rather than static measurement—we are subjectively aware of time passing, a present perception. In this moment, there is nothing but the present: The past is a present memory; the future is a present anticipation. We are subjectively aware of time passing, a present perception. We never directly experience the past or the future; both are constructions from our current mental state. However much we may remember the past or anticipate the future, we live in the present.

We've become familiar with time from clocks, as well as from our own internal experience of it. Clocks provide a convenient fiction, implying that time moves steadily and predictably forward. Yet experience tells us that it often does the opposite, to stretch, compress, or stop, depending on our state of mind.

Time seems to move only in one direction, the physicists claim. We have no moments to hold, only the memory of what happened in a segment of time. Time flows continuously, and we can never have it back. We know time, the container, only by what occupies it. From before there were words or even a language to the present moment, the interstices of memory hold experiences invisible to the radar screen of time.

Time's silent passing dominates our lives, yet its various signals simultaneously impart structure. Time, the most abstract of notions, is nonetheless precisely measured and subdivided, calibrated by clocks and calendars. The measure of time is not the thing itself, just as the map is not the territory.

Time has many frames of reference, each imparting its own meaning. Time may be gauged in the number of questions with which we have danced, by the lessons we have learned. In the unconscious, there is no binding, isolating, or organizing sense of time. Time is not a sequential arrow marching forward, but a circle always coming back on itself. Always being in the present moment occurs in a world in which time is a cycle, and each experience may be repeated, though we can never step in the same river twice. The future, ever a stranger, is an empty space that chance forfeits or plans generate. We can strategically plan, but the only way we can absolutely predict the future is to make it a replica of the past.

The Landscape of Time

The whole life of man is but a point of time; let us enjoy it,
therefore, while it lasts, and not spend it to no purpose.
— Plutarch

Time not only measures our days, it also gives them form and dimension. The bookends of personal time, birth and death, remind us that we measure time subjectively, relationally, always referencing some fixed, often intangible point. We divide time for a scaled map of personal geography to depict our history, our present, and even our future. Time offers continuity, a predictable illusion of the future.

Because we cannot freeze time, we encase icons of the present moment, a never-again moment collapsed into a simple souvenir of preservation—future memorabilia of the past to register memory. These gray weathered images weave together the texture of time past, a former life that crosses the bridge of artifact to present time.

We can use time to free or imprison, to dictate or liberate. Assumptions are our individual ways of stopping time. How we love, fear, lose, gain, organize, or waste time creates a life seemingly encased within time. Our lives, our subjectivities, our emotions, cannot be captured by moments, clocks, or calendars. Love and sleep, work and creativity, all the essentials of our psyche and spirit, can neither be computed nor legislated by time. Yet each in its own way is an intangible prison.

Each of us has our own personal time housed in memories of how we thought, felt, perceived, and processed a particular segment of our lives. Yet when we open a time capsule, the memory emblem changes because we have subsequent experiences to shape how we regard ourselves and that particular past. The repetition inevitably unfolds on a present stage, illuminating change. Time passes, transforming even our metaphors. Recollection of an incident or moment within a stored experience has its own prologue and epilogue. Remembering, an act of present construction, an imagination synthesizing a current experience with one of the past, invariably alters the drama with each remembered recreation. Time's dimension of history includes the density of a relationship, its depth, intensity, and frequency.

The nodal points of significant change in life, such as a birth, a death, a loss, or a new relationship, are the skin of time, the surface events of continuous processes. A model of perception recording surfaces and segments constitutes reality for the user of that model; an observer alongside seeing the continuity of segments, the heart and soul beneath the skin, creates a quite different experience. Each is right; each reality becomes the true and consistent one for its believer. Just as memory is a filing cabinet for incidents, with a creative reconstruction at each retrieval, time is also the tick of a clock's hand in a personally constructed context. Time takes its own revenge if we lack respect for it, fail to be aware of its continuity, defy its measured segments, or oppose our internal authority. *Time is money* may evolve through age, maturation, trauma, or other determinations to the simpler *Time is time*, and *Money is money*.

Remember your first realization that you don't have forever?

Time, like nature, is an unforgiving editor. The inescapable continuity of our future can best be lived by learning from the past, not segmenting it from the present. Every present moment has a past and future dimension: the system of time rather than the line of time. Our recognition registers this moment in time by an ongoing dialectic of repetition and current creation. Past and future are personal, present compositions.

Action forecloses other options; an action symptom—such as impulsively using a substance like alcohol, drugs, or food—collapses past and future time into this moment's urge. The past is encoded in the choice of action and item to change the way one feels, such as the symbol of food as proxy for a nurturing, soothing parent. The future (what is in one's best interest, or even what happens after what happens next) is lost. In impulsive action, neither past nor future can be constructed in the present moment, as it is occupied totally by the driving urge. Impulse dissolves the potential space of time between urge and action, for it is in this potential space that judgment resides. In this impulsive state of mind, the only future is in planning what, where, and when the action will occur.

Bargaining with oneself to stop the addiction at a designated point creates an illusory future. An action metric is used for time calculations. The alcoholic determines the future in terms of present urge: *How long until my next drink?* Even in recovery, the alcoholic may measure time by the drink. *How long have I been sober?* The compulsive eater will measure the future in pounds: *I'll lose 20 pounds by the class reunion.*

The self that is without present cohesiveness cannot construct a meaningful continuity in future or past time. Goals and ideals also require a formulation of a concept of future time. When external structure ends, such as school, work, or a relationship, one may feel lost, unable to envision the future, even to see oneself in future time. And because time is dependent on a continuous sense of self to perceive continuity, different states of mind create different time perceptions.

Intense emotion also may eliminate the future. Our wiring and storage system is encoded, filed, and retrieved by affect. A specific emotional stimulus activates the neuronal networks and pathways associated with that affect, triggering a memory. *Why did you do that?* from a parent may trigger a scenario of hurt, anger, and perceived criticism: The past and present fold into the procedural memory of the relived past. When he hears a car backfire, a combat war veteran surrenders all the time between when he was under fire in Vietnam and the present instant of startle.

When an internal point of reference is fully established, all the self-derivatives of esteem, confidence, coherence, and continuity are present and can be envisioned in a future landscape. The particular moments that collectively feature in our life, unsummoned and perhaps indistinct individually, nonetheless compose the journey of life. These incidents may attain their full awareness or meaning only retrospectively. At these particular junctures, implicit knowledge creates a new meaning, a process that at the time may elude interpretation and evade verbal explication.

Our Story of Time

*Time is a companion that goes with us on a journey. It reminds us to cherish
each moment, because it will never come again. What we leave behind
is not as important as how we have lived.*
—Jean-Luc Picard, *Star Trek*

What kind of relationship do we have with time? Is it something that
needs filling? Or something that tends to get wasted? Is there never
enough? Do we have a lot of it to kill? Do we feel that we have plenty, or
that it's running out? Do we spend a good deal of time planning how to
use time?

Transference and repetition are ways of encapsulating time, to seal it
off and isolate it, thus preserving it.

Our beliefs and expectations of the future can determine what happens in the present. Our perception and processing depend on the filters of both belief and mindset. Our expectation influences our current
behavior. Expectations—which are about the future—are determined by
past experience but reside in the present to influence our current behavior.

Less present stability makes future prediction more questionable.
Present stability is required to make reasonable estimates of future consequences of behavior. And the less trusting we are of the context we're in,
the more we tend to focus on the present moment.

Like silence, time is known by what inhabits it. Yet a process fits
only retrospectively into a dimension, such as time. In the landscape of
time, the middle distances of weeks and months may escape close scrutiny, while the short spaces of minutes and hours, and the longer intervals of years, may be subject to significant review. Though time cannot
be stopped, a cycle or season can be closed, such as by a birth or death,
a graduation or divorce. The end of an era, it is said, occurs when all its
fundamental illusions become exhausted.

We use time perspectives to register, encode, store, and recall our
experiences. Not only do these downloads determine how we regard
time, they play a fundamental role in the way we live.

Most broadly, how we focus on the past, the present, and the future is a highly individualized perspective of how we write our stories. *Past-oriented* people likely have more negative memories, often inhabit a museum of regrets, and archive injustices. *Present-oriented* people engage in more pleasurable experiences, tend to take more risks, and may rely more on substances such as alcohol or food. *Future-oriented* people tend to be more successful academically and professionally, take better care of themselves physically, do things such as regular physician visits, and save more for the future.

The tendency to focus on the past, present, or future becomes a binding frame of reference that then determines perceptions and thus more positive or more negative viewpoints.

Each memory is a current creation, and involves some revision in the process. Each decision and action in the present instantly becomes part of our past. Mastery of the present allows us to determine our past in an ongoing way, and to minimize the need to retrospectively rewrite the past.

On any day, at any moment, each choice may seem insignificant, but taken cumulatively, they determine a life story. As a whole, these experiences define who we are, who we were, and who we will become.

Finite Time

> *What you are, they once were.*
> *What they are, you will be.*
> —Inscription at the crypt of the Capuchin monks,
> Santa Maria della Concezione church
> above the Spanish Steps in Rome

Each of us shares a journey that we simultaneously embrace and deny, yet we know that, inevitably, our time here is finite. We share an ultimate destiny that in the blink of a cosmic eye will end uniquely, definitively. Time reminds us to live more passionately, to prepare less for death.

The paradox of time is the same as the paradox of money: Our attitudes toward both have a profound impact on our lives, as well as on our world. Yet for the most part we are unaware of our own stories of both time and money.

We often become aware of time by momentous events and tragedies, such as the death of a loved one, 9/11, or the birth of a baby.

Unlike money and things of value, we can neither possess nor accrue time. Once a moment has passed it is gone forever. Time is our most valuable commodity. Yet we may give little thought, if any, to how we spend it. We are finite beings, so time matters. We live our life in moments of time as we write our life stories. How we spend our time is always a choice, just as there are always opportunity costs to consider. An attitude toward time is essentially learned, and then how we relate to time becomes basically unconscious and subjective.

How we spend our time is a decision worthy of great consideration. If we find it difficult to say no and give our time to someone else as a default decision, we may later feel resentment for sacrificing time that we did not really want to spend in the way we did. In fact, we may spend our money more wisely, and with more deliberation, than we spend our time.

Spending money is tangible. Spending time is intangible. We can save money, yet we cannot save time. Time passes however we choose to spend it, whether or not we are subjectively and objectively aware of our choices.

How we think about time is ultimately how we think about the meaning of life. Measurable wealth may be accrued by someone who spends all of his or her time making money but may not take time to enjoy life. There are experts who can advise about personal investment, but what about the investment of personal time?

At every moment of our life we are spending our time. An economic principle of opportunity cost offers a perspective on time expenditure. If I spend $100 on Apple stock, I have opted to not invest that money in another company, to not otherwise spend or save the money. What I choose to do costs the opportunity to do something else. This opportunity cost acknowledges that resources are finite, and that there is an expense of one sort or another associated with choosing one option over another.

Like our money, the opportunity cost of our decisions about time is omnipresent. Whatever we choose and how we invest time eclipses other possibilities of the use of that time. Unlike money, we can't make more of time.

You can't entirely let go of an old story until you have a new one to inhabit. This is, after all, the way scientific theory works. Thomas Kuhn, the science philosopher, summarized it: *A scientific theory is declared invalid only if an alternate candidate is available to take its place.*

Time Elasticity

The present is not just something which comes after the past. . . .
it is what life is in leaving the past behind.
—John Dewey

We experience the elasticity of time, in which a moment of anguish seems like days, and the hour of pleasure or joy seems momentary. Our sense often is that time speeds up as we get older. Our days go slowly, yet the years go fast, especially if we are raising small children. When everything is new and we are young, we pay more attention, and time seems to expand. With age, new experiences diminish, landmarks become more familiar, and time seems to pass more quickly.

Two essential elements of our experience of time are *memories* and *markers*. Days fly by on vacation and then, when we get home, the other element comes into play—our memory. In retrospect we feel we have been away for a longer time because so many new experiences have happened that we have a good deal more new memories than derive from a usual week.

The unfamiliarity of an initial trip seems to stretch time with its linear series of unknown landmarks. Time seems to pass more quickly on the return trip, as in the later phases of life, as we have created more markers and points of reference. Traveling in the dark exaggerates the perception of time, as only the immediate is illuminated. Having a framework, seeing the big picture, seems to embrace time. Another factor appears to be the clarity of memory. As our memories fade over time, we may assume an event happened longer ago. When we telescope personal memories and have less distinction of specific memories, we tend to assume it happened longer ago than it actually did.

The subjectivity of time is captured in the 11th book of St. Augustine's *Confessions*, where he declared that the past and future are mental constructions that we can only see through a window of presence.

We create our own perception of time, based partly on the neuronal activity in our brains combined with the physiological input from our bodies. Yet time is not simply chemical, not only perception. We can propel ourselves into the future or time-travel through our past.

Our relationship with time is anything but straightforward. We have no specialized sense organ for time. Such experiences as anxiety, unhappiness, boredom, isolation, and even rejection have all been shown to slow our perception of the speed of time. Time perception, highly subjective in our minds, is also warped by tiredness, age, emotion, and life-threatening situations. In life-threatening situations, time is remembered as a longer span because the experience is more vividly recorded.

Time expands, rather than flies, with enjoyment. When we enjoy music we listen more carefully. When we have a good time on vacation, we pay more attention and perceive longer intervals of time. Time seems to stretch out the more we immerse ourselves in the enjoyment of it. Time flies when we aren't paying attention to the clock, and slows when we do.

When we look at an analog watch, the second hand seems to freeze for longer; on a digital watch, it seems to stay on the same number longer before moving on. We usually think that this is because we happened to look at the start of the second, but this is an illusion. What actually happens, scientists tell us, is that when our eyes move from one point to another, our perception of time stretches slightly. It actually stretches backwards and our brain tells us that we've been looking at the watch for slightly longer than we really have. The illusion is that the second hand or the number is frozen for more than a second. This happens every time our eyes move from one fixed point to the next; it's just that we notice it when looking at a watch. Our brains usually fill in the gap while our eyes move from looking at one thing to the next, but we can't do that with a watch.

Conscious efforts of trying to either enhance or suppress our emotional reactions change our perception of time. When people try to regulate their emotions, time seems to expand. This stretch has been demonstrated in experiments where participants were asked to remain emotionally neutral while watching a film clip, while others were told to act naturally. Those who tried to suppress their emotions estimated that the clip lasted longer than it really had.

States of mind impact the perception of time. Altered states of consciousness, such as under hypnosis or the influence of drugs, distort time perception. People under hypnosis underestimate the time they are in a trance by up to 40 percent.

Writer Vladimir Nabokov supported the straightforward mathematical theory that a year feels faster at the age of 50 because it is only 1/50th of your life, whereas at the age of 10 a year forms a far more significant proportion. This proportionality theory impacts autobiographical memory in a way, but it's certainly not the only explanation. The same space of time, as we grow older, seems shorter, but does not account for how we experience time at any one moment. We hardly judge one day in the context of our whole lives. Our subjective experience of time is the only way we can experience time, and this is never easy to measure.

The ultimate paradox of time may be that the pain of growing old lies specifically in the recognition that a part of us does not grow old. In an article contrasting young and old professional basketball players, Jeff Zilqitt wrote, *The young don't always grasp the concept of time and the speed in which it vanishes.*

If you think back on your life and recall experiences that made you especially happy and those that made you particularly sad or afraid, there's a good chance that most of them will have occurred between the ages of 15 and 25. Psychologists call this the reminiscence bump. This reminiscence bump of more memories occurs not only with life incidents, but apparently also with scenes from films, passages from books we read, news events that occurred.

The key to this reminiscence bump, as Claudia Hammond proposes in *Time Warped*, may be novelty. We remember our youth so well because we had more novel experiences then than in our 30s, 40s, and later, as experiences became repetitious. First experiences including sexual relationships, jobs, travel, and living away from home are all novelties with strong impact on memory. In one study of first-year college memories, 41 percent were found to be from the first week, the time of the greatest number of new events.

This same period of late adolescence and early 20s is a time of identity consolidation, and vivid memories serve to organize our core sense of identity. We need these events as a coherent organizer for who we are, to help us reflect back to make sense of who we have become. While we're searching for meaning, we're also seeking to cement our individuality. Finite events become anchors.

How much we need these memories as anchors is exemplified by Victor Frankl, who found comfort when in Auschwitz by vividly recalling his past life, of taking the bus to his home, walking to the front door, unlocking the door, and turning the lights on in his apartment. The memory of these ordinary times could occupy him, remind him who he was, and lessen his pain while providing the groundwork for the greater purpose of transcending his immediate experience. He resolved to use his time while imprisoned to study the human mind. He observed that the days passed slowly, yet the months rushed by. For him, a small unit of time, say one day, filled with torture and fatigue, seemed endless. Yet a larger time unit, even a week, seemed to pass quickly. He observed, *My comrades agreed when I said that in camp a day lasted longer than a week.* When days are very similar to one another and we become accustomed to routines, even when those routines are daily horrors as they were for Frankl, still, one is left with few new memories to register.

Our brains, from an evolutionary perspective, conserve energy by hardwiring repeated behaviors into neuronal networks and pathways so that they become a default mode; we record each subsequent event along the same pathway as a simple repetition. We become accustomed to a large number of similar memories traveling the same highways and villages of our brains, compressing the experience of time. When experiences are repeated and travel the same neuronal circuits, the repetitions don't register as distinct entities of time with the same intensity as a new experience. William James, the father of American psychology, wrote of this in 1890: *. . . the foreshortening of the years as we grow older is due to the monotony of memory's content, and the consequent simplification of the backward-glancing view.* Referring to time, he said, *Emptiness, monotony, familiarity make it shrivel up.*

A common phenomenon is that time drags when we're ill. Yet, when we look back, the hours of feeling bad barely feature in our memories. We remember that we were ill, but with little novelty for the week spent at home being ill.

These paradoxes are everywhere. Time has an impact on our memories, yet our memories also create and shape our experience of time. Our past perception shapes our experience of the present. Our memories create the elastic property of time, giving us the ability to conjure a past experience, to sense ourselves existing across time, and allow us to re-experience a moment in time and concurrently step outside that event to consider its accuracy.

A present experience overwrites a past experience, continually altering both, just as ancient civilizations built cities on top of other structures.

Writing a Story in Present Time

> *History doesn't repeat itself, but it rhymes.*
> —Mark Twain

Past

During World War II, beginning in 1938, Nicholas Winton, a Londoner, went to Czechoslovakia and saved an estimated 669 children, mostly Jews, from almost certain death at the hands of Hitler's armies. He told no one what he had accomplished for 50 years. At the age of 105, finally honored for his feats by knighthood, he said, *I'm not interested in the past. I think there's too much emphasis nowadays on the past and what has happened.*

What we believe about the past influences how we think, feel, and behave in the present. People who have positive attitudes about the past tend to be happier, healthier, and more successful than people who have negative attitudes toward the past.

The past has its influence as an ongoing story, and that story, as we know, can evolve and change. People are affected by the actual past but do not have to be determined by it. We can write new stories that do not involve a past template. Our attitudes toward events in the past matter more than the actual events themselves. Our attitudes toward the present are most important. We can't change what happened in the past, but we entirely determine what we think, feel, and experience in the present.

The full appreciation of the present moment may be the greatest for those who recognize the distinctions of past, present, and future—those who have their tenses straight. To repeat the past, to project it onto the future, or both, is to become a prisoner of time.

Present

We can be locked in time by continued repetitions, by recreating the same process occupied by the same characters, though perhaps with different faces. Unaware of temporal cycles and unconscious scripting, we seem to be taken by surprise with a repetition that is unconsciously intended for prediction. There is no future in repetition of the past; hope and change are both supplanted by predictability. Though rimmed by prediction and informed by the past, the timelessness of the uncertain future can prove so daunting that we project the past onto it, trading creativity for safety. Since we know the outcome, repetition can masquerade as effectiveness. Repetitions provide the illusion of preserving—even freezing—time by continuing the old story in the present. A search for elusive love and unsatisfied past needs fuses *then* with *now*, so that one can relive an old story with the same people though they have a thousand different faces.

Past need cannot be filled by present symbol. And you can never get enough of what you don't need. The food binge to fill the emptiness of emotional hunger, or the spending spree to counter feeling depressed, only works for a little while, never long enough or well enough.

Future

When we focus on the present, we tend to make different choices from those we make when we focus on the future. The gambling industry exploits this fact. When one enters a casino, a timeless world of present pleasure beckons. The temperature, lighting, and noise level remain consistent 24 hours a day. There are no clocks and no last calls by bartenders.

Stanford psychologist Laura Carstensen found that anything that compromises our sense of the future shifts both motivation and priority away from future goals and toward present emotional satisfaction. Old people who anticipate a limited future are more apt to do what presently feels good: speaking their minds, traveling, even becoming victims of get-rich-quick scams.

Time Perspectives

> *I've given up all hope for a better past.*
> —Dudley, a member of Alcoholics Anonymous

There are a number of life experiences and studies that can help us better understand ways to reset our time perspective clocks to significant benefit.

Visualization of the future can have significant, practical benefits. Princeton researcher Emily Pronin found that those who are able to visualize the future—to see their future selves at an older age—save more money for their later years. A study from Stanford University revealed that computer-enhanced images of an aged future self motivate people to double their retirement savings. A Stanford study also showed that computer-enhanced projections of the results of choices including smoking, nutrition, and regular exercise influences people to make better choices.

In *Timelock*, Ralph Keyes makes this recommendation: *Trying to increase one's menu of possibilities contributes to over-choice, a key source of "timelock." Reducing the range of options makes it possible to narrow one's focus and concentrate better.*

A reminder that time is our most precious possession suggests that we practice giving and receiving the *gift of time*. Remember, some of that gift needs to be for oneself, for life enhancement, growth, fun, exercise, and play. Clearly separating the time for professional life and personal life—and keeping the two distinct—is a fundamental component. Work hard during work time; play hard during play time.

Our time is brief. It will pass no matter what we do. Spend it so that it matters to you and to those whose lives you touch.

Analogous to wanting the elusive "more," many spend the present "waiting for Godot," whom no one seems to know, and whom they wouldn't recognize if they saw him. And yet, despite this inability to know Godot, they have chosen to trust him with their time.

Consider whether each person is worthy of your time. If someone does not give you joy, at least do not let that person take it from you. Consider whether each endeavor you choose is worthy of your time. Is it of worth, of purpose, of significance, a component of your life's mission?

Clarify what you are waiting for: purpose, specificity, and direction about how you spend your time. Time is passing. Embrace time fully, passionately, purposefully, while you realize that it is fleeting.

Whatever time is for you—love, money, work, play, friends, children—it, like life, is what you make of it. Make your time matter.

The true currency of life isn't money. It's time.

Memory

Old and New Stories

We do not know the true value of our moments until
they have undergone the test of memory.
—Georges Duhamel, *The Heart's Domain*

When I look at a photograph of one of my children, I see more than a flat image of an instant in time. I see the past behind that moment, and remember the hopes in front of it. I propel the image from its quiet, even plane into the foreground of a vivid, three-dimensional drama. My experiences are different with each of my children. They cannot evoke internal pictures of their infant and toddler selves; their mind's camera did not yet have permanent film. Yet they will remember those experiences in the process of instinctively recreating them with their own children. Each picture is an enigma, another piece of life that I will never live again, yet a ghost that will inhabit my memory forever.

These pictures, trinkets or memorials are a brief but necessary magic. We most appreciate present time by understanding it in relationship to the past, as well as to the future. Pictures represent a monument of our identity; their silent responses ratify our history. Fossilized insignias confront us with the passage of time. The pictures are testament to change, just as the birthday notches of my children's height on our file-room wall climb upward.

We look at our watches to see time and perhaps, occasionally, we may look at the arm beneath to see a different notation of time—the gradually changing skin lines and coloring. Pictures may not be so much a reminder of the past as a measure of the line of time marching forward.

Stories live forever—but only if you tell them. We keep souvenirs of an earlier era to help us remember, to prompt the stories. We grasp the handles of stories to keep us from feeling lost, to ensure that our remembered past is preserved yet contained so as not to intrude on either our present or our anticipated future. Some individuals search hungrily, longingly, for memories; others are trampled by them. Our autobiographical memories are complex constructions of forgetting, remembering, and reorganizing. We continue an internal dance with those truly important memories from our past, those with echoes of unique voices.

Memory Is a Verb

> *What is remembered is what becomes reality.*
> —Patricia Hampl, *Memory and Imagination*

Memory as a videotape playback system is a misleading metaphor, since there is no such recording device in the brain. Memory is not an entity located in a specific place in the brain; there are no designated neurons to store or retrieve a memory. Memories are created as part of the associative learning system to make connections of experiences and events. Repetition and recall strengthen these associations; disuse weakens them.

Unlike a computer template, memory is constructed when a current stimulus activates a neural network. A memory is a current creation, more active and fluid than retrieval of a computer file. We have many memory systems, and more than one system may be involved with each memory. While memory is a process, the retrieval cue can be any entity that activates one of those systems.

Recollection of a twelfth birthday is a combination of an actual experience, parents reminiscing about it, a picture taken then, and subsequent reviews of that time in life shaped by subsequent events and recollections. Memory changes each time we tell its story. Many of our memories are not of events that actually took place but records of our own stories.

Lived experiences record both implicit and explicit memories. The patterns of needs and caregiver activity are encoded as procedural memory, with icons of episodic memory. Memory is an attempt to impose order on the environment, to ensure sighting of a familiar face in a foreign country. We continually engage in categorizing and reordering experiences and events as we perceive them in the world.

Inside each of us resides a personal historian, a ghostwriter from earliest memory, who pulls together the images and events of a life into a story. Stories are how we understand and how we remember. Separate clusters of similar experiences form patterns that become meaningful landmarks in memory's landscape. This ghostwriter, unconscious and unseen, whispers meanings and generates connections to make sense of our lives, as each of us gathers our own medley of experiences into a coherent story of identity.

Memory is a stock of material that is always available for revision, subjected to rearrangement according to new circumstances. With each retranscription, the memory itself is changed. Perhaps the idea of memory and the notion of forgetting are just artifices we employ to help us keep the past and future apart.

Memory reflects our selective attention. I have no memory of my default decisions of driving each November to the French Quarter cottage in New Orleans for my month of writing sabbatical, but I vividly recall the audio books I listened to on each trip. The stories were most salient, the drive was automatic.

Einstein spoke of needing a theory in order to understand. Our number of theories expands to include more, allowing us to see what previously was invisible. A farmer and an archeologist pass through the same terrain of undeveloped land. The farmer sees the soil and envisions growing crops. The archeologist sees signs of an ancient civilization and reconstructs its history. The data viewed validate each individual's story. What is gathered as evidence and as proof is fashioned by the theory, which then determines meaning.

Engaging an unconscious myth to exchange it for conscious autobiography transforms neural software. Our myth, this created life story perceived as fate, gives shape and meaning to our lives. We are always successfully reaching our goals; it is helpful to know consciously what they are.

An incident or moment is set within a stored experience of unique individual history; recollection synthesizes stored experience with present emotion and perception. We remember something in the way we experienced it, so the only way we can retrieve it is the way in which it was recorded. Memory's meanings are aligned with the plot of an evolving story, transformed over time, progeny of both mind and brain. Not only does emotion enhance experience and its memory, it also edits and sculpts it. Some memories with the scent of authenticity are misremembered; some are totally fictitious events.

Retrieving a memory is an act of reconstruction, like conceptualizing a dinosaur from bone fragments. The reconstructions of the dinosaur and of the real dinosaur are not the same thing, though they bear a resemblance to each another. A present moment resonates with a past experience, and the two form a stereoscopic amalgam to connect neural networks as a memory construct. The emotional retrieval keys the old engrams to be enacted on this moment's stage. Remembered feeling is present feeling. This stereoscopic view changes both the past and present as memory continuously evolves with its own storyline.

Because recalling a memory also shapes it, our memory is anything but a passive storage vault. To record every fact and encounter is as impossible as it is undesirable. Our effective neural machine selectively disregards or deletes certain reminiscences to bring a desirable peace. Memory has many hiding places.

Freud was a psychological archeologist, excavating the minute detail, the childhood incident, the night thirty years ago. To him, the analyst partnered with the revenant, revisiting the moonlit past. We now know that the mind is not layered memory, like stacked artifacts or onionskin. Present stimulus resonates emotionally to activate a neural network in the brain, and we compose a memory story.

When certain themes, familiar patterns, and central organizing concepts transform, the past and the present changes. This is not an *Aha!* experience, but a process of looking back and looking forward, and both past and present look different because we have moved to a new place.

Memory Stories

When I was young, I could remember anything,
whether it happened or not.
—Mark Twain

Facing different directions, both memory and imagination construct images from what is not physically before us. Each is divorced from time, yet each exists in time; both memory and imagination transform and influence the other. Proust knew that the greatest experiences of his life came in memories, and his reminiscences of the past occupied most of his present; Flaubert looked the other direction, saying that anticipation is the greatest pleasure.

Some memories linger in a persistent way, like snow in shadowy places, until they achieve an order and meaning in a larger context, such as understanding why something happened. Memories are all we have left of our childhood, of our younger selves. Our memory shapes those moments of experience, recontouring them each time we revisit. Yet we may yearn for the original experience itself, for those times of undiluted joy and uncomplicated love, the moments of magic and mystery. Nostalgia is memory's bias to airbrush the image and set it on an idealized stage. Some of these special experiences reside in a unique place, a room all their own, seemingly protected from being reassembled by subsequent reality.

We remember in various ways, some of them without shape or form. Our bodies may remember, as do our feelings, even when our mind has forgotten—or never knew. A particular scent may open an entire scene of memory. Proust smelled a madeleine, a French cake, and tens of thousands of words later couldn't stop remembering.

We often remember by recreating a process, by sad or happy anniversaries such as a birthday, deathday, or particular holiday such as Christmas. A new framework of understanding can create new meanings of the same experience, as well as illuminate patterns and designs of memory's threads not visible at the time. Some of the most moving moments of our lives are often found without words, perhaps with an understanding now that was elusive then. As we come to terms with who we are, and who we once were, we make sense of our lives and our world in ways not earlier fathomed.

Our experiences are linear, a series of episodes that have their own daily order. Our memories are not. Instead, they seem like random occurrences that surface depending on how an experience or sensation resonates with a memory snapshot.

The past is an immense sky of darkness in which a few incidents, seemingly remembered at random, glimmer.

Memory keeps time differently. Each moment in time will never happen again, but the acoustics of memory can yield it at will. We have a consortium of past memories as well as future expectations residing in the present moment. Memory, our resident historian, runs our past through filters of emotion, belief, and prejudice, sometimes failing to acknowledge the role we played to originally create and now recreate what we remember.

Keeping Memories Alive

> *Memory is a complicated thing, a relative to truth, but not its twin.*
> —Barbara Kingsolver, *Animal Dreams*

Mind and brain are not just partners in a dance, they are more like Siamese twins. Yet any attempt at analogy falls short in depicting their complex interaction. The brain is an atlas of the mind. The nervous system develops its own pathways. When a usual neural pathway is blocked, an alternate pathway is created. Nature's imagination is rich; alternative compensatory programming and adaptations occur simultaneously. The mind and brain actively construct a sense of self from the myriad experiences of the past harmonizing with a present moment. The adaptive human mind creates an organization and order from the most diverse circumstances.

For emotional stimuli, input comes via the senses to the thalamus, which crudely filters it and passes it to the amygdala. The amygdala gauges an emotional significance from the storehouse of personal emotional memory. The message then passes to the hippocampus to assign specific meaning. The hippocampus, the primary residence of the unconscious process, creates and retains the factual memories and patterns about an emotional experience. From the hippocampus, information then proceeds to the left and right hemispheres of the frontal cortex. Here in the conscious mind, emotions, associations, and meanings link with the reason and logic of working memory. Note that the logical, conscious mind—where we make sense of things by having it focus on the tangible—is the *last step*.

Our memories gradually degrade over time when we do not use them. The part of our brains which governs memory formation, the hippocampus, engineers the restoration of fading memories in response to specific experiences. This commonly happens when we have not encountered the name of an object or a recollection of the thing for a while and may not be able to recall the name, even though it has been stored in Broca's area, a region of the brain that houses names and labels. When we see a picture of that object and are told its name, the hippocampus swings into action to recreate its memory and former associations. Along with governing initial memory formation, the hippocampus also engineers the restoration of fading memories in response to experience.

Numerous recent studies have shown that cognitive function can improve with age, especially when we expose ourselves to new and ongoing experiences, engage in social situations to activate a language-related facet of memory and others. Repeated use can also prevent the deterioration of certain areas of expertise, such as public speaking, playing the piano, or chess—for example, continuing to practice or play. Exercising the hippocampus keeps us young. It also crafts new memories to replace degraded recollections.

The meaning that we give memories determines our behavior. We can change our behavior when we change the meaning of the memory. We can reprogram our associations and rewire our brains.

A woman wrote to me about how frustrating therapy had been for her during several years with different therapists after reading my book *Destiny: An Uncommon Journey*.

Destiny could be a profile of my life. I'm sure a lot of other people experience the same thing. I don't want to relive this pattern over and over again. There seems to be this circuitry that I keep entering, reliving the same memories even though I try to repair them. Destiny had to trust in order to learn. When will I learn to trust? I keep peeling back more layers. How many layers to these distortions are there?

I wrote back the following response.

We each have a personal story with a plot and storylines. Our beliefs ghostwrite that story. When you peel back all the layers of the onion, what's left is not a pure, unadulterated onion, but nothing, since you've destroyed the object of the quest. Instead of the model of layers going deeper to discover the next layer, consider generating a new story. Going forward rather than backward, focusing on possibilities rather than problems, on visions rather than memories. You can even assess when you're rewriting an old story and plagiarizing an earlier version of yourself. Then, you can edit the repeating storyline. Or create a new one.

Memory's Language

> *The years teach much which the days never know.*
> —Emerson

We can remember what never happened.

My dad and I would plant plots of our farm for the cattle to graze at different times of the year. When a new feed plot was ready, we would put up an electric fence around it to contain the cattle. I found it fascinating to learn that once a cow touched her nose to an electric fence, every offspring from that cow, as well as succeeding generations, would never need to touch the fence again. They would just know to avoid it. Every offspring imitated the parent's behavior to avoid touching the fence. How in the world was that possible? How did that behavior—the belief in the danger of the electric fence—get passed from one generation to the next?

It fascinated me, though I did not understand until later when I learned of mirror neurons that propagate patterns, and the epigenetics of mutual influences—that beliefs and behaviors can turn genes off or on. Memory can be passed from one generation to the next through genetic code.

The mind and body speak in various ways, using many languages. Memory, emanating partly from that reservoir of neuronal downloads, is both selective and misleading. What is recorded and what is distorted are both highly subjective. Because it is a unique construction by each individual, reality is negotiable. Reconstructed and revised with each recollection, memory is an ongoing dialectic of past experience and present construction.

To respond to someone in a categorical or stereotypic way as if he or she were a figure from one's past, called transference in psychoanalysis, is one of the ways that memory speaks. What we expect in the present tells us instantly what has happened in the past. Attachment patterns and behavior models downloaded from important others become the cartographer forming the shapes and shadows of the map's terrain. These templates, stored in the brain's neural networks, travel neuronal pathways to shape subsequent relationships and self-perception. Unless the old story is revised, repetition simply ensures a new edition of it.

Expectations not only predict the future, they determine it. Our experiences are always consistent with our theories. Our beliefs shape and give meaning to what we perceive and construe. Can we ever be totally objective, free of bias and value? A computer cannot work without software packages to receive and process, or it would be empty, unable to function. Everything that we experience is inevitably taken personally, construed with various significances, and assigned personal meanings. This active construction of a personal map becomes a highly unique set of beliefs about self and expectations of others.

A traumatic memory is one where the past is too present, intruding to overtake the present. The challenge is to transform the past into history, to regulate the state changes that instantaneously activate a traumatic memory.

Memories of trauma and emotional pain may be reviewed as insurance against their intrusive return, as reassurance of no longer being in residence there, of having come to the end of the past. They are the evidence of how far we've traveled, like the scar proudly shown by the combat veteran, a reminder of the life he didn't lose. Ironically, someone may recreate a traumatic process hoping that the past won't return, unbidden. The recreated trauma may be specific, as similar a replay as possible. Yet the repetition only ensures its continuity, just as when our tongue cannot stop touching the painful place in our mouth.

One can become stranded in the past, a captive of memories, seemingly powerless against history and its repetitions. The mind may partition unconquered trauma, relegating it to the hinterland of dissociation, much as the body walls off an abscess to protect the system from contamination. Even though deleted from conscious awareness, the disregarded trauma exerts powerful influence. Being a victim can become an identity, an organizer of experiences, the paradox of an old ghost wandering down roads not yet traveled, rewriting the same storyline.

With experiences of trauma, memory imposes itself with certain unpredictable and unforeseen triggers. The triggers may be subtle, linked symbolically rather than explicitly. A visual or sensory cue may trigger traumatic memories. These flashbacks as well as flashbulb memories, such as remembering where we were when we heard of Kennedy's assassination or when the Challenger exploded, are etched as freeze-frame memory. These deeply etched memories, especially ones of highly charged experiences, may intrude, unbidden, as an unwelcome replay.

Psychology and neuroscience have taught us that flashbulb memories actually fade significantly over time, even though they seem so vivid that we hold an unrealistic confidence in their accurateness. We also know that emotion produces a tunnel memory, enhancing recall of focal objects but blurring the surrounding details.

Of the body's eleven systems, only two, the immune and the nervous, store memories. Both have a central role in distinguishing and preserving self from nonself. The immune system remembers what the body has forgotten. Immunological memory, as specific as for one tiny virus, lasts a lifetime. Lymph nodes, the hard-drive storage site of the immune system, have a large capacity as the repository of infectious and immune memory. If the immune system fails to distinguish self and perceives part of the body as alien, autoimmune disease is the result.

While the immune system can only store memories of previous encounters, the mind can create memories of events that never occurred, memories unknown even to itself.

Explicit Memory

We spend much time on explicit recall, the short-term memory that links perception with stored information, as well as remote memory that attempts to preserve time or place. The incident of explicit memory may represent an era whose time has passed, or it may be a token of an entire process, expired or ongoing. The associations and concepts underlying our general knowledge of the world—our explicit memory—make up the fund of knowledge that is independent of contextual cues for retrieval. Recalling content from a general fund of information, such as the number of months in a year or who was president during the Civil War, is not predicated on the context or the particular episode of the learning situation in which the information was acquired.

Implicit Memory

Implicit memory (procedural and associative) combines skills and processes linked to meaning from our bank of working knowledge. Implicit memory expresses, largely unconsciously, specific operations and the repetition of a process. A motor skill, such as riding a bicycle, can be remembered by recreating the process many years later without subsequent cues or relearning. Another procedural memory involves behavioral patterns, such as repeating with our own children the same type of attachment scenarios we experienced as a child.

Autobiographical memory is not about accurately remembering what happened but is rather an active construction of the self. We are constantly reminded of memory's fallibility, that we can never actually know in fact what happened during a childhood, yet the procedural memory blossoms within a current context. Rather than being retrieved as in an archeological dig, the past is continuously reconstructed. Procedural memories are simultaneously activated and subjectively reconstructed. We often co-create memory in the presence of another. One illustration of this mutual influence was a statement a physician patient made to me many years ago: *My mother of this analysis is different from the mother of my first analysis, and both are hardly recognizable from my mother in childhood.*

We perceive, encode, store and organize experiences and perceptual images by the emotion associated with them. Core memories of early formative experiences are more powerfully linked with a greater intensity. Although we spend much time on explicit symbolic memory, these procedural memories of attachment patterns form the infrastructure of relationships.

Associative, procedural, and implicit memories have various labels depending on the perspective: For habit, transference, repetition, or personality, each is the imprint of implicit memories determining perception, regard, and relational patterns. Change and developmental growth call for revising the exigent model to create new ones, upgrading the software. Implicit memory, present from birth, informs and directs relationships with self and others. These implicit memories are sustaining and organizing, incorporated into self-concept. Change may feel unsettling, disrupt familiar cohesiveness.

Intangible Memories

You seem to be devoting your entire vacation to the construction of memories. Perhaps you should put away the camera and enjoy the moment, even if it is not very memorable.
—Daniel Kahneman, *Thinking, Fast and Slow*

Catherine, a professional coach I was mentoring, spoke of how her client Sara talked profusely of various activities and relationships with no apparent feeling or engagement. Catherine had become frustrated that she could not get her client beyond a superficial recounting of events and external matters, such as decorating her house and going various places to find the material and items. Catherine felt ineffective to help Sara formulate goals or even find a focus. She was exasperated with Sara, viewing her as hopelessly resistant to the coaching process.

Her client seemed empty and treated every subject with equal monotone. Catherine described relentlessly trying to find the plot of Sara's experience, but continuously felt lost and ineffective, frustrated that she could find neither thread nor theme.

I asked Catherine for the detail, emotionally and physically, of how she experienced talking with this woman. Catherine mentioned how restless she felt, that she found it barely tolerable after a period of time when she could find nothing that Sara would focus on in a meaningful way. Catherine felt disconnected from her body, alone in the room, unable to formulate anything that seemed to make a difference.

Knowing her considerable skill and sensitive attunement, I suggested that we might consider that Sara was inducing an empathy in Catherine for exactly what Sara was experiencing herself: questing hopelessly for some focus, some organizing container. That is, the *process itself* was the *implicit memory* communicating the helplessness and ineffectiveness that the client experienced in trying to get some recognizable form and definition to her experience. In this unconsciously recreated memory process, her client was teaching Catherine *exactly what it was like to be her*, hoping unconsciously that Catherine could help her make sense of it and co-construct a new experience.

When Catherine recognized this conveyance as meaningful communication and found a way to put it into words, Sara began to describe her preoccupying efforts to figure out what others wanted from her. She would then try to give it, or be it—yet "it" always seemed elusive and had been so all her life. Sara was then flooded with *explicit* memories of what it was like to try to elicit responses from her husband and earlier her mother, how busy she made herself to try to be perfect, yet how frustrated and empty she felt as both people seemed preoccupied and impossible to engage. This experience, so pervasive in Sara's life, was "remembered" currently with her professional coach by recreating the process of the emptiness, boredom, and drivenness, all the while unable to crystallize an external focus to make things make sense.

Catherine was able to help her client generate a new story by focusing on the choice architecture of each moment: for Sara to recognize that her current thoughts, feelings, and experiences were entirely her creation. And to gradually co-create a new story.

We teach the past at least as much as we are taught by it. The past is made tangible by our specific recollections of its instances and incidents, as well as by its reconstruction. We habitually take the old road, not always for the illusory mastery of repetition and the security of familiarity, but at times to see the same thing in a new way, revisited from a present life experience. And at times, perhaps, just to see how far we've come. The same thing now looks and feels slightly but surely different.

We are always remodeling our memories, revising as we recall. The stories we tell about our past become our past. The dancing midnight shadows of memory pause to pay homage to the present moment, both necessary to transform the future.

Memories are the evidence of being able to forget, testimony of extracting oneself from procedural memory to create a new story.

We gather the experiences of each moment as parents to hold deeply in our hearts as family archives. There are no unimportant encounters, as each of us leaves some of ourself in the other. Brevity of time teaches me now, as some unexplainable premonition did earlier, to appreciate each moment.

For, all too soon, gone too fast, today will be a memory, too.

Nostalgia

Revisionist of History

Nostalgia is a seductive liar.
—George Ball

Proust smelled a cookie and launched tens of thousands of words of nostalgic remembrances.

In the army, nostalgia was my dad's only available comrade all day long on Christmas Day 1943 in Kodiak, Alaska, as he shoveled coal. In his homesickness he recalled earlier times, old friends, holiday gatherings. Family togetherness was my dad's cookie. For this gentle man, nostalgia was a constant companion, a composition impersonating memory, with its sepia glow replacing the original reality, most certainly better than the harsh light and sharp edges of that cold, lonely Christmas Day. Family memories warmed him and fueled the many stories he continually shared.

At the time, I appreciated nostalgia's passion; later I would learn of its ubiquity and complexity. Nostalgia remembers things not as they were, but as we wished them to be. Nostalgia recalls the ideal rather than the real. Has anyone become *less* popular in memory replays? Or gotten *worse* in high school and college sports as the years go on? (I'm very close, now, to being all-state in basketball *twice* in one season. Probably by next year. And that was the season—as best I recall—that we were undefeated.)

We remember our past as it was, and also as it would have been, for nostalgia is a revisionist of history. Nostalgia, generally thought to refer to positive reflections about the past, to memories infused with pleasure and warmth, occurs universally. Often accompanied by an expansive mood and infatuated state, it adds something to the memory not there in actuality.

Memory Is a Verb

I have spent a large portion of my life in the shade of a non-existent tree. It was without meaning, though my feet took a remembered path. In sixty years the house and street had rotted out of my mind. But the tree, the tree that no longer was, that had perished in its first season, bloomed on in my individual mind, unblemished as my father's words to me: "We'll plant a tree here, son and we're not going to move anymore. And when you are an old, old man you can sit under it and think how we planted it here, you and me, together." The memory of the tree was part of my orientation in the universe and I could not survive without it.
—Loren Eiseley, *The Brown Wasps*

Loren Eiseley writes of a particular tree that had taken root in his mind as an image of home. He discovered that the sapling cottonwood had for sixty years been growing in his mind, though not in reality. His memory was nostalgically revised, remembering the past as better than it was, even the remembrance of things never past. Memory has its own imagination.

Nostalgia is an instrument of forgetting dressed in the attire of memory, framed by the idealization and hope of a former period. It is still a memory, but a memory of what never was, even at the time. We remember gratifying times in adolescence, former loves, school or sporting experiences, and nostalgically resonate with the expansive, hopeful, idealized aspects of the era. The enigma is that changing one's past may have significant consequences on the future.

Nostalgia bridges the present to a better past, airbrushed memories informed by yearning, backlit by retrospective idealization. Memory is about what happened, the register of perception at that moment in time; nostalgia seems more about what didn't quite happen, though it came so close as to record a near miss, circumscribing fantasy while igniting hope. Memory's longing and past incidents speak with the same voice in the moment of nostalgia. The ideal becomes the real of remembered experience, defending against too-painful actual reality.

Nostalgia attends to archaic longings by filling in the memory, while altruism does so by proxy. In nostalgic reflection, there is no mourning for missed or lost experiences, for the fantasy *is* the memory, a pretend satiation of primordial hunger. While nostalgia recognizes that the past can never return, it elevates the idealization to past reality, a memory newly tailored to fit a wish or perceived need.

Nostalgics collect memories, but only ones that have been edited, reshaped, possibly even recast, and set on a different stage. Often cued by particular music, a certain smell, or the resemblance of a person or object to past experiences, real memories and real fantasies blur. A nostalgic portrait as reality, such as an idealized picture of a parent during childhood, may substitute for the disappointment of repeated empathic failures.

Nostalgia is aesthetically crystallized and enshrined in art, antiques, and memorabilia. The bittersweet elation of nostalgia reminds us of what was missed and, at the same time, engages the absent experience, to be remodeled by wish's archetype.

Nostalgia's river of sentiment is never to be followed back to its spring, for it would lack something, or worse, at its source might be discovered the contamination filtered from memory over the years. The dedicated nostalgic remembers the colorized, augmented version of stark, black-and-white experiences or, in more extreme instances, of the missed experiences as unapparent at the time as they were impossible.

Fictive Past and Hopeful Future

People cannot discover new lands until they have courage
to lose sight of the shore.
—André Gide

Nostalgia remembers a time when the future was viewed with idealism, without the restraints, disappointments, and limitations reality would later impose; the idyllic was as close as the imagination, hope limitless and passions grand. The time capsule of adolescence is opened to revisit its omnipotentiality. It is the memory of hope, of a future that had not happened, of desire combined with expectation at a time when both reason and adulthood were simply blind within childhood's possibilities, with no disapproval from childhood logic.

Like the verbal tickling of teasing, nostalgia also lies alongside the truth, not at the center of it. Nostalgia binds up and packages past hope in that space of unfulfilled longing, keeping it alive yet knowing deeply that it can never be filled now any more than it could then. The nostalgic contract defensively counters disillusionment and painful disappointments by preserving idealizations, perhaps at the time of the experience, certainly in retrospect. (Nostalgia derives from the Greek *nostos*, to return home, and *algia*, a painful condition; the German translation is "homesickness.")

More extreme nostalgia longs for the past without accepting that it is over: The past is not irrevocable, for it is recreated as ideal. Blind to the paradox that hope exists presently within a past context, an obsessional attachment to the past may impoverish current experiences. The particular missed experiences, woven into the plot of nostalgia as dreamy remembrances, become part of one's identity, often paralleling and defending against emptiness and hurt. This investment in idealized memory filters all that is inconsistent with the plot of the pleasant past, defensively camouflaging painful aspects.

Nostalgic Resilience and Adaptation

> *The present is not just something which comes after the past. . . .*
> *it is what life is in leaving the past behind.*
> —John Dewey

What cued your mood to watch an old movie, or an old episode of *Cheers* or *Friends*? Are there triggers that will prompt you to crave a piece of candy you ate in childhood?

Marketing taps into nostalgic experiences. It's easier and faster to associate a product with idealized memories than to create a new product identity. A nostalgic trigger is coupled with new information. Arnold Palmer and that old tractor—two classics—preserved by one particular motor oil.

A consortium of neuroscientists examined situations that led people to prefer nostalgic products—those that remind them of the past—over contemporary products. A series of experiments found that the key to preferring nostalgic products is the *need to belong*. Their studies found that a situation in which people feel a heightened need to belong to a group, or a need to feel socially connected, will prompt a preference for nostalgic products.

In one study participants were excluded from a ball-tossing computer game, which prompted their choice of vintage products that had specific emotional ties for each person including movies, TV shows, food brands, and cars. The scientists discovered that when participants were excluded, not only did they feel a higher need to belong, this need was "cured" by eating a brand of cookie that had been popular in the past. Their nostalgic moments were about feeling left out.

Chinese psychologist Xinyue Zhou studied hundreds of migrant children who moved from remote rural areas to a major city; their average age was 11. This emotionally disruptive experience and the adjustment to their new world prompted nostalgic memories, which, for them, salved the pain of loneliness. Nostalgia was self-protective.

All of us, regardless of age or circumstance, protect ourselves from emotional pain by conjuring romanticized memories of the past. We summon nostalgic experiences to buffer loneliness. In fact, psychologists know that the most resilient people—those with emotional hardiness—are more likely to use nostalgia as a coping strategy.

Nostalgic reflections often intensify in middle age with the recognition of both the passing of time and the illusions of timelessness and immortality. The earlier assumption of timelessness carried less urgency for nostalgia, because then there seemed to be unlimited time to acquire what never was. With recognition of the finiteness of time, though, awareness dawns of what was, what never was, and what can never be except in nostalgic creations. Nostalgia may then be enacted in various middle-age modes, such as revisiting adolescence via affair or sports car or, perhaps more adaptively, by an increased focus on health and exercise and reviewing goals and ideals.

Nostalgia takes on increasing significance in older age, as elderly adults are more vulnerable to social isolation and disconnection. Nostalgia counters feelings of loneliness by providing a link of continuity between past and present.

Memory vs. Monument

> *Reality has a way of hiding from even its most gifted observers.*
> —Loren Eiseley, *The Unexpected Universe*

Recent studies have shown that nostalgia occurs in all cultures and age groups. Some common features include nostalgic thoughts that feature a person we are close to, a significant event, or an important place. As writer and director of our nostalgic scenes, we usually play a starring role (why not?), and as casting director place ideal witnesses of family and friends (what better for them to do, anyhow, especially if they didn't pay enough attention originally?).

The nostalgic there-and-then serves as proxy for a bereft here-and-now, to purify the hurt, to supplant the absent, and to achieve the unattained. *If only* fantasies abound in this nostalgic place, inhabited perhaps by reminiscences of the heartmate of a past time—a time in which, truth be remembered, *someday* fantasies occupied that same space, leaving little room, even then, for the present moment. *Someday* fantasies look ahead to an idealized future, establishing the model for later looking back to an idealized past.

The nostalgic moves between the idealized past and the romanticized future, while the obsessive alternates between the minute detail and the globally abstract. Both miss the present moment. Driven, obsessive nostalgia selectively demands filtering out all but the ideal, without concurrent recognition of loss or impossibility.

The nostalgic may search perpetually for lost omnipotent figures of the past, editing and annotating reality to retroactively claim that sought in the past to fuse imperceptibly what was and what never was. The longing comes to life in various nostalgic pursuits of the present, such as collecting memorabilia.

Nostalgia benignly and innocently restates and reinstates the past, creatively blurring memory and monument, seduced by the longings masquerading as nostalgic remembrances. The past dances with the fantasy of attainment, keeping both alive. Proust's pleasurable reminiscences used much of his available energies, so that, on the one hand, he lived little in the present, but on the other achieved immortality by encasing these recollections in his writing.

Blended in the recipe of nostalgia may be a regret that both devalues the past and falsely idealizes it, for the memories are often bittersweet, an amalgam of deification with despair. Nostalgia desperately holds onto hope of change or relief by filling in missed experience, countering the dismay of resignation. As such, it is a substitute for mourning, clinging to love's (predisappointment) hope. Missed experiences, woven into the plot of nostalgia as sanitized remembrances, become part of one's identity.

Investment in the constructed nostalgic memory may organize around only those memories consistent with the plot of the pleasant past, defensively camouflaging painful aspects. We remember that which fits into a plot. We also search an infinite sea of possibilities to perceive what we believe, even if it involves seeking memories that distort (enhance, edit, fill holes, buff sharp edges) to construct a better past. Selective perception and memory, at one time perhaps a necessary developmental adaptation to vault us into a more hopeful future, may compromise the present.

A Psychoanalytic View of Nostalgia

Those that do not have power over the story that dominates their lives, the power to retell it, or think it, deconstruct it, joke about it, and change it as times change, truly are powerless, because they cannot think new thoughts.
—Salman Rushdie

As the following vignette will illustrate, while nostalgia grasps the imagined and the ideal as real, it also freezes moments or selective aspects of relationships in time, perhaps because they would never have gone beyond the point at which they are frozen, as necessary elements were missing. Nostalgia, in addition to defending against disappointment, resentment, and loneliness, becomes its own attempted developmental remedy and compensatory self-restoration.

This vignette from my former psychoanalytic practice illuminates the distinction from professional coaching, spotlighting someone who needed therapy rather than strategic coaching.

Emily, a 43-year-old child special-needs therapist, began her analysis with a vagueness that permeated her life and relationships, aware of her own uncertainty in the way obsessionals are aware of detail. She beamed a perpetual smile, and her eyes gazed radiantly upward as she spoke of her life, her children, and her professional work in glowing terms. As I reflected her pride of accomplishment, she allowed a brief excursion into her own disillusionments and accounts of people who had disappointed her. However, showing the cautious restraint that she developed in all her encounters, she would not allow either of us to empathically enter her obviously painful experience.

In her quiet, admiring way, she seemed to demand my absolute attention to share and validate her nostalgic portrait of her past. I tried to extend our focus from her broad romanticized images to specific detail and feelings. During a pause when her longing seemed quite vivid, I asked if she might be experiencing more than she was allowing herself to feel, such as sadness about missed experiences. She reacted allergically to my urging her toward feeling and detail, as if I were inserting a toxin in her cherished nostalgic system.

She quickly moved from lying on the analytic couch to sit in the chair opposite me. She could not explain why she wanted to move. Sensing that she wanted to see my facial and expressive reactions to her, I suggested that it hurts not to be seen, not to have experiences validated. She cried and spoke of how profoundly sad she was when she became aware of the childhood that never quite was, of the little girl she could never be.

As we spoke of her sadness, I said, *Perhaps because you didn't feel fully seen by your parents . . .* and she finished my sentence by adding, *And I couldn't see myself until you did first, and I have to see you seeing me for a while*. I acknowledged this need and how I had not appreciated it fully until she told me her specific experience.

I asked how long she could hold in her mind the image and feeling of herself in my presence, and of our work together after she left the sessions. She indicated that initially it faded just after she left the office, then later it remained for an hour or two, but about four months into the work it persisted for many hours, up to a day.

Emily enshrined lost innocence by keeping her little-girl qualities, including its cognitive model of good or bad, all or nothing, seeing only the loving aspects of an interchange. Preserving closeness with the past, she vulnerably relied on idealizing responses to maintain a positive self-esteem. Adhering to the attachment patterns of caution as she did with her alcoholic mother, combined with unrelenting attempts to please others, she presented herself as childlike in interactions and in dress. She wore stylish but baggy clothes, dresses in which she felt small, often ones that specifically had little-girl tailoring, such as sailor suits.

She saw her childhood family as five characters in search of an author. Both parents were preoccupied with social pursuits in their nonprofessional hours, and she felt lost and uncertain about parenting her two younger siblings. In her caretaking of her two brothers, she was informed only by her own needs projected onto them. She imitated the ideal parent she longed for.

During a Christmas visit by her mother, she spoke flatly, without feeling, of the visit and highlights of the mother's non-attunement to her. She spoke of her mother's friend who came along for the drive, then lapsed into reminiscences of the friend's daughter and their shared teenage adventures.

I stopped her to ask for the details of what exactly happened when her mother drove up for this Christmas visit. She was vague, indicating that her mother stayed in her car in the driveway talking to her friend until Emily walked out to greet her. She then spoke of having to always initiate telephone calls to her mother, and how her mother lacked spontaneity and affection.

I asked what she felt as she approached the car and saw her mother, to tell me her experience, frame by frame. She described how her mother sat in the car, still engaged in conversation with her friend, seemingly not excited to see Emily. She had to open the car door to get her mother's attention, even though it had been almost a year since they had seen each other. I asked what she experienced at that moment. Emily hesitated, cried, sobbed, then talked about how lonely she felt in her mother's presence, how hurt and angry she was as she waited for her mother to come to her. When she recounted how the mother finally got out of the car and they hugged, I asked her specifically what she experienced during that hug. She shed burning tears as she described how stiff the hug seemed, how much more connected her mother seemed to the friend than to Emily, how this felt exactly like her loneliness and emptiness as a little girl.

Similar focus with Emily on specific detail of aspects of her encounters and memories, and of her romanticized childhood, illuminated her nostalgic purification of experience and memory. Emily's nostalgia, the present fantasy as memory for a past that never quite was, and a future that had not yet happened, had become a style, infusing her entire life. In the bittersweet sadness of the romanticized childhood and adolescent memories she created, nothing ever seemed so perfect or so ideal as when refined in remembrance.

She allowed, gradually, the detail of her painful reality to be experienced without nostalgic copyediting and annotations. The disappointments came alive in the analysis for her to mourn missed experiences, to come to the end of the past, with its present illusions. She no longer had to split off the experience she had paradoxically continued to engage by nostalgic denial.

Emily recognized her disappointment of perpetually seeking the past in the present, ensuring continued disappointment in both; she allowed herself to feel the painful losses embedded in both. She had created revisions along nostalgia's idealized storyline, repeating what was disappointing, yet keeping hope alive. Her nostalgia was about her fantasies that had never taken place. Her remembrances were better than the events, as she recalled wishes rather than the actual experiences. She had found substitute gratification in parenting her daughter, as well as in her love of doing special-needs therapy, where she worked with learning-disabled children who responded dramatically to the care and affection she bestowed on them in her work that she conceptualized as *reparenting*.

In the analysis, she allowed a gradual unmasking of this defensively romanticized, fuzzy filter that had let her avoid painful detail and mourning. She had nostalgically cropped deprivation and loneliness from her pictures of childhood. She ultimately recognized that reentering her old story to try to rewrite a different ending, edit imperfections, and fill in a multitude of missing spaces only served to recreate the past. Mourning the past, rather than continuously writing better endings to her old story, allowed her to focus on creating a new story.

Like new geese migrating to the warm South from the coming barren cold of Canada, nostalgics can also go back to the place that they have never been. Nostalgia's wistful adhesion to old familiarity is for the hope, rather than the actuality, a fantasy that never took place but is recalled as if it did.

The only thing harder to give up than what once was, is that which never was.

We glance backward and look forward to view a world shaped by both desire and experience, simultaneously creating memory and anticipation.

The pile of coal that my young, healthy, almost indefatigable dad shoveled seven decades ago on that cold, lonely Christmas Day cast a long shadow, inhabited nonetheless by his future hopes and dreams.

Perhaps even I was conceived there.

Belief

The Software of Life Stories

A belief is not merely an idea the mind possesses.
It is an idea that possesses the mind.
—Robert Oxton Bolton

The Neuroscience of Reverse Truths

The doors we open and close each day decide the lives we live.
—Flora Whittemore

While my children's adolescence cured me of most of my theories, a few fundamental ones survived, perhaps even more boldly illuminated against the backdrop of passing years. One of those survivors is the principle of reverse truths. In traditional science, truth is arrived at by proffering an hypothesis, then accumulating data to prove or disprove it; the data force the conclusion. Reverse truths work just the opposite—the hypothesis or belief *creates* the data.

A vital reverse truth is our belief in our children. They look to us as a mirror of who they are, and they become what they see. If we trust and respect them, they become trustworthy and respect themselves.

Some parents have this reverse truth backwards, thinking that they will trust a child only after he or she has proven to be trustworthy. There are forward truths, but this isn't one of them. Our belief in our children is taken in by them and metabolized into their own belief in themselves. We convey to them an unspoken message: *I'll believe in you until both of us do.* When that affirmation isn't there, they may spend their lives looking for that elusive approval.

A corollary of believing in my children was to believe their words, their truthfulness. When both my children were very young, I told them that I would never lie to them and would always believe everything they told me as well. I knew then the responsibility that placed on them to always tell the truth.

On a Father's Day many years ago now, my son's last before leaving home to start college, I found a letter from him at my bathroom sink. A passage in it offered a progress note on this reverse truth:

> *You never lied to me and I have never lied to you. Sounded stupid at first, but as time passed, it became more important, and I realized that I never would. This is a relationship few others have ever had.*

The philosopher Carlyle had it right: *Tell a man he is brave and you help him to become so.* As a parent, the trick is that you have to believe what you say, for feigned praise and inauthentic interest are forgeries immediately discernible to a child's expert eye. I see this reverse truth professionally as well. When I work with practicing professionals and executives, I have to believe in them so they can believe in themselves. Which is why I only work with clients in whom I really believe. A belief of immense success personally and professionally may be difficult to conjure, since people can only imagine from within their own systems.

The Geography of Belief

> *There is no doubt that right hemisphere intuitive thinking may perceive patterns and connections too difficult for the left hemisphere; but it may also detect patterns where none exist. Skeptical and critical thinking is not a hallmark of the right hemisphere.*
> —Carl Sagan, *The Dragons of Eden*

A baby elephant can be trained from birth to be confined to a small space. The trainer ties a rope around its leg and stakes the rope in the ground. The baby elephant will initially try to break the rope, but the rope is too strong. The baby elephant has to stay in the area determined by the length of the rope.

When this elephant grows to a mammoth adult size, it could easily break the rope, but it doesn't try, because earlier, as a baby, it wasn't able to do so. The five-ton adult elephant is constrained by an assumption based on earlier experiences. Putting a little rope around one leg has activated a *belief system* that determines its behavior.

Beliefs, what we consider our basic truths, ghostwrite our experiences and results in life. Our beliefs write the software of our behavior.

Beliefs drive both perceptions and behaviors. Beliefs are the seedlings of reality: the oak that sleeps in the acorn; the bird that waits in the egg. We come to believe what we repeat to ourselves, whether it is true or false. If a lie is repeated, it is ultimately experienced as truth—the teller ultimately can't discern the difference.

Appreciation, an anlage of belief, attunes the unconscious mind to repetitions that will contribute to forming a belief. Any thought that is repeatedly passed on to the unconscious mind will ultimately be accepted.

Our assumptions select what we perceive in the world and determine what meanings we attach. Not only is believing necessary in order to see, we also bring about what we expect to happen. A belief creates a reality. A placebo is an inert pill, plus a story. The patient is prescribed an expectation that, in the vast majority of cases, manifests. The belief generates a truth so powerful it can even *reverse* the pharmacological effects of the real medicine. The placebo's story is a white lie, a fiction that becomes a truth. A recent MIT study showed that a more expensive placebo worked significantly better than a much cheaper one—same placebo, different stories. By anticipating an experience, we can create it.

The brain generates beliefs and reinforces them as truths. Our brains process complex sophisticated information better than any machine in existence, while at the same time being capable of understanding the process of understanding—of mentalization.

It's an illusion that we carefully consider all decisions through logical analysis and rational reason. For at the same time we are quite capable—more than any other species—of self-deception and creating illusions.

We fool ourselves, while thinking we can logically avoid being fooled.

Since beliefs come first, we can believe something that defies logic, and we can find reasons to confirm. We have susceptibility to beliefs. A belief comes quickly and naturally, skepticism slowly and unnaturally. We have a low tolerance for ambiguity. Our minds desire closure, and our brains strive to end dissonance—especially dissonance stemming from the unknown—so these two ineffable forces join in collusion.

To a large extent we view our beliefs and assumptions as the truth, as reality of the way things are. We validate our beliefs by experiences that affirm them, and we surround ourselves with others who share our values and hold similar points of view. And we live those assumptions by communicating to others how to respond to us. If you firmly believe you will be rejected or abandoned, you will either choose someone who will enact it, or you will act in a way to generate that response. Because your belief system contains what you see as inevitable, without insight the only degree of mastery you can exert is to determine how and when the inevitable happens.

Our assumptions are often in evidence but not always in our awareness, because they are so basic to who we are. If you want to find out what you believe about yourself and the world, look around at your life. Your life is the self-statement, the mirror, of what exists inside you. When you feel chaotic or disorganized internally, you likely will notice that your house or office reflects that experience. You have created, promoted, and allowed everything in your present experience. All that you say, in the syntax of thought, feeling, and behavior, is about yourself. To find out someone's belief, simply ask, *So, how do you really know?*

You may regard your past as a series of episodes at times, seeming to lack a theme or continuity. What you remember and how you remember it, however, fit into the plot you earlier incorporated and now accept in yourself and others. Your unconscious filter omits from perception or forgets any incident that doesn't fit comfortably into your plot. Like the words of an unknown foreign language, these happenings are not recorded for later retrieval or reference. Because of that filter, the episodes you recall of your past are not at all random. In fact, the incidents of your past are variations of a recurring plot, consistent with one another. Without insight and change, new editions of the same story place a thousand different faces on the same central characters to repeat the same themes.

The Anatomy of Belief

> *If it is a miracle, any sort of evidence will suffice.*
> *But if it is a fact, proof is necessary.*
> —Mark Twain

A life story contains silent assumptions and emotional scripts. From an infinite sea of possibilities, our beliefs and assumptions tell us what to look for and how to perceive and process experiences, thereby ghostwriting our stories. Each of us has a personal story with a plot and storylines. Some of our beliefs and patterns may be invisible even to ourselves. We make a story out of events in order to infer relationship and assign causality. We personify the economy or the stock market as if each were a story of its own. Marketers have also figured this out, which is why we see so many stories in advertisements.

The brain needs a story. It will infer one, so it's helpful to know the lexicon. A story can define possibility. In centuries of recorded time, no one ran the mile in under four minutes. It was impossible. Roger Bannister broke the four-minute mile in 1954. Within the following eighteen months, a dozen other runners broke the four-minute mile as well. The obstacle of the impossible could no longer be constructed. Today this achievement is commonplace. When the mindset of what is possible changes, reality then changes as well.

We believe and remember only that which fits our plot. What we expect to happen in the present reveals instantly our experience in the past. Our expectations help us see—in fact, they determine what we see. But they may blind us to other things that we aren't looking for. At the end of class, a professor who is fond of telling stories asks his students if they have time for him to tell them a story before they leave. They look at their watches and say yes. He then immediately asks them what time it is. They have to look at their watches again, because the first time, they checked to see how much time was left—not what time it was. If we look for one thing, we may miss another.

We only see what we believe. Our beliefs are the software that writes our behavior. Our experiences are always consistent with our assumptions. And we're always right—because we write the story. *Believe in someone and then he or she will show you why you do.* Neuroscience has demonstrated that authentic belief in someone activates his or her brain to create a state of mind that transcends usual thinking and performance. Statements of belief are not always equal. Belief statements in science are based on principles that can be confirmed or disproven with more data, and a better theory—better beliefs—can be substituted. A belief in a flat tax, a belief in Santa Claus, and a belief in multiple personality disorder are not equivalent; believing doesn't make them so nor does disbelieving invalidate them.

Our own determination of belief and confirmation has a specific location in the brain. What we believe—what we have constructed as possibility—is determined by our perception. We then perceive exactly what our radar already has coded as possibility. The hippocampus in the midbrain, the brain location of the unconscious, connects perception with existing association to assign meaning. That belief then determines behavior. If we do not believe, we simply do not see, so we neither perceive nor process.

Inattentional blindness is the tendency to miss something obvious and general while attending to something special and specific. It is perhaps the most powerful of all cognitive biases. The classic experiment of this bias has subjects watch a one-minute video of two groups of three players passing two basketballs back and forth. They are assigned a task: to count the number of passes made by the white team. After 30 seconds, a gorilla enters the room, walks across the screen, stops, turns to the camera, thumps his chest, and exits. Psychologists Daniel Simons and Christopher Chabris found that 50 percent of subjects did not see the gorilla, even when asked if they noticed anything unusual.

Errors in Belief

Well, as with anything, if you want to believe, you can find reasons to.
—Tom Hanks's character in *Extremely Loud/Incredibly Close*

People do not hold entirely accurate and unbiased perceptions of themselves and the world. People can, however, live into (create) stories based on positive belief systems. By driving both perceptions and behaviors, beliefs can serve as a powerful motivating system.

We originally construct beliefs to make sense of our experiences in the world. The beliefs then become predictors and confirm the reality that generates them.

Two anthropologists were chosen to enter separate, essentially identical ape colonies to live and observe for a year. They had remarkable similarities of personality, philosophy, and education.

When the two anthropologists emerged to compare notes, they expected essential similarities, but instead they found remarkable discrepancies. One anthropologist, after an initial period of transition, was accepted by the apes, integrated into the colony, and achieved a unity and comfort with the apes. The other anthropologist never got beyond the social periphery of his colony, remained careful and vigilant, always seemed right on the cusp of a conflict, and never reached a harmony.

The anthropologists could not understand the discrepant results or find any reasons for them. They and their teams puzzled for months, until they finally found one difference. The anthropologist who was the uncomfortable, careful outsider carried a gun. His gun never showed; he never used it; the apes never knew he had it. But he knew he had it; he knew that if things got tough, he had an "out." The anthropologist who had no gun had a commitment: He knew from the beginning that he would either make it—or not—on his own.

In retrospect and reconstruction, each of their assumptions created the reality that they experienced.

We tell our story. Then our story tells us.
Our experiences are always consistent with our assumptions.

Perception, an individual reading of current input or stimulus, is determined by expectation. Expectation, based on cumulative experience, means that we have an individual, preprogrammed radar screen. What we perceive is based on what we believe as possibility, and the hippocampus, the brain location of the "unconscious," links perception with particular associations and assigns meaning.

The tendency to predict that past events will repeat in the future (extrapolation), and the desire to achieve mind and brain closure regardless of true cause and effect, at times preempt accurate understanding. The different biases that have been shown to be operative illustrate this process of inaccurate predictability and false attribution of cause and effect. Our brains are wired for narrative, not statistical certainty. We tell ourselves simple stories to explain complexities that we can't know.

Each of us writes our own personal story and makes sense of things by fitting incidents and events into our unique plot. This story fills in the blanks and connects the dots to complete the picture of who and what we are. Events, images, and experiences form the patterns and storylines of that plot. We construct meanings to make sense of our life, and determine what is remembered as narrative in a coherent story of our identity. Reality validates and affirms those assumptions as we live out our expectations.

Using our beliefs and assumptions, each of us creates our own personal story and the themes of that story. The plot defines and orients us in the present and guides us toward the future. The stories we tell about our lives become our lives. The stories we tell about our past become our past. Until the story is uncovered, questioned, and reevaluated, the default model continues. That we are always right about our assumptions never comes into question; it only further etches those beliefs as reality. And we are always creating our own story, so reality self-validates. We perceive and remember what fits into our plot, which is our internal model of the world and ourselves. The plot—the core beliefs and assumptions of each life storyline—informs what we look for and how we attribute meaning to what we find. We then create narratives of self-statement according to that plot, as brain and emotions are both programmed to ignore facts that contradict our assumptions. We ignore, mistrust, disbelieve, or more likely don't notice anything that doesn't fit into our pattern. These notions, prejudices, fears, and expectations construct a self-concept. Some aspects are conscious and some are not.

Without knowing how to examine and change them, it is difficult even to challenge these assumptions. In fact, any departure or change from a well-traveled plot line, even a positive one, may initially create anxiety and uncertainty. Beliefs must be in conscious focus before we can revise the ones that don't work and create new ones to enhance a life storyline. When we recognize the plot of each storyline, we can discern the hidden assumptions and emotional agendas that ghostwrite them. We can then revise our stories to live them fully and successfully. When we stop telling ourselves all the things we *should* say and cease listening for what we *ought* to hear, we can begin to recognize our own stories more fully.

How do you form a new belief? Many of the ways by which we try to facilitate change are contrary to the way the mind and brain works. Changing our belief system changes the neurophysiology of our brains, making it both an art and a science to create a new story. Regardless of whether the content of the belief system is about life possibilities, money, or other personal stories, change is challenging.

We often change, not because we seek transformation or enlightenment, but because what we've been doing doesn't work (often dramatically so). And we begin to look for other possibilities and options because it is lonely and unpleasant inside our own stuckness. The ability to admit that we are wrong depends on our willingness to tolerate the unpleasantness associated with being wrong. For guys only: Remember being hopelessly lost, yet stopping for directions was *not* an option? C. S. Lewis addressed this challenge by saying, *If you are on the wrong road, progress means doing an about turn and walking back to the right road; and in that case the man who turns back soonest is the most progressive man.* (Notice he even singled out *man.*)

Being wrong is, first and last, an emotional experience. Our mistakes become a moment of actual alienation from our sense of self. The ultimate challenge: To not believe everything we think. Our sense of self is composed of a number of beliefs, any one of which can be mistaken. All of us have had ideas about ourselves—beliefs—that have evolved over time. A few of those beliefs may have collapsed abruptly. Remember when you thought you didn't want children, or knew you would grow up to be a lawyer, or reasoned that you would be happy only if you lived in New York City?

Adventures in Error

> *For those who believe, no proof is necessary.*
> *For those who don't believe, no proof is possible.*
> —Stuart Chase

Don't Believe Everything You Think

Derren Brown did an experiment on London's Regent Street in which he placed on the sidewalk his wallet, with money clearly sticking out. He drew a circle with yellow chalk around the wallet—much like the crime scenes on TV. Then he walked away, leaving the wallet lying there. Hundreds of people walked past this wallet. Most saw it, many stopped to look at it, but no one would pick it up. The yellow chalk circle created a barrier—an assumption that limited people from simply picking up the wallet. Belief systems are both powerful and enduring. Beliefs come first, expectations follow. We form our beliefs from various personal experiences with family, friends, colleagues, and culture. After forming those beliefs, we seek to validate, even to justify and rationalize them. We then confirm the beliefs by cherry-picking data to support, and become blind to data that diverge. Our perceptions of reality rely on the beliefs we hold of it. The brain is fundamentally a belief engine. Beliefs are the software that organizes both what we perceive, from an infinite sea of stimuli, and how we process, and the patterns we deem meaningful.

We can't entirely let go of an old story until we have a new one to inhabit. This is, after all, the way scientific theory works. Thomas Kuhn, the science philosopher, summarized: *A scientific theory is declared invalid only if an alternate candidate is available to take its place.*

Some change is slow. Consider how, at an earlier age, you were adamant about a particular point of view. A dozen years later, you look back and may even mock your former position. In between, a gradual process of transformation lets go of a belief, to take on a new one. This is the stuff of time-lapse photography: slow and gradual, imperceptible in any moment or month.

Our sunk costs in a belief determine how loyal we are to it. The more emotional currency we invest in a belief, the harder to extract ourselves from it. We leave the security of our known stories, and the certainty and predictability of how those stories—and we—will turn out. It feels like a lack of control, so we're motivated to avoid new information. Especially if we expect bad news. The ultimate mistake is to avoid the truth about ourselves.

One woman said to me as her last child was about to depart for college, *If I'm not a parent, then I'm not sure I know who I am.* I heard a man say, *If I don't believe that every word in the Bible is true, I don't know what to believe.*

When we embrace change by recognizing the limitations of a belief, or admitting the wrongfulness of a notion, various emotions come with it. Initially we can feel lost, alone, perhaps scared. Neuroscience teaches us that a fundamental belief is an anatomical reality in our brains; to change it can feel like an amputation, even tampering with our identity.

No matter how psychologically minded or resilient we are, facing up to mistaken beliefs challenges us. Since the past can't be changed, restitution involves admitting mistakes, then using them to inform a different story.

The Challenge

> *There is nothing either good or bad, but thinking makes it so.*
> —Shakespeare's *Hamlet*

The challenge is to recognize, own, and assess certain aspects of our own stories. We tend to seek information that confirms our beliefs rather than disproves them. New information may cause unpleasant feelings and a departure from our comfort zone. Different behavior disrupts our default mode. People are afraid to go to the doctor. They're not afraid of doctors; they're afraid their denial will be confronted.

Growth and change begin with personal story ownership: the recognition that we are the authors of our own stories. Taking ownership of a life story begins the process of inquiry. Only by accepting ownership can we proceed to assess the storylines and decide what to change.

We become what we think and feel. Our beliefs become our reality. The beliefs *within* us—our own internal map of reality—determine our perception of what surrounds us, including what and how we select, register, and process.

We construct our storylines from these premises. We have to bring each of our beliefs into conscious focus to assess how well they work in present time. We choose the beliefs we operate on, write each element of our life stories, and in so doing sculpt our brains.

Hope

Fuel for the New Story

Sandy consistently handed Farrell one club too short to make the green.
His caddie was handing the club to the stronger golfer latent in Farrell,
and it was Farrell's job to let this superior performer out,
to release him from his stiff, soft, more than middle-aged body.
—John Updike

When Pandora's curiosity overcame her and she opened the box sent by the gods, uncrating calamities into the world, the whole point of the story is that once you open it, you can't close it again. And yet, last to emerge, as the legend has it, was hope.

Hope focuses on a better future, a wishful expectation that tomorrow someone, some event, or perhaps even time itself, will bring fulfillment. In extreme instances, hope is not *what* the future is but *that* it is.

Hope's blueprint is mastery; its reverse image is ineffectiveness. Hope maintains motivational fuel—purpose—as central theme in the plot of a life story. In childhood, hope is the gaze into the parent's eye for the approving reflection of "good enough." The original inspiration for hope is for a significant other such as parent, mentor, or teacher to believe in us, so that we can import that belief and metabolize it into belief in ourselves.

Hope is guide to the void, sentinel for the unrecognized, and promise of what can be.

Hope, ambition's daydream, lives in a duplex arrangement with the uncertainty of actualization. Optimism, the anticipation of the best possible outcome, is a neighbor to hope, as hope is built on a foundation of desire with expectation of fulfillment.

The search for a good story can lead to miscalculating and under-estimating risks. Optimism bias, a positivity illusion, can also benefit its holder, by allowing one to address tasks not usually engaged.

Over time, disappointment and disillusionment transform idealized hope to attainable reality.

Hope gives shape to the impossible. By blaming and perceiving fault in one's self, a possible remedy for hopelessness is created. To believe that one caused an event constructs an antidote to passivity, reverse engineering potential effectiveness.

False hope survives as long as the destination is just out of reach, as the illusion collapses upon attainment of the goal. The maintenance of the illusion *requires* impossibility.

Hope's Origins

> *When I started the company, I was 52 years old.*
> *I had diabetes, lost my gallbladder, and most of my thyroid gland.*
> *But I was convinced that the best was ahead of me.*
> —Ray Kroc, founder of McDonald's

There are miraculous moments in the creative process of parenting, such as when the toddler takes a first step forward. The parents cannot walk for the child, but their faces beckon encouragement, excitement, hope. The child walks alone with eyes fixed on the parent's face, not on the difficulties in the way. Surely this must be the earliest model of how to proceed in the world, of what to look to, of being focused on an ultimate destination.

The parents and child continue to live in a hall of mirrors, seeing themselves in each other. Children look to their parents to define who and what they are, to find and stand firmly on the bedrock of self. Each parent, hopefully empathically attuned and responsive, can accurately give the child back a sense of value and worth. In this creative exchange, the child develops a sense of self, becoming less and less dependent upon parents over time.

The most powerful motivation that any of us have is a desire to be effective, to experience mastery. Looking into the accurate mirror of a parent is the earliest experience of effectiveness, of being a cause, of having the pleasure of empathic connectedness and validation of feelings and responses. The child and parents co-create this mastery, the experience of home as a secure place. This safe haven becomes a foundation from which the child launches into the world. And it is here to retreat to, whenever the world outside turns confusing or threatening.

The creative parent quietens the thunder and lightning of tears to the calmness of smiles without manipulating. A time of intense storm is not a time to learn the principles of weather, but a time to find a safe harbor, and the parent understands and accepts the child's feelings rather than demanding a different response. (The most common thing that gets in the way of understanding is trying to fix.) If a child has a nightmare or a fear of monsters, mastery is robbed if the parent must chase away the monster or check to ensure there are no monsters in the house. This only verifies that there may, indeed, be monsters whose absence has to be assured by the parent's routine check of all possible hiding places.

Our young child hopes we have magic, authority, knowing answers, and courage to triumph over their absurdities. And all the while not shirk from their idealization of us. By adolescence, our children need—but do not want—authority, to instead have us witness, often silently, as they triumph over their own absurdities.

Our children need us to enter their childhood without becoming children ourselves, to hold their hands, mingle our souls, join their spirits. They wish for us to sense their trepidation as they face bold new ventures without adding our concerns to theirs, lest the blending of both might crowd out their playfulness and expansiveness. Our encouragement helps them cross the nebulous line from fear to excitement. They want our love, but there is something beyond love for which no words suffice.

Our children hope for some iteration of this ineffable:

Get inside my experience and be here, totally with me, but not all the time, just enough to experience what it is like to be me, to know that my childhood is unique. See my childhood as a poem, as both reality and metaphor, not as a task to do or piece of machinery to maintain. Don't be afraid of contact and availability. Exchange your art with me for mine. Know that I have to learn jazz as well as love—the improvisations of my music rather than the rote tune of another's words. Accept and enjoy me, and later, I will be free to do more of what you would really hope, because I have been my true self for me and not a false self for you.

In the absence of affirming, empathically attuned caregivers, the child may package hope in a container of perfection, offering a perpetual series of occasions for fulfillment. Perfection is elusive, an unattainable quest to be ultimately and reluctantly mourned; the antithesis of perfect is real. Bidding farewell to that which never was is perhaps surpassed in sorrow only by having to give up what has already been taken away. Indifference is a less specific, though far greater pain than death.

Hope and Irrational Neuroeconomics

> *Hope is the thing with feathers,*
> *That perches in the soul,*
> *And sings the tune without the words,*
> *And never stops at all.*
> —Emily Dickinson

Rainbow fantasies idealize the future. *Some day, winning the lottery,* and *the perfect person* promise possibility. This defensive hope, perhaps necessary at times to help one vault beyond despairing ineffectiveness to a better future, renders one a prisoner to hope's rose-colored fantasies, agnostic to self-deceptive falsehoods. And, if we find the right person (the one we've longed for, that one we *wanted* to want), we have to give up longing—that familiar fantasy of what may, but really cannot be.

An ancient part of our brain gets excited about the hope of making money. This deep midbrain area, the nucleus accumbens (a.k.a. the pleasure center) can trump the rational forebrain and even collectively influence entire economies. Mirror neurons and active amygdalas contribute to the social contagion of everything from tulip bulbs to housing prices. Most of the factors influencing these decisions are outside conscious awareness.

But there's one area where it's all in the open. Everyman's game: the lottery.

Each year Americans spend $7 billion on movie tickets, $16 billion on sporting events, $24 billion on books, and $62 billion on lottery tickets. The lottery is the most popular paid entertainment in the country.

What fuels our national pastime? Why do people continue to play the lottery?

The anticipatory excitement mounts when three of your six numbers are called—or when two of the three scratch-off symbols match, and a third is *still possible*. The near miss, as when the first two cherries align on the slot machine, ignites brain kindling. *Walk away,* says the rational forebrain. *No way,* counters the midbrain, *I almost won—just one more time. The third cherry was only one notch away.*

Why not spend $1 for a brief time of (irrational) hope? This buys a significant number of minutes of pleasurable fantasy, of thinking about what might happen if you suddenly won. Where else can you dream so fancifully for $1? Escape to a better life for a buck? Or transcend usual limited thinking in exchange for a fanciful *What if . . . ?*

Does hope come any cheaper?

We know from studies of the brain that it is the *anticipation* of pleasure or a win, rather than the win itself, that creates excitement and the release of dopamine (a chemical very appropriately named). When someone approaches a slot machine, there is a spike in dopamine *before* the machine is actually touched.

In all situations of bias and inequality between rich and poor, in *one arena* everyone has an equal chance: the lottery. Never mind that a win is almost impossible. Never mind that it is fanciful and illogical. The lottery is the Great Equalizer, it is impartial, and for a brief, shiny, emotional moment it lights up an entire neighborhood in the brain. Not one, however, where good business practices prevail.

The truly elite spend time concealing their wealth, while those without spend time aspiring. On average, in state lotteries, households that make less than $12,400 a year spend 5 percent of their income on lotteries. A Carnegie-Mellon behavioral economics team explained why poor people are so much more likely to buy tickets: They *feel* poor. Sad, since playing the lottery, a massively losing proposition, exacerbates the poverty of those with low income.

Our helplessness inspires us as a catalyst to create both effectiveness and autonomy. But it is an ersatz mastery, since a temporary illusion such as the lottery, drugs, alcohol, or risk is self-limited and carries the danger of being used again. And again.

Alone on a desert island, Tom Hanks's character in "Cast Away" attempted repeatedly yet unsuccessfully to start a fire, until his hands were rubbed raw and bleeding. He then constructed Wilson, the volley-ball with painted face, as an imaginary companion. Wilson could counter the abject loneliness, affirm his existence, and listen to him. Hanks's character could see Wilson seeing him. (It is, after all, what we do every day in our crowded civilization, to make self-statements projected onto another to either validate or expunge aspects of our selves). A needed companion serving as mirror, Wilson had to be enough. Within moments of creating Wilson, glancing repeatedly at his new witness for encouragement, Hanks successfully began a fire.

Fear and hope both predict the future. The only certainty of the future is to repeat the past, for repetition promises predictability, the security of known terrain, even if it has a limited result. Repetition contains the anti-thetical hopes of forgetting vs. fulfilling, recreating vs. changing. There is no future in repetition, as predictability supplants hope. The pull of the old and the fear of the new inform invisible decisions that become cam-ouflaged in habit, our collection of repetitions. Other choices and pat-terns remain unseen, outside the usual and familiar. We repeat because we know the outcome, creating the illusion of effectiveness.

Hope imprisoned in the past becomes hostage to the familiar; the dread to repeat dances untiringly with the desire to change. At times, we repeat to master belatedly, to detoxify past traumas. Purpose is not derailed, but successful in a journey on the wrong tracks. We fear change, and may be loyal to attachment ties of the past hoping for the exhilaration of winning the affirmation and love (by proxy) that before may have been elusive. Hope then remains deadlocked within an earlier context and mission.

At times we repeat just to see, in relation to a fixed point of reference, how much we've changed. Each time we return to the chorus of a song, those same words are different, for more of the lyrical story has unfolded, and we see more of the unfolding journey at each juncture of repetition.

Hope's tired legs may give way to despair and, going forward, to anticipatory fear, creating a menu of potential harm. Just as each individual uniquely localizes internal anxiety in a specific designer fear, so also is hope created with its own personal geography.

Tangible, specific effectiveness gives oxygen to hope.

Symptom as Hope Embodied

All right, you'll ask me questions and I'll answer them.
You'll clear up my symptoms and send me home.
And what will I have then?
—Hannah Green, *I Never Promised You a Rose Garden*

Valiant efforts to remedy ineffectiveness, to temporarily dissipate tension or fill emptiness, may include such compulsive activities as sex or exercise, or such substances as food, drugs, or alcohol. The chosen substitute addictively deployed works (for a while) to end tension, to distract.

A symptom can be clothed with the essence of a personality (such as bulimia or paranoia), even as the protagonist in a story of fear and pathology, rather than as a sentinel in a story of hope and desire. When my former colleagues pejoratively give nicknames to clusters of symptoms, such as borderline or narcissistic, they sometimes miss the person and his or her hopeful attempt to bridge the missing link to self.

Every psychological symptom carries hope, a mission of simultaneous defense and restitution. Symptoms serve as a splint to navigate necessary developmental passages: to cure an absence, to remedy helplessness, to apply local anesthetic for emotional pain. Constructing a symptom embodies enigmatic hope in sustaining engagement with what is feared, devising the object of yearning and dread to be *the same thing*. Fear guides toward, yet obfuscates what is longed for, a fugitive of desire. Like Jacques Lacan's narcissistic lover, the subject of desire's vigorous pursuit is icon of the ideal self, yet only temporarily (but excitedly) staves off emptiness or deadness.

The diversity of action symptoms involving any addictive activity, substance, or person renders hope finite. Additionally, to choose one side of a conflict or ambivalence and act on it creates the perception of resolution.

Illusory hope reenters an old story and revises a better ending; true hope writes a new story.

Hope's noble intent may create the malignancy it intends to counter. When one's veil of safety and invulnerability is pierced by trauma, or ripped apart by physical or emotional tragedy, hope has to be more carefully preserved, more deeply protected. It has to look forward and see a better future. In extraordinary pain, the idea of suicide may be the only available promise of an end to suffering. This ultimate option transforms helplessness into potential reversal, a choice perhaps sufficient to allow its creator to go on living. Alternatively (or additionally), the voice of suicide may coerce others into making consolation responses, for even the emotionally obtuse respond to a crisis of sufficient proportions. It may only be after the idea of suicide, silent or proffered in word and gesture, fails to redeem hope that the suffering one chooses that final act.

In deep distress and abject aloneness, it may seem that the only way to build a common ground with another is by inducing a similar experience. Helplessness, hopelessness, or anger enlists the significant other to articulate some version of *I can't stand it anymore*. Only then can the originator unconsciously wink, *Finally, you've got it. That's what it's like to be me. (And I can know it better when I see it in you)*."

The adolescent who feels entirely misunderstood, alienated, and alone may rouse in parents a state of anger and helplessness akin to what he experiences: *I'm going to show them how it feels*. He is carrying all the hope*less*ness, the parent the hope*ful*ness; the adolescent shifts some of the hopelessness over to the parent and vice versa, a more equal balance. These attempts to induce empathy create *similar* but *parallel* experiences rather than true empathy, resulting in alienation rather than connection.

The act of sharing hopelessness with another is a very hopeful act. It conveys the need to further the search for its meaning.

And who would want a guide who's never been lost?

Mourning and Fulfillment

Writing a novel is like driving a car at night.
You can only see a little distance ahead,
but it is enough to make an entire journey.
—E. L. Doctorow

Barbara, at age 43, was hitting her business stride as her company had just gone public. We had worked together strategically in Mentor Coaching to bring this about. Yet Barbara experienced a glass ceiling on the enjoyment of her good fortune. As soon as she lost her excitement, her usual state of mind returned. If she felt *too good too long* she engineered a takeaway, such as to worry about some upcoming task, to reinstate the familiar. She had always made sense of this dynamic by reasoning that she didn't dwell too long on a victory but needed to prepare for the next step.

She recognized that feeling good made her anxious and uneasy, the trepidation of being in new territory, devoid of familiar landmarks. Yet her current anxiety felt different, more expectant, even exciting. She had been interpreting the new anxiety in an old way, assuming it meant that danger was imminent. Like putting new wine into an old bottle.

We reframed her uncertain anxiety into a current model of affirmation that she was beyond the familiar, a signpost of being in new territory, a reminder to celebrate each step to acknowledge and enjoy the present victories.

At one particularly difficult point in our early work, after an unexpected setback in her business, Barbara said to me, *You've just been lucky, protected, that you seem so full of life. Life is suffering. There is no hope.*

I responded, *Your paradoxical hope may be that if you can't convince me life is suffering and hopeless, then there's hope for you. A purpose.*

She added, *I recognize that you've been optimistic and hopeful for me at times when I couldn't see it at all. I've needed you not just to empathize and strategize with me, but to stick up for that part of me that's not coming through—or that I don't even know yet.*

Of course.

We have to believe in order to see.

In its transformation to present context, hope's illusions—viewed prospectively through rose-colored glasses and retrospectively by nostalgia's memories—must be mourned. This chimney-sweeping may recover lost love, and balance remembered hate. And, by so doing, awaken an original hope not ensnared by illusion or obstacle, the antithesis of both fantasy and dread.

The risk and vulnerability of making use of a significant other in one's life to resume developmental growth becomes hope personified, awakened in a current context. Hope must be freed from limiting assumptions and compromised relational patterns of earlier times.

To remember by repeating disallows forgetting. Memories are the evidence of being able to forget, emblem of where we no longer reside. We use memories in order to forget. Innate hope, developmentally unfrozen and currently embraced, moves to a present context.

Hope devises many designs. A truly intimate relationship personifies both hope and purpose. It is a partner dance, the co-constructed mix of two real people, handing each other their souls, their best feelings, with the expectation that each will give it back, enhanced. Each to be catalyst for what the other needs to grow more of.

How surprised we are to learn that our terror lies not in the dim shadows of the past's unknown, but in the hopeful light of this moment's change.

Story

The Creation of Self

We can understand the known only through metaphors attached to what we know.
—James Thorpe

One Boy's Story

Imagine a four-year-old boy—no brothers or sisters—isolated on a farm three miles from the nearest town (population 720) in central Texas. Just three and a half feet high and unemployed, with an active mind and not much to do with it. The unemployed part would change in the next couple of years, though, when farm chores began. With very little reading material, even if he could read, that little cowboy made up a lot of stories. Dead outlaws all over the place.

On the wall in the dining room was a telephone, a big wooden box with a cone receiver and a hand crank to call the operator and tell her the number you wanted. In the country, you shared a party line with four to six other families, each family with a different ring. Ours was one long and one short.

And then I made a major discovery. The kind that James Hillman speaks of in *The Soul's Code* as the spark that ignites a life's calling. I learned, accidentally at first, that you could *listen to stories*. Miss Dessi lived about two miles further down the caliche road, but she was only two short rings and one long away. She had the best stories by far. Hers were even better than the ones I could make up. Her currency was information. And she was one rich woman.

Later, when we became one of the first farm and ranch families in Miles, Texas, to get a television, *As the World Turns* had nothing on Miss

Dessi. She and her friends expanded my world view. The only downside? It shrank my story-making time—I had to stay close to the phone. She single-handedly saved a lot of West Texas outlaws from an early death.

But even with my imagination I never dreamed that I would have to go to school for the next twenty-three years to learn how to listen to stories.

Later, one person's story changed me and my world view. He said the most important thing anyone has ever said to me besides *It's a boy, It's a girl,* and *I do.* (Not necessarily in that order.) He said, *The mind is the most powerful thing in the world.*

I really listened to my favorite athletic coach. I believed that he knew. He taught me daily for four years how to use my mind to perform, to succeed, to be part of a team. And I saw that it worked. We won games and championships in three sports.

I was reunited with him three decades later when my daughter located him to come to my surprise 50th birthday party at my weekend ranch. He'd become the superintendent of one of the largest school systems in Texas.

I told him how right he had been. His smile was still slightly asymmetrical from tearing off miles of athletic tape with his teeth to wrap ankles. Still the smile of ancient wisdom.

That lesson from my original mentor has since been verified by human science research and neuropsychology. And life experience.

More than any other person or experience, my coach's story guided my decision to specialize in psychiatry, subspecialize in psychoanalysis, and later make a full transition to Mentor Coaching. *The mind is the most powerful thing in the world* became my story.

Over the years I learned to listen to different kinds of stories. In medicine, each symptom is a story, needing, begging to be listened to rather than silenced or disregarded. In Mentor Coaching, I co-construct successful new life and business stories with my clients.

I now do almost all of my work with Mentor Coaching clients, as well as training Specialty-Certified Mentor Coaches by telephone, and I collaborate on fascinating stories with people from all over the world.

I'm still careful to not breathe into the receiver, but these days I get to talk back. And the big difference now is that the person knows I'm on the other end of the line.

Examining the Narrative

If you don't know the trees, you may be lost in the forest,
but if you don't know the stories, you may be lost in life.
—A Siberian elder

On a recent skiing trip I saw a woman purchase a ski jacket for $2,400. While she'll stay just as warm as one that costs a fraction of that amount, it's part of her story to purchase the one she did. It's easier for her to buy that jacket than it would be to change her story. It's harder to change a habit when we incorporate it as an identity, yet a habit is simply a series of choices, a collection of repetitions.

Each of us has the ability to write a new story. Every day is a fresh page, and that page is blank until we write it. Whatever we think, feel, and experience is what we create each moment.

We literally change our brains by retelling our story so that it includes new understanding, insight, perceptions, and especially new conclusions. As we rewrite our story, we rewire our brain by building new, more functional neural pathways. As we continue to retell this new story to ourselves and others, we strengthen and deepen the pathways, making them more automatic each time.

Did you wake up fresh today, a blank slate for a new start? Or is today another day of living out the narrative that you've been engaged in writing, largely unconsciously, for years? The reason it's the latter for each of us is that our minds and brains are not blank slates but are preprogrammed to process things in the way that we have done before. We are our story. Not the story of our life events, but the story we tell ourselves about the events of our lives.

A life story is a continuously imaginative act. When it ceases to be imaginative, that is, when it's a repetition of the same storylines generating redundant themes, it moves from creation to repetition. The faithfulness to ancient traditions becomes a present redundancy. The geography of the imagination is an ever-changing map.

From an evolutionary perspective, our brains have created neurons and neural pathways to make our repeated behaviors default decisions. This collection of repetitions, our habits, efficiently conserves energy.

Neuroscience helps us know more about that story that we write daily, and even specifically how we write it. Every choice we make is consistent with that story. Whenever we buy a new car, a trip, or a ski jacket, it fits with the story we tell ourselves and activates the part of the brain that determines our sense of self. This invented self is a composite of all experiences and attributions, especially the downloads of influences from others, over a lifetime.

Our identities are the stories we tell about ourselves. This identity is a composite set of beliefs about what we can and can't do, what we will and won't do. One of the strongest forces of our psyches is that we remain consistent with that self-definition. We each have a model of how we get our needs met, and how we feel life should be. This personal blueprint—our story—governs how we perceive and process things, and the meanings we attach to whatever happens to us. When we encounter something that doesn't fit our story of how we feel life should be, we have to change either the blueprint or our story.

The Tao teaches us that nothing is meant to be. There is no predestination, no cosmic puppeteer at work. We are solely responsible for our own actions. When we construct circumstances and a story, such as helping others, the good lasts for a long time. When we construct circumstances and a story that is not beneficial, such as falling far into debt, the bad will also last for some time. Both lasting situations arise from our own actions—a causality, not a destiny. It is not destiny at work but causality. At each moment we create whatever we think, feel, and experience.

Story as Cartographer

If stories come to you, care for them.
And learn to give them away where they are needed.
Sometimes a person needs a story more than food to stay alive.
—Barry Lopez, *Crow and Weasel*

Tens of thousands of years before books and computers, we transmitted our essence and principles by story. Story linked to the past, organized the present, and illuminated the future. Story allowed us to connect with each other's humanity in the paths crossed on the long journeys out of Africa to populate the rest of the world. Then the anatomy and physiology of our brains grew by putting thoughts and feelings into stories. Stories informed, instructed, inspired, governed, and organized.

Priests and shamans knew what psychology would later confirm: If you want a message to burrow into a human mind, work it into a story. For millennia before the innovation of writing, story occurred when a teller came together with a listener. In more recent times with the printing press, and still more recently with technology, story continues its ancient function of binding people together by reinforcing values and cultures. Story makes us citizens of a global village, the glue to define and hold groups together.

Story is the most powerful way humans communicate. Story gives birth to possibility. Stories provide a way to resonate with our earlier selves, connect with others, and create a roadmap to proceed.

It has been said that the secrets of great stories are the secrets of the mind. Unlocking these secrets awakens the power of story in us. Work with that power, James Bonnet tells us, and we can steal fire from the gods.

A story can transcend language, time, and culture. Our brains are wired to need and enjoy stories. And a story has both an emotional and cognitive influence on our beliefs and decisions. Stories motivate and persuade, appealing to our emotional capacity for empathic connections with others.

Our stories orient, guide, instruct. The narrative we construct steers our lives.

Storytelling

Personal stories and gossip make up 65 percent of our conversations.
—Jeremy Hsu

The magical incantation of a beginning story immediately seizes our attention. *Once upon a time* . . . is essentially irresistible at any age. Engaging a story activates hardworking parts of both our minds and brains.

We all love stories; we are born to them. They affirm who we are. We want these affirmations of who we are, these validations of our being, that our life has meaning. Nothing has greater affirmation than when we connect with stories. Story both crosses the barriers of time and creates unity between ourselves and others.

Every word is a dab of paint on a pointillist canvas; each alone has no meaning, but the evolving image becomes captivating. The analogy is imperfect, for the information of the scene is not on the canvas: The color, shading, texture, and nuances are in our minds, co-created by the catalyst of the author's evolving story.

We supply the emotion. When young Petya is killed in battle in *War and Peace*, Captain Denisov walks slowly away from Petya's warm corpse, puts his hand on a fence, and grips the rails. We are not told by the storyteller that he is sad; we never read of his tears. But we know. It is our sadness, our mirror neurons that resonate with the unspoken tears of Denisov. Our imagination as a reader serves as catalyst.

Storytelling is one of our most powerful techniques to communicate and to motivate. The simple story is more successful than the complicated one. Our brains learn to ignore certain overused words and phrases that previously made stories compelling.

Storytelling is about connection, a connection between the teller and the listener. Rather than a fixed form, storytelling offers a series of choices of how to connect the narrative with the listener. The listener is drawn into the story because he or she can see the teller seeing the images, feeling the feelings, and experiencing the process.

The challenge of a story is to be fully present in the story, in the moment, as you tell it. When we visualize our stories, and see them unfolding in front of us, a number of things happen. The listener's brain activates in the same way that physically perceiving something does. The audience sees the same vision the teller does, to engage in the experience as it is presented. The storyteller moves from image to image rather than word to word.

We speak of a problem, and changing a problem. We speak of changing the story, but the creation of an ineffective story *is* the problem.

Some innovative scientific studies suggest that we daydream about 2,000 times a day for an average of fourteen seconds each. That means we spend almost half of our waking time spinning fantasies. These daydreams include past content and context: things we might have said or done, recalling victories, failures, admirations, and grudges. We imagine different ways of handling conflict, create different storyline endings. And, going forward, we spin fantasies of what may be, of opportunities, possibilities, and visions.

Story touches every aspect of our lives. We use story to understand, to make sense of things, and to remember. Stories are the most effective way to persuade, to provide emotional transportation to move into action.

Attorneys know that they need to develop a story in order to be believable. As does the child standing next to a broken vase. Stockbrokers don't sell stocks, they sell stories. And the best story wins.

Our Brains on Stories

When the woman spoke English, the volunteers understood her story, and their brains synchronized. When she had activity in her insula, an emotional brain region, the listeners did too. When her frontal cortex lit up, so did theirs. By simply telling a story, the woman could plant ideas, thoughts, and emotions into the listeners' brains.

—Uri Hasson

Our brains want to find patterns in our observations, particularly cause-effect relationships. An effective story can take over our brains to the point where we disregard more valid information, including reliable statistics and the opinions of true experts. When we want something to be true, or believe it to be, we gather information that supports that desire or belief. This confirmation bias affects not just the information that we cherry-pick, but also what we actually notice, what registers in the first place.

We know now from the science of storytelling that a story is the most powerful way to activate our brains. When we are being told a story, it activates both the language processing areas and other areas used in experiencing the story's events. Someone tells us how delicious a peach is, and our sensory cortex lights up. If it's about action, our motor cortex fires. A story puts our whole brain to work.

Stories affect us mentally as well as physically. Anne Krendl at the Dartmouth brain lab showed how viewers' brains resonated with the specific emotion enacted on the screen. When the central character was angry, the viewers' brains registered anger as well. When the scene was sad, the viewers' brains corresponded. Whenever we seen a scene of disgust, it triggers the brain region of our disgust, the anterior insula.

Neuroeconomists find that we make a purchase when the product activates a part of our brains that orchestrates our sense of self—our identity.

Scientists viewed the brain function of subjects on an fMRI while they read an exciting passage from various books. The scans showed that the subjects' brains lit up in specific areas corresponding to the description in the passages. For example, when the story characters were grabbing objects, motor neurons were activated; vision-related neurons fired when the characters were observing their environment. We aren't passive when we read, and our brains turn on "scripts" based on real world experiences, so that reading is like remembering or imagining a vivid event.

We are designed by nature to enjoy stories. Evolutionary psychologists find that our brains have a hardwired affinity for stories. This capacity provided early humans a significant advantage over other species. Humans can describe their experiences, and others can learn from them. Fiction simulates human problems. But mostly we want story simply because we enjoy it.

As many scholars of world literature have noted, stories revolve around a small handful of master themes, universal predicaments of the human condition. They are about sex and love, fear of death and challenge of life, power and subjugation. Everything that happens from making coffee to having the flu ties to the great predicaments.

Dream stories work on resolving matters while we are asleep. Even in nighttime language, dreams are self-stories with plot, theme, scene, character, point of view, and perspective.

The first rule of telling stories is to give the listener an emotional experience. The heart is always the first target, meaning the portal of entry is the amygdala. Metaphor and analogy, the most effective ways of doing that, are building blocks to evoke images and activate memory with all its rich synergy and emotional associations. This brings the listener into the story as co-creator.

As recently as 1996, neuroscientists at the University of Parma in Italy noticed that certain neurons fired when a monkey performed an action, and they also fired *in exactly the same way* in another monkey who simply observed the action. This revolutionary finding of mirror neurons provided a brain basis for understanding both empathy and social connection.

Mirror neurons are not specific cells, but are a function of actual networks in different parts of the brain that reflect the behavior and feelings of others.

Mirror neurons help us directly and indirectly imitate actions and create experiences. Stick out your tongue at a newborn baby, and the baby will immediately return the gesture. A baby smiles and her mother smiles back. Mirror neurons are instrumental in acquiring empathy, language, and social behavior. This mirroring activity explains how children download beliefs and behaviors beginning in the first years of life. Later, for example, we experience and download models of various behaviors, including how our parents handled money, the behaviors, messages, attitudes, biases, meanings, and regard of money.

Mirror neurons help us to understand emotional and social contagion. If we see a person being poked with a needle, our pain neurons fire as if we were being poked. Our neurons fire at the exact location as those in the protagonist. We unconsciously resonate with what we witness, ranging from movement, to behavior patterns, to yawning. Movies and novels allow us, because of mirror neurons, to have empathy for the characters, know how they feel, and experience the same feelings ourselves.

When we hear a story, we simulate it in our heads. When we imagine events or sequences, we evoke the same area of the brain that is activated in the real physical activity. When people imagine someone tapping on their skin, they activate the tactile receptive area of the brain as if it were actually happening. When people drink water but imagine that it's lemon juice, they salivate more.

Mirror neurons enable us to empathically understand, to appreciate another's point of view, and see ourselves as others see us—a form of self-awareness. Stories become virtual reality that parallels the joys and dilemmas of human life.

Peter Pan stays in Neverland, refusing to grow up. Although we're not as flagrant as Peter Pan, we never stop pretending. We simply change how we do it. We read novels, have dreams, see films, dodge bullets with Jack Ryan, get wide-eyed with a magic trick.

Narrative is more than a literary device; it's a brain device too. We create ourselves through narrative. Vividly narrated stories activate the same brain areas that process various components of real life experiences. Brain imagining technology shows that we borrow from our own knowledge and experience to resonate with the sights, sounds, and movements described in a narrative.

Princeton researchers monitored brain activities in pairs of subjects while one told the other a story. When the subjects were empathically connected, neural activity in their brains became synchronous. As soon as the listener ceased to pay attention or there was an empathic rupture between the two, the synchrony immediately stopped.

Studies have shown that a story's power provides the knowledge of *how* to act as well as inspiration and motivation *to* act. A *creditable* idea makes people believe; an *emotional* idea makes people care; a *stimulating* idea prompts people to act. Stories are highly correlated with entertainment. When a child says, *Tell me a story,* the request is for entertainment, not instruction or information.

But the audience is not in a passive role. They are drawn into the author's world, or the cinematic story. We identify with the protagonists. An idea is a fact, but when emotion is added, it makes people care. We feel something.

The Storytelling Mind

It is important to realize that what one neuron tells another neuron is simply how much it is excited.
—Francis Crick

The storytelling mind is as allergic to uncertainty and randomness as it is addicted to meaning and causality. In creative and imperfect ways, we find meaningful patterns in the world. Even if they do not logically exist, we will impose them. We will churn out a story, or manufacture one when it's not there, to explain the perceptions originating in the midbrain.

Our hunger to find meaningful patterns can create false links of cause and effect. Our minds seek closure to end uncertainty, and our brains pursue completion to end dissonance. Never mind that it may be coincidental rather than causal. Many studies have shown how we automatically create stories from the information we read; even if there is no story there, we invent one. *The market is feeling expansive on the heels of news from the Fed. The economy is contracting its outlook until Mideast tensions settle.*

Neuroscientists postulate that the primary reason for existence of the conscious mind is to find or create data to make a logical, acceptable sense of the perceiving mind, the midbrain.

Psychologists asked a group of shoppers to choose among seven pairs of identically priced socks. They inspected the socks, made their choices, and were asked to give reasons for their choices. They explained their choices on the basis of color, texture, and quality. In reality, all seven pairs of socks were absolutely identical. The pattern and their preferences that they were unaware of is that they tended to choose socks on the right side of the array. Rather than say they had no idea why they chose the socks they did, they invented a story that made their decisions rational. The stories were confabulations, honestly told lies.

Those with short-term memory deficits make up stories to fill in the blanks of memories. This confabulation creates continuity and a sustained story without any stumbling points or holes to fall into.

We are storytelling animals. Wherever we go, we want to leave behind not an empty space, but comforting trail markers of stories. We keep making up stories to orient and guide us, to make us feel secure with our ignorance. As long as there is a story, it's all right. In our last moments, even if it's in the split seconds of a fatal fall or when drowning, one sees the story of a whole life passing rapidly in review.

Story as Personal Construction

> *A story is the only way to activate parts in the brain so that*
> *a listener turns the story into their own idea and experience.*
> —Uri Hasson

Our memories are not precise records of what actually happened, but reconstructions of our experiences of what happened. Many of the details, both large and small, are unreliable.

Although unreliable, memory is a self-serving historian to soften sharp edges and airbrush the pores and blemishes of harsh realities. We become the heroes of our own epic story. So much so that we always look less attractive in photographs than we do in mirrors. In mirrors, we can selectively focus, unconsciously pose, raise our eyebrows, and lift our jaws to obviate wrinkles and bags. We arrange ourselves until we are a flattering image of ourselves.

Thomas Gilovich surveyed a million high-school seniors to find that only 2 percent thought they were below average. Academically, 60 percent thought they were in the top 10 percent, and 25 percent thought they were in the top 1 percent. Invincibility bias—that seemingly inextinguishable sense of immortality that peaks in adolescence—still has whispers in adulthood. Some adventures in this error include that 19 percent of people believe they're in the upper 1 percent income bracket; 75 percent of people believe they are healthier than average; 90 percent of people believe they are better drivers than average; 94 percent of university professors think they are better than average at their jobs.

Stories featuring positive illusions keep us from yielding to despair.

Studies have revealed that those who perform better on tests of empathy are more easily transported by a story. This ability to put ourselves in another's shoes allows us to discern the intent, motivation, awareness, and mental states of others. Children develop mentalization—the theory of mind and the ability to think about thoughts—around age five. Once we develop a theory of mind, we can imagine minds in others, and make stories of things. This means that we attribute intentions and motivations to people and to things in the world around us. A study by Jonathan Gottschall at Washington & Jefferson College found that stories of people around the world possess universal themes that reflect common underlying biology.

Stories are vital to learning, as well as for developing relationships. We keep tabs on people, understand them, and spread information by storytelling. A story makes a comprehensive and complete narrative of both mind and brain. We practice social skills and promote social cohesion by stories. People more readily accept ideas when their minds are in a story mode versus an analytical mindset.

We tell ourselves stories to convert events and observations into an integrated whole, to give meaning to what we experience. The processor in our left brain seeks to explain events to make sense of scattered facts. These explanations are actually rationalizations based on a miniscule portion of the things that make sense in our consciousness.

This interpreter function, our built-in storyteller, generates explanations about our memories, perceptions, and actions—and the relationships among them. The result is a personal narrative, a story that confers an experience of unity, a sense of self.

There's a significant comfort being inside a story arc. At times we can tolerate the anxiety of a challenge because we know a resolution will come. Stories both move and motivate us because we see in them the echoes of possibility for ourselves.

One of my storytelling mentors told of an encounter he had at a Chicago airport. A woman stopped him to tell him how impressed she had been four years earlier when she attended a presentation he had made, saying that it had stuck with her and made a significant difference in her life. He asked her to remind him the subject that he had presented.

Her response? *Oh, I don't remember what you talked about, but I'll always remember that story you told.*

One of the most successful ways to get someone's attention is to begin with a mystery story, or a question that invites the reader or listener into the material to engage the question or solve the mystery. Curiosity happens when we feel a gap in our knowledge. Good marketers know how to begin with the listener's pain points, the challenging, unanswered questions. And then move to the product's benefits.

When we raise a question, we ask the participant to join in a journey whose ending is unpredictable. This sustains interest. Curious to answer questions and close open patterns, the listener wonders, *What will happen next?* and *How will it turn out?* Mysteries create a need for closure. The brain strives to end the dissonance, while the mind strives to bring closure to the story.

This gap theory of curiosity says that our tendency to tell people things and convince them of something should begin with opening a gap: a question to illuminate a gap in knowledge, a challenge to predict an outcome.

To communicate more effectively, we may need to shift our thinking from *What information do I need to convey?* to *What questions do I want my listener to ask?* Curiosity and interest stem from gaps in knowledge. But to emphasize that knowledge and gaps exist, some known knowledge often needs to be highlighted first: *Here's what you know. Now here's what you're missing.*

I recently read a story about psychoanalyst Dr. Kurt Lewin, a well-known and published clinician. It immediately got my attention, because he is my psychoanalytic grandfather. In psychoanalytic training, a subspecialty of psychiatry and psychology, each psychoanalyst has to undergo his or her own psychoanalysis as a component of the training. Kurt Lewin was my training analyst's psychoanalyst. (My analytic great-grandfather was Freud, but enough digression and genealogy.)

One day in 1927, Dr. Lewin finished a meal with colleagues and called the waiter over to ask for the check. The waiter immediately told him how much his group owed. A few minutes later, on a hunch, Dr. Lewin called the waiter back and asked how much their bill was. At that point, the waiter had no idea. His curiosity piqued, Dr. Lewin and his colleague Dr. Bluma Zeigarnik then ran experiments in her lab to follow up.

She had people perform a number of little tasks, such as solving puzzles, interrupting some of them halfway through. She then asked all of her subjects which activities they remembered. Her conclusion was that people tend to remember incomplete or interrupted tasks better than completed ones. This observation is now widely known as the Zeigarnik effect.

This effect has been used both in academia and advertising. It helps us understand why unsolved problems are so addictive, the allure of mysteries, how suspense keeps audiences interested, and how marketing can be more effective. Leaving something incomplete makes it more memorable.

The most effective speakers leave the audience with a question, something to think about. This keeps the process of inquiry alive.

This has even been known to induce readers to . . .

The Clues to a Great Story

Frankly, there isn't anyone you couldn't learn to love once you've heard their story.

—A statement TV's Mr. Rogers always carried in his wallet

The greatest story commandment: Make me care. Intellectually, aesthetically, emotionally. We scroll across scores of movie channels and suddenly stop on one. Something about it is compelling. We care.

All good stories give a promise in the beginning. A promise that it will be worth our time. We invite the listener to join the campfire of the story.

Storytelling, like life and life stories, has guidelines, not rules. A strong theme always runs through a well-told story. All well-drawn characters have a spine: an inner, dominant, unconscious quest that they're striving for—an itch they can't scratch. Michael Corleone in *The Godfather* wanted to please his father. And there are other spines, not all of which lead someone to make good choices: to find the beauty, to prevent harm, to do what is best for my child.

The brain has a feedback mechanism that rewards the acquisition of knowledge. We are programmed to quest for new information. The University of Southern California's Irving Biederman found that pleasure receptors in the brain fire when people process new visual stimuli. Seeing something new increases activity in that area of the brain, stimulating the reward system. We unconsciously seek things that are rich in information, and that are novel. *People experience a neurochemical reward when they acquire new information.*

We learn best and respond best to *specific* stories, such as testimonials, much more than data compiled from many people across a wide range of situations. The brain's preference is for *trusted* stories. If someone we know tells the story, it will be even more credible and potent than a celebrity or a paid endorser. An anecdote is far more interesting and relevant than statistics.

Mother Teresa said, *If I look at the mass, I will never act. If I look at the one, I will.* A story is inherently more persuasive than statistics. An anecdote capitalizes on the power of narrative and holds more sway over us

For a story to be powerful, persuasive, and memorable, it needs to induce empathy in us. Donations increase, both in amount and percentage of responders, when the appeal moves from the abstract to the specific. Response to an appeal for "A famine in Ethiopia" was enhanced by 25 percent by a photo of "Rokia, a seven-year-old who faces a threat of severe hunger or even starvation." *Donations increased 66 percent* when the story and photo appeared without the famine data. Statistics reduce empathy and interest in giving. A study from Princeton found that people give less when they're thinking analytically.

Life As Story

*Caring for people often takes the form of concern for their stories,
not for their feelings.*
—Daniel Kahneman, *Thinking, Fast and Slow*

Consider the danger of having a single story of anything. The danger is the illusion that it is the only story, rigidifying perception into a finite container.

When author Chimamanda Ngozi Adichie recently spoke at a university, a student told her it was a shame that Nigerian men were physical abusers like the father character in her novel. She responded by telling him she had just read a novel called *American Psycho* and it was a shame that young Americans were serial murderers.

She could give this clever, facetious response because she had more than a single story of America.

If all facts or characteristics are compressed into one story, the process can create racism and prejudice, a stereotypy both incomplete and inaccurate. A single story can dispossess and malign; multiple stories can empower and humanize.

We think in stories and tell stories throughout the day. We frame our narrative in terms of supporting characters—spouse, children, colleagues, and friends. At times, adversarial characters also occupy positions.

We classify our lives in chapters of past and present, getting married, raising children, current career, and relationships. Tragedy and triumph are events as a well as plot lines.

Despite being natural storytellers, with brains wired for stories, a few of us actually tell our stories to ourselves—step out of our stories to figure out what they're about. To recognize that we are actually writing the script, that whatever we think, feel, and experience, we create at each moment. To understand the rules we've chosen to guide that writing. To reflect on the challenges we face, and how we can turn them into possibilities and strengths. To plan the next chapter.

It's hard to be objective about our own stories. An internationally known figure was discussing this topic with me when he said, *You know, Dave, I don't know how to tell my story to myself in order to know what to change.* Additionally, people may be afraid to question their storylines because of what they may discover.

Ample evidence shows that changing a strongly held belief has little do with facts, even with logic. The best method, whether we're changing our minds or someone else's, or leading a group, is emotional, persuasive storytelling. Stories are more powerful than data because they allow us to identify emotionally with ideas and people otherwise disregarded or seen as outsiders. We tend to align with people who share our identity, even if the facts disagree. Once we care about a character in book or a leader, we will find a way to fit that character or leader into our identity.

We now know that our minds are not designed to be changed by evidence and argument presented by a stranger. Ideas will be considered much more readily when there is emotional, persuasive storytelling and when we can identify with the storyteller.

Writing a new story doesn't change the past, its facts, or narrative. The most powerful component of writing a new story is the mindfulness to be fully present in each moment.

A Final Challenge

Write the truest sentence you know.
—Ernest Hemingway

If your life were a nonfiction book, what would the current chapter be called? What would be its theme?

Write your genuine life story. Write the truest story possible. Who you are is what you're creating this moment. Your story is yourself, your life, and what will survive you. At some point in the distant future, all that will be left of you, all that will survive you, is your story.

Make sure it's the best one possible.

Serendipity

The Invisible Bridge

The princes were always making discoveries, by accidents and sagacity of things, which they were not in the quest of.
—*The Three Princes of Serendip*, a Persian fairytale

The three princes of Serendip (known today as Sri Lanka) were sent by their father, the king, on a journey to test their suitability to reign. Along their way, they met a camel driver who asked them about his lost camel. Each of the three was able to describe a camel in significant detail: *Your lost camel is blind in one eye. It is missing a tooth. It is carrying butter and honey.* So accurate was the description that it raised suspicions, and the princes were thrown into jail. Later they were pardoned when it became clear that they had merely connected many separate observations together to produce an uncannily accurate story.

On their travels, the princes had seen grass eaten from one side of the path and reckoned an animal blind in one eye must have been responsible. Grass was scattered unevenly, so a tooth must have been missing. The ants on one side of the road indicated the presence of butter, the flies on the other side of the road honey. The story continues along similar lines as each twist sees the clever princes combine seemingly casual observations—things that most people take no notice of—into something meaningful.

The word *serendipity* surfaced two and a half centuries ago when Horace Walpole, son of an English prime minister, mentioned *The Three Princes of Serendip* who made happy, unexpected discoveries by accident. However, anything but chance or randomness is responsible for the outcome in the original story.

The Science of Serendipity

In the field of observation, chance favors only the prepared mind.
—Louis Pasteur

Although discoveries at times depend on chance, an essential component is that the chance observation is viewed by a receptive eye and considered by an open, informed mind.

What may look like luck or a happy accident in reality is the result of depth experience—casting a broad net in a hard-working synthetic process to generate conclusions or findings not necessarily predicted. Serendipity and innovation are siblings, almost twins.

Serendipity corresponds more, however, with innovation and hard work rather than happy accidents. The ingredients of innovation include determination, informed work, intuition, and openness to relationships not necessarily sought or immediately explained by cause and effect. A thread weaves its way through all four: Keep an open mind. And never stop believing in yourself.

One of the greatest serendipities of history occurred when Columbus planned to reach the Indies and happened upon America.

One day in 1945, Percy Spencer was touring one of the laboratories he managed at Raytheon in Waltham, Massachusetts. It was wartime, and this laboratory supplied radar technology to the Allied forces. Spencer was standing by a magnetron, a vacuum tube that generates microwaves to boost the sensitivity of radar. He felt a strange sensation and checked his pocket to find that his candy bar had melted. Both surprised and intrigued, he decided to send for a bag of popcorn and held it next to the magnetron. The popcorn popped. Within a year, Raytheon applied to patent the microwave oven.

The history of scientific discovery is laced with breakthroughs that came about by accident. In 1928, Alexander Fleming noticed how a mold that floated in a Petri dish killed off surrounding bacteria. Foreseeing the significance of this stray spore, Fleming turned his observation into innovation in the discovery of penicillin.

Fortunate, possibly accidental discoveries abound in the history of medicine. In 1630, an Indian laborer in Peru accidentally ingested quinine, a liquid from the bark of a cinchona tree while suffering a malarial fever. It cured his fever. Similar discoveries produced smallpox vaccination, x-rays, the treatment for anaphylactic shock (resulting in a Nobel Prize for Charles Robert Richet, a French physiologist), the role of insulin in diabetes, and the Papanicolaou smear for cervical cancer. Each medical discovery occurred when two aspects were concurrent: the active pursuit of a question, though unrelated, coupled with keeping an open mind.

In pursuing the science of serendipity, innovation consultant Matt Kingdom has found that until members of an innovation team recognize their expertise, biases, and knowledge gaps, they will find it difficult to listen openly to others.

Engineering Serendipity

The seeds of great discoveries are constantly floating around us, but they only take root in minds well prepared to receive them.
—Joseph Henry, American physicist

Serendipity is often interchangeable with innovation, as they are very similar concepts. Serendipity, the synthesis of seemingly unrelated points, is the useful and innovative application of connections. Innovation is the creation of new value, with a very similar meaning. Serendipity may simply be how the innovator's journey feels from the inside. One of the first steps is to approach with a beginner's mind, to not be bound by conventional wisdom or expertise, to *unlearn* all that may limit thinking in order to immerse in provocative stimulation. What may seem like a lucky series of coincidences is really the result of a great deal of hard work.

There is a high level of cooperation among different parts and systems of the brain to orchestrate a process that produces creativity. When an external system parallels this process, innovation can result. Unintended outcomes can be engineered by planning the encounters and interactions of people from disparate areas and disciplines.

Technological innovators have recognized the role of serendipity and sought to engineer it by designing buildings and workspaces to foster chance interactions. A Google real-estate chief described how at Google they sought to maximize *casual collisions of the workforce.* Google attributes the genesis of projects such as Gmail, Google News, and Street View to engineers' fortuitous conversations at lunch.

Yahoo and Google see serendipity as largely a byproduct of social networks and interactions. When close-knit teams who do well at tackling the challenges in front of them expand to connect to others, complementary ideas can emerge. Steve Jobs designed the Pixar headquarters with central bathrooms so that people from around the company would run into each other.

Thomas J. Allen, a professor of management and engineering at M.I.T., found that setups with colleagues unable to view each other led to a state of out of sight, out of mind. He found that people are four times more likely to communicate regularly with someone sitting six feet away than with someone sixty feet away, and almost never with colleagues separated by floors or buildings.

Companies are no longer leaving serendipity to chance. Their managers are thinking of new ways to encourage interactions among employees who normally don't traffic together. The hope is that increased contact, including face-to-face chats among people with different skill sets and experiences, will spark new ideas and lead to new solutions.

National Public Radio now holds Serendipity Days in which about fifty employees from different departments volunteer to come together and think of new ideas and projects over a two-day period.

A New Beginning

> *Serendipity is looking for a needle in a haystack and*
> *finding the farmer's daughter.*
> —Julius H. Conroe

Sometimes a new beginning arises from careful and conscious effort, but at times, although we think we take charge of our lives and plan carefully, important new beginnings have a mysterious and sometimes serendipitous quality. Some of the most important beginnings take place in the darkness outside our awareness.

Two years after my divorce I was at an authors' conference in Austin, planning to leave on Saturday after the last session. I had just enough time to drive to my weekend ranch between Austin and Houston to catch the sunset. One of the principle measures of the quality of my life is the number of sunsets I can enjoy at the ranch—on the porch with a cigar and single-malt scotch in the late quiet of the day, watching the sun set over the lake and trees.

For no apparent reason, I decided spontaneously to stay for the social hour at the conference, a wine and cheese event. Nothing in particular was binding me. I had already met and conversed with everyone I intended to see. And I knew the quality of the wine was not a compelling feature.

There, I met my future wife. Two years later, with her children and mine attending, we would marry on that same porch I never made it to that evening, at sunset.

It's the ending that makes the beginning possible.

There will always be things we don't plan that change our lives: things we don't want to happen but have to accept; things we don't want to know but have to learn; people we can't live without but have to let go; things we can only get ready for after they happen.

Synchronicity

The Hard Work Miracle

In between two or more people lie a foundation of archetypal truth, and a tribal, relational field where psyches intersect in a mysterious yet rather common way.
—Tess Castleman, *Threads, Knots, Tapestries*

Synchronicity is a synthesis of meaningfully connected events that may not be logical, conscious, intellectual, or explainable by science or physics. Yet, with exact correspondence, these events may no longer be relegated to pure chance but considered as meaningful arrangements without clear reason or causal explanation.

In Jungian psychology, synchronicities refer to meaningful coincidence as evidence of the collective unconscious. Jung believed that people as well as all animate and inanimate objects are linked through a collective unconscious. This is not a garden-variety coincidence that can easily be explained and thus dismissed, but a manifestation of the tribal psyche. In quantum physics, Einstein referred to the unified field theory: Each person is a bundle of energy and interacts with the energy field of another person, as well as to the energy field of the group as a whole. That each of us, through our energy fields, interacts with the other includes the awareness that the researcher affects whatever he or she studies, even at the particle level, just as the observer interacts in each moment with the events being observed.

The manifestations of an interactive energy field, synchronicities, appear regularly when we are alert for them, when we have coded our radar for their possibility. This intangible energy field is elusive to conceptualize and define, yet there are certain methods to examine possible meanings and connections involved in a synchronistic event.

Western science, via sophisticated and complex methods, addresses the same barely comprehensible solitary meditation of the eternal Tao. Both share common themes: the unity and interrelationship of all phenomena, and the essentially dynamic nature of the universe.

Synchronicity, a meaningful coincidence, finds expression in our daily lives. To live in harmony with our purpose and depth—to align needs and ideals—creates a path for synchronicities to occur.

To consider the connections in our daily lives among others, the universe, and ourselves offers a larger and more encompassing possibility than logical reasoning and concrete facts. Events, dreams, and happenings that may seem to contain deeper meanings provide confirmation that we are on the right path, as well as to provide information when we are not.

While there are no rational explanations for these situations, often a thought, dream, or inner psychological state coincides with an event. As an example, a researcher, stumped at a crucial point, needs some obscure, highly technical information and at a fund-raising dinner is unexpectedly seated next to a person who happens to have that information.

To recognize and accept synchronicity may allow us to feel connected rather than isolated, part of a dynamic interrelated universe, rather than only engaged in an individual journey.

There is a privileged access to participate in a synchronistic event. It is a special challenge for the intellectual and the scientific mind, as patterns of underlying oneness are neither visible nor logical. Yet consider how the stars are not visible in daytime, yet are still in place. If we consider not favoring a certain kind of consciousness at the expense of another, we may allow that we have different ways of thinking, perceiving, and experiencing, just as we have, globally, two brains, a right and left, emotional and logical.

Goethe observed that we murder what we dissect. We kill the vitality, the spirit, and deny the soul of something that we require to be processed through our left hemisphere's logical, intellectual workings.

In a very oversimplified and general way, synchronicity is a tendency toward patterning in the universe whose essential profoundness and importance may not be fully grasped intellectually.

Essays on the subject are difficult reading, beginning with Jung's initial paper on the subject, *Synchronicity: An Acausal Connecting Principle*—a concept impossible to grasp by intellect alone, requiring an intuitive facility. Synchronicity was initially a descriptive term for a link between two events connected through their meaning rather than explained by cause and effect.

A synchronous event is one that is simultaneous, events that occur at the same moment. Clocks and schedules are synchronized. To really appreciate a synchronistic event would be to personally experience an uncanny coincidence and feel a spontaneous emotional response, with accompanying feelings such as chills, awe, or warmth. Additionally, there is no way to account for the coincidence rationally or by chance.

The Uncommon Journey

The intellect can understand any part of a thing as a part, but not as a whole.
It can understand anything which God is not.
—R.H. Blyph

There are three types of synchronicity. First is when there is a coincidence between mental content, such as thought or feeling, and an outer event. An example is when someone anticipates an unspoken wish or need, and suddenly the wished-for object, such as the specific food or flower silently desired, appears.

I had the experience, as soon as I began my faculty position at Baylor College of Medicine after my residency, of wondering what my original anatomy lab partner was doing, planning to contact him and catch up with his parallel beginning of an ophthalmology practice in another state. When I was taking an elevator at the major teaching hospital, the doors opened and there he stood. He happened to be there to be evaluated for a specialized medical procedure known to this hospital, and was planning to contact me.

Second is when someone has a dream or vision that coincides with an event taking place at a distance and is later verified. An example includes knowing when a child is in trouble in a distant city, or when someone has died, and receiving a confirming call.

Third is when someone has an image, such as a dream or vision, about what will happen in the future, which then occurs. An example is when a parent knows what gender an unborn child will be and prepares accordingly.

We fully appreciate a synchronistic event when we personally experience an uncanny coincidence and feel a spontaneous emotional response to it. We remark about the event, and experience the awe of there being no way to account for the coincidence rationally or by chance. Causality, having to do with objective knowledge including observation and reason, does not apply or explain synchronicity.

To appreciate cause and effect, we need to observe outer events and think logically. Causality is distinguished by logically explained and essentially repeatable sequences of events. To appreciate a synchronistic event, we need to notice an inner subjective state, such as a thought, feeling, intuition, vision, or dream and to intuitively link it with a related external event. Synchronicity is this co-incidence of events that are meaningfully related to the individual.

An American psychiatrist who had lived and practiced in Singapore for a number of years because of her husband's business position was moving to Houston and had decided to seek psychoanalysis. She initially consulted me and began analysis after settling in and beginning her own practice.

As the analysis unfolded and we worked on issues that included aspects of her body self and image, she mentioned a book she had used in a teaching course to healthcare professionals in Singapore. She described how helpful this book was to her in dealing with some initial body image issues for herself. She mentioned the title of the book, *Integrating Body Self and Psychological Self: Creating a New Story in Psychoanalysis and Psychotherapy.*

I asked her if she knew who the author of the book was. She said, *Yes, it was David . . . Oh my God, that was your book I was teaching from! Here I am in analysis with you. I don't believe it.*

We discussed this synchronicity and her recognition while in analysis, and only after my question did she consciously link her previous and current experience, and the common denominator.

Synchronistic occurrences become mirrors to reflect back to us an aspect of ourselves. We need to look and see what it is, what the pattern tells us, and what the promise is. As we have drawn certain people and events into our lives, we may then be able to complete the story of their connection.

The Group Field

The whole is greater than the sum of its parts.
—Fritz Perls

The process of groups and the development of group wisdom is a widely appreciated phenomenon, especially with well-chosen group members coupled with an experienced and knowledgeable group leader. The development of a working alliance and group cohesiveness allows the wisdom to emerge.

The power of groups can be magical, as many professionals have observed. When people come together to share a common goal, work on problems, and support one another, they find that their power is greater than any of the members has individually.

A significant aspect of this phenomenon is that the group forms a field—a collective energy in which ideas, focus, creativity, and passion emerge. Often while we focus on content, this field of energy is the process that becomes powerful in and of itself and allows everything else to be held in its container. Within this crucible, the energy field develops a power of its own. I have experienced this in doing Mentor Coaching groups and Mastermind groups, and it occurs equally when done by telephone, where all of the group meetings occur by teleconference. The group itself, this crucible of the energy field, is often taken for granted and ignored because the focus of the group is on the collective problem solving.

In the simplest concept, we are affected by one another. When people come together to form a group, the group itself forms its own entity, its own personality, which is to say an invisible energy field. This field establishes a foundation that can become an essential theme, like having a personality of its own. And each group is unique. It seems not to matter what the purpose or mission of the group is, or its composition, for this unifying strength to solidify. The group can be composed of leaders who want to make a difference, or it can be composed of significantly wounded people with disabilities or tragedies wanting to support each other.

Tess Castleman, a Jungian analyst, wrote in *Threads, Knots, and Tapestries* of one form of synchronicity whereby group members consistently had an uncanny habit of dressing in the same colors or the same clothing for their meetings, without ever discussing or planning to do so. A commonality or theme becomes ubiquitous in a close group, where, for example, her groups who did dream work would come to dream along similar thematic lines. Castleman noted an uncommon number of coincidences and interweaving of the members of her groups that defied conceptualization. These synchronicities became very real as a single event, or at times as overarching themes and common experiences.

Group phenomena such as mass hysteria, herd mentality of buying or selling stocks, social contagion of ideas and behaviors, product adoptions, and this collective energy field and its dynamics can explain mass movements.

A group process is always at work, whether that group is a coaching group, a fourth-grade class, a neighborhood, a church, or a family. The group process is evidence of the collective energy field—the tribal field at the unconscious level—that has a purpose and intent, as well as an evolutionary movement. Just like the individual human psyche.

Messages Delivered

We are something we can't know.
—Michael Eigen, *The Psychoanalytic Mystic*

The individual unconscious is often aware of one's own energy field in a way to know something before there is conscious awareness. Someone can have a dream, often initially in symbolic form, that depicts awareness of what is happening in the body totally outside of conscious awareness.

An example from my psychoanalytic practice many years ago is one patient, a woman executive, who dreamed of having an infestation in her garden of a particular type of bug that was invisible, yet these bugs implanted themselves in her larger plants and would infest the plant, unseen by the human eye, until the plant became symptomatic. At the point of her reporting this dream, I inquired about any physical symptoms or unusual happenings in her body that she might have dismissed. She mentioned a slight soreness in her chest below her left breast that was barely noticeable except when she moved her left arm in a particular way when she worked out. She had dismissed it as a muscle strain. I suggested, on a hunch, that she have a mammogram. Although neither of us could come up with any logical explanation for this, she both trusted my judgment and believed enough in my hunch to do it. When she did, a very small nodule was found that, when biopsied, was cancerous. This nodule could be successfully extracted because it was in such a nascent phase.

Another woman revisited me almost two years after we had done a few months' work on performance enhancement for a professional sports competition. Thriving in her sport, with recent lucrative endorsements that were both exciting and demanding, she now wanted a brief booster shot of our previous work for an imminent international competition. Once in her presence, I experienced a barely perceptible flatness about her that seemed slightly different from what I recalled as my previous experience of being with her. She was vaguely aware of the same experience but had dismissed it as caused by the extreme demands of time and energy from both the competition and her expanded schedule. She had had a recent physical exam that showed glowing health, yet this barely perceptible flatness manifested as slightly less than the vibrant enthusiasm with which she usually approached her life and her sport, where she had an international presence. Although her present enthusiasm for life was what most people aspire to, yet in her, something felt different to me.

Simply on the basis of an intuitive hunch, I suggested that she consult with a neurologist with whom I had worked closely. The neurologist was an astute diagnostician, especially in areas of the interface of mind and brain, that border between the neurological and psychological occasionally crossed by some happening to become manifest. We had referred patients to each other a number of times before, and respected each other's hunches that at times could barely be approximated by scientific explanation.

In his first studies of the athlete, the neurologist discovered an ependymoma, a small growth in her right forebrain. After further investigation he indicated that it was the earliest detection of an ependymoma in any published study in neurology. Neurosurgical intervention could be done quite successfully with no residual issues for her.

Both these cases, solely based on an intuitive hunch, are examples, I believe, of this energy field that can exist between two people when one is attuned to the possibilities of reading subtle signals and believing even more subtle intuitive blinks.

In psychoanalysis, dreams are usually considered internal dramas in symbolic ways, as well as that the dream components represent aspects of self. Another consideration is that dreams prepare for the following day, to prepare one ahead of time for things that are not known in usual, logical, and conscious ways. In this way of thinking, the unconscious can collectively perceive and assimilate information from the energy field that is not consciously known, and help in preparation for dealing with upcoming events.

As a research tool, Castleman and her followers recorded every dream each one of them had for one year. Then, at the end of the year, each of them would read the dreams, noticing patterns, recurring images, and people with whom the dreamers interacted. The dreams were reviewed for clues ahead of significant events, and clues ahead of time about relationships and transformative events over the year.

Tess Castleman reports an example of this phenomenon. An analyst and friend of hers had the following dream: *I am in the bayou in Louisiana and two crabs jump out of the water and each bites one of my hands.* Shortly afterward, she reports, the dreamer discovered he had cancer in both lungs.

A reported example of the unconscious power of an energy field giving rise to a new creation was the not uncommon phenomenon of a patient in analysis having either dreams or fantasies of pregnancy and of giving birth. For men, it was usually of simply having a baby. Regardless of age and life circumstance, these individuals were able to discern their metaphor for the birth of a new, healthy, viable self with nothing missing—their experience of creating and nurturing a new beginning through the analytic work.

Dreams also represent aspects of the dreamer's self and developing new story. They incorporate the tribal energy of relationships in the dreamer's circle of peers and colleagues.

Patterns Woven by Synchronicity

No one can stand in these solitudes unmoved,
and not feel that there is more in man than the mere breath of his body.
—Charles Darwin, *The Voyage of the Beagle*

Each of us has a natural resistance to patterns and forces of the unconscious, which is often a necessary aspect of the evolution of our life force. We want to deny or minimalize negative possibilities and want to live each day believing, at one level, that we will live forever, though logically knowing, at least in an abstract way, that this is not true. We believe in the abstract notion of death, but with the caveat that it is not something we'll deal with now or have to come to terms with until later. We often disregard even relevant and instructive messages, from intuitive hunches and dreams, to actual physical symptoms, especially if they counter our positive, even omnipotent and omniscient fantasies.

A common example of the awareness of an energy field from another is to be inexplicably aware, at an event, of *feeling a person's stare.* This can happen from across the room, and when you turn to actually catch the person staring, the unexplained sense is validated. This common human experience is often dismissed because there is not a viable scientific explanation for being able to feel a person's curious stare. There are no measurable brainwaves or logical sequences to explain such a phenomenon.

This unified field theory, or tribal field, of energy of people and groups emphasizes our connectedness to others and to ourselves. The intersection of mind, brain, and psychic energy happens in an unexplained way to form a force field as real as it is logically undefinable.

The collective energy of a group, when specifically focused and directed, can explain why professional sports teams, no matter what their current record, lose over twice as many away games as home games playing the same opponents. Away games subject them to a huge force field of negative energy, in the same way home games do to positive energy.

At certain presentations and retreats, I have done an exercise to request a volunteer to come in front of the group. I will ask the volunteer to stand with his or her left arm extended, parallel with the floor, and to resist my efforts to push the arm down. With sufficient force, I am able to push the arm down with my hand. I then ask the group to send this person totally positive energy, good thoughts, and wishes for a powerful physical presence. When I attempt to do the same thing, I cannot push the arm down with one of my arms. I then ask the group to send this person negative energy, negative thoughts of any nature, and when I ask the volunteer to resist me pushing the arm down, it is so weak that I can push it down easily with one finger.

This communal field and synchronistic contact with one's self and others is experienced by many people, often simply noted and dismissed, yet very real. Two people sensing a distress or a positive synchronicity serve as common examples of this phenomenon. It explains how someone we haven't spoken to in years suddenly calls at the very time we are thinking about the person and wondering what they've been up to. Or the parent who calls a child at college in the middle of the night with a sense that something is wrong, at the very time the child is experiencing a specific distress or unusual circumstance. Sometimes we label it intuitive or package it in other ways that allow us to believe we understand it, in order to dismiss it.

Those who have psychic experiences are often more attuned to this tribal field than the average person. Often the people who have psychic abilities have had a window of opportunity opened early in their lives, sometimes by some significant psychological traumas, which have activated a portal to this ancient and fundamental aspect of their psyche.

This collective energy field interweaves minds and psyches at a layer below and beyond ordinary consciousness. It is how a good friend can sense that something has gone wrong despite a thousand miles of separation.

A Collective Voice

Every person,
All the events of your life
Are there because you have drawn them there.
What you choose
To do with them is
Up to you.
—Richard Bach, *Illusions*

A group, however defined and constituted, serves as both a container and a focus for the individual and collective energies of the members. The group can be for any purpose: training, support, coaching, entertainment, education.

Carl Jung indicated that synchronicity in itself is neutral and reflects the amount of energy that we have for an endeavor. The energy is not positive or negative, good or bad, but present as a force field. Synchronicity does not itself predict outcome, but the energy when directed can significantly *affect* outcome. The energy is neutral and functions as a natural force without judgment.

In a group, one person may subliminally sense what is not spoken and become the voice of that collective unconscious.

I have seen this phenomenon occur at some boards of directors meetings in which a negative feeling would exist about a situation or person, though no one was actually explicitly expressing it. What was not being discussed was almost palpable, yet nevertheless unpoken. Finally, when one member of the group would speak for this position, it crystallized the awareness of other members so that they then could oppose this person without being consciously aware that they were opposing part of their own disavowed position. The person who spoke for the collective unconscious of the group would then be extruded or marginalized, as a way for the group to deal collectively with a point of view that they did not want to own.

A close knit and well-functioning group, whatever its type and purpose, often finds how members' processes intersect and interweave like notes in a symphony, and their experiences as well as their energies function in harmony and with congruence.

There is a well-known dynamic in family therapy in which one person in the family plays the role of the identified patient. This person captures and enacts unconscious and thereby unspoken aspects of others in the family as an accurate and often exasperating mirror. The same dynamic can be seen in groups of all sorts.

One's inner desire, collectively manifest in the communal field, is the energy of the self. It emerges in uncommon and unplanned ways, often not linear, logical, or intellectual. Because it is subtle, it is inherently difficult to describe and may manifest in very quiet ways as slight sensations, intuition, or the most subtle of perceptions. These soft inclinations, the brief insights of small moments, are often how we discover our essence, of who and what we are.

These energy fields are fertile grounds from which can emanate meaning and fulfillment. Synchronicity confronts our linear understanding of the nature of time and space. A benchmark of appreciation consists of an openness to consider and receive, to break out of preconceived notions. It can help us make ready for things, or be aware of things previously unregistered.

From one perspective, this is our instinctual brain, not bound by linear time or external reality, continuously contributing to a tapestry of energy from which we can grow and develop. This internal force consistently pushes toward greater awareness and our understanding. Its instinct, to survive and thrive, is a life force of powerful energy.

Synchronicity Emerges

> *The only thing I know for certain is that something is moving.*
> —Albert Einstein, when asked if he knew anything for absolute certain

People in a group can increase their chances of health and wellness more than through a singular effort, for example, through such support groups as Alcoholics Anonymous. The power of a group, through the assimilation of a collective energy, can do significantly better things than any member of the group could do alone. Astonishingly evil and astonishingly heroic acts are examples at either end of the spectrum.

A group, especially one with a common purpose and focus, can embody an otherwise mysterious element of power by the collection of energies and the resulting synchronicity.

An illness can signal trouble or disruption, but it can also inform about unconscious developments that are significant. A number of times I saw young women develop anorexia nervosa at a point when they perceived their parents were on the verge of divorce. Though unconscious and unplanned, this common focus on a daughter's wellbeing served to unite the family.

Synchronicity illuminates how our human behavior both reflects our internal reality and mirrors the energy of the relationships in our larger field as we interact with one another. This connectiveness internally and externally contributes to the interrelationships in ways that sometimes defy words and concepts.

At the heart of synchronicity is the unknown, the mysterious that puzzles us because it transcends our rational and logical approach.

We often find that things become much easier, with more internal synchrony, when we follow an inner wisdom. The necessary component of following this flow is to have a compass rather than an aimless lack of orientation and purpose. To consider synchronicity is to see ourselves as far more interconnected with one another. The meaningful coincidence of synchronicity, the mysterious correspondence of seemingly unrelated events, not explained in usual scientific ways, nonetheless has its own principles.

The collective energy field is all the relational energy that we feel, energies that form the foundation of our sense of self.

Self

The Bedrock Story

What is the ultimate truth about ourselves? Various answers suggest themselves. We are a bit of stellar matter gone wrong. We are physical machinery—puppets that strut and talk and laugh and die as the hand of time pulls the strings beneath. But there is one elementary inescapable answer. We are that which asks the question.
—Sir Arthur Eddington

Body Self

The mind had to be first about the body or it could not have been.
—Antonio Damasio, *Descartes' Error*

The infant searches swirling, formless surroundings for a knowing touch, a lock with parent's eyes, affirming a fortifying form and confirming a grounding presence, the essence of human attachment. This hope is relational, linked with soothing flesh and satisfied mouth, to become the building block of the psychological regulation of physiological needs and the foundation of trust. Later, from this foundation of affiliation and effectiveness, excursions of exploration and assertive curiosity occur, allowing separation with affirming rapprochement.

The gentle whisperings and soft murmuring echoes of sensation are outlined and contained as the infant's body is held in total suspension by the strong hands of another who knows that safety and passion are no paradox. To be wrapped in an encompassing cocoon of gentle vitality is simultaneously intense and calm. These sensory experiences (or their unmet yearning) are reactivated throughout life; the desire evolves but never evaporates.

Significant caretakers define the infant's body by interactive attachment, mirroring, outlining, and resonance with both surface and interior. This relational matrix organizes and gives meaning to body self. From before birth, there is an intersubjective dialogue, a fantasized relationship unfolding that already begins to fashion the nascent self. Later, the child's body shapes and co-authors the relationship with parents, and they to the child.

The foundation of the early body self is formed by contact with the surface of the caretaker's body, including skin, voice, and eyes. All five senses bridge from one body to the other, as later these same senses create an internal bridge between mind and body. The shaping and containing of the infant's body creates the initial experience of embodiment, the fabric and shape of body self. The embodied self evolves in psychic representation to a psychological self, ultimately an integration of mind and body.

In the beginning of life, there are no words. Words are not necessary for the original self of the infant—the body self—or for early communication. Before language exists, we communicate nonverbally: facially, posturally, gesturally, affectively, and kinesthetically. Sensations are first bodily experiences, and only later shaped into words.

Earliest developmental needs speak to state changes, desires, hungers, satisfactions, and actions. These undifferentiated bodily experiences, largely engendered and nonverbal, imperfectly translate. We acquire verbal language ontogenetically and phylogentically relatively late.

The self and emotional processes are always and inherently embodied, co-created within a relationship, continuously revised. There is no realm of thought, feeling, or action that can be conceived without bodily engagement and expression. Even purely verbal exchange involves the gendered body, the body self, and the senses. The extent to which we experience feelings within a mental state rather than solely as body sensation depends originally on primary caregivers facilitating, identifying, and accurately labeling feelings and somatic experiences. To do this, the caretaker must take the child as point of reference, rather than projecting himself or herself onto the child.

The regulation and alignment of states is dependent on accurate parental attunement to the child's signals and sensitivities well before verbal language. This attunement and engagement at a preverbal/nonverbal level is a foundation for internal connectedness of mind and body, of human-to-human relatedness. These attachment patterns create the procedural (implicit) memory of self, self-states, and self-in-relation to another.

In the adult, nonverbal communication accompanies every word: posture, gesture, countenance, body rumblings, voice changes, and quality. Even silence expresses loudly. The body has its own dialects, its own channels of memory. The body of memory, the body of fantasy, the body we create, and our actual body may each be different, and each may be determined in part by issues outside the body. Fundamental emotions may remain embodied, the perceptions communicated in concrete physical terms.

The body appears in the narrative of dreams, metaphors, symptoms, symbolic visions of inner landscapes, mysterious structures and configurations, and geographical terrain. An idea as well as a fact, the body contains and serves as conduit for the emotional, a visible Rorschach blot onto which we project fantasy, meaning, and significance. Our internal self creates and houses our body image, the map within the actual territory of the body. We regard our bodies through a gender filter, a default perception that operates continuously.

The unconscious is inscribed just as it is embodied. While the unconscious is located in the medial limbic structures of the brain, it originates from the skin, from the appearance of the body, and from the perceptions of notable others about one's body, including attractiveness, functioning, and abilities. Body and body image are the mutual creations of meaning and flesh, revealed and constructed in relationship, inscribed by original caregivers and important others, then subjectively articulated. Gestures, needs, somatic affects, and attachment patterns belong to the depths of time when there were no visible islands, no shore as boundary, only shadows, yet living simultaneously in each present moment. The distinction between creation and discovery ever remains overlapping.

Psychological Self

Moments when she came home to her body in ways she never had before—
moments when she felt its aches, varicose veins and wrinkles so intimately and
gently that she groaned with a happiness she could never describe. Fleeting
seconds when Vivi knew that her body, and all its imperfections, was her own
lived-in work of art. She lived there and she'd die there.
—Rebecca Wells, *Divine Secrets of the Ya-Ya Sisterhood*

The self that seeks embodiment and the body that yearns for a residence
in the mind integrate throughout life. The subtleties of mental states are
interwoven with inchoate bodily states. For our entire compass of experiences, words alone aren't important enough. The mind and body murmur,
whisper, shout to each other; their mother tongues speak many dialects.

The compass of registered feelings assumes their developmental recognition and differentiation. The child looks to the parent to see the
parent seeing him or her. The accuracy of the empathic attunement by
caretakers is crucial, as it is the initial linking of mind and body experiences. If the caretakers are not accurately and consciously attuned to the
infant, the basis for a mind-body division (nonintegration) is formed,
inhibiting one's ability to "see the world feelingly," as Gloucester indicates in *King Lear (IV.6.151)*. An emotional literacy evolves with its own
language for feelings and internal experiences by accurate labeling from
essential caretakers, developing roadmaps of internal and external experiences throughout this developmental journey.

The interactions with caregivers continuously define body self and psychological self-awareness. Inadequate or inaccurate empathic attunement
by the caregiver lessens subjective and self-reflective awareness. When
aspects of a child's experience are invisible to a primary caretaker, the invisi-
bility extends to the child. The child who does not see parents seeing her has
difficulty seeing herself. For example, boldness in a little girl may be actively
shaped into submissive cuteness by critical suppression, or indirectly by
subtle cues to subjugate assertiveness. Talents may not register on the radar
screen of a parent, or may even be actively inhibited by criticalness.

A sense of having a boundary between the self and the world, of being within one's skin, with a solidified sense of self is established through interaction with attuned others. As a cohesive sense of self evolves, the boundary between mind and body dissolves into a seamless integration. In present time, empathic attunement and accurate labeling of physical and emotional states are necessary to identify, differentiate, and desomatize affect, to develop an emotional literacy, and to experience effectiveness and mastery.

Superordinate Self

The self is our only natural means to know the mind.
—Antonio Damasio, *Self Comes to Mind*

The brain composes a sense of self from a consortium of facts, sensations, and experiences. We add pieces as the self evolves organically, continuously fashioning a unity built on the foundation of body self, constructed by the psychological self, and furnished by illusions. We have a medley of different selves that always accompany us. Each of those individual selves, as well as the superordinate overarching self, is all-important.

A specific region of the left forebrain specializes in personal self-narrating actions and thoughts: the brain coordinate of our sense of self. This interpreter function is the glue that keeps our stories unified to create a cohesive sense of self.

Our minds synthesize an autobiographical self that is capable of reflective self-awareness and of continuously gathering knowledge. For this synthetic wisdom to be both understandable and transmissible, storytelling provides the crucible. Whether something fits a personal storyline—the identity theme of the autobiographical self—determines its permanence. That which doesn't fit the narrative thread gets extruded (*not me*), or more probably just doesn't register on our personal radar.

The self consists of both the conscious and unconscious minds, of psychological self and body self, and the superordinate self to integrate all components. We continuously evolve, change, and add new information.

Earlier selves remain housed in a container of time and place, preserved carefully to avoid rearranging. Some traumatic memories may remain imprisoned in that capsule of time and space, bound within the invisible container of a specific state of mind originally designed to sequester toxic experiences. Like the immune system that erects a wall between self and nonself, a traumatic memory is cordoned off to preserve the purity of the remainder of the system from contamination.

Our brains and our immune system know who we are and, at least equally important, who we are not. A stressful experience can trigger hormones that suppress the immune system to create vulnerability to invasions of nonself such as viruses, or to turn against the self at times to blur recognition of self versus nonself to create an autoimmune response.

(In)Visibility

> *The mind does not dwell entirely in the brain.*
> —Diane Ackerman, *A Natural History of the Senses*

When the caretaker, through nonattunement or incorrect reading, renders a child's feelings invisible, subsequent aspects of the child's internal world remain silent and undifferentiated, or confused and conflicted. Emotional experience may then have to be defined in outlining its shadow by obsession, or illuminating its reverse image by denial. At times we may engage something the first time by denying it.

When essential others in the caretaking environment have not resonated with or responded to these fundamental needs, regions of experience remain undefined for the child, awareness muted, the body self and sensations unsymbolized. These missed experiences and unmet needs become an abiding question, and nonidentification can fashion an organizing yet unconscious assumption of defectiveness, or of shame. Shame results from failing to live up to parents' ideals, and later to one's own. Parents must co-construct the ideals to be internalized by the child by praise, affirmation, and validation in defining *good enough*. Failing this process, *good enough* then remains elusive, not internalized as one's own ideal.

Children do not have to be possessive of the mother if they already truly possess her. They only become possessive when they recognize that, indeed, they do not possess her, that she does not respond as if the child is entitled to her. This sense of belonging, then, cannot be taken for granted or metabolized as an internal secure attachment.

The failure of empathic attunement by a caregiver leads, in the child, to non-awareness of nuanced feeling. Psychosomatic symptoms can temporarily splint an otherwise unintegrated mind and body, as well as effectively elicit care and responses by a parent. These limitations of articulating and communicating feeling then compromise reflective self-awareness and affect regulation.

Every child attempts to make his or her parents normal. The child of the depressed parent will try to fill and fix the depressive emptiness; failing that, a palpable problem may be offered to the parent who can now feel effective. Someone can become symptomatic in order to accomplish this mission. When essential developmental needs are invisible to parents, a core belief of inadequacy fuels a continuous quest to affirm value and worth, to create mirroring and validating experiences of the self. Later, even when that child has become an adult, validation and affirmation through remarkable and consistent success does not eradicate the core organizing assumption of defectiveness. The seeming validity of defectiveness etches even more firmly when positive, affirming responses and successes do not change the basic unconscious assumption. The vertical nonintegration remains, as the internal disavowal becomes, *If they only knew who I really am*, or *They just don't know the real me.*

The parent may be unable to resonate accurately and consistently with the infant's internal experiences, or respond to the subtleties of emotional and physical experiences, movements, and affects. Given the caregiver's empathic unavailability, the child's experience does not become a point of reference. When the caregiver responds inconsistently or selectively to only certain aspects of the child's experience, and when touch and secure holding do not accurately define body self, the child cannot develop a reliable body boundary and sensory awareness. Later, the child's body self development and awareness is incomplete, and body image is distorted.

The projective drawings of body image of such individuals are distorted, without shape, with blurred boundaries, and excessively large. Their body images often fluctuate with their mood and state of mind, oscillating several times a day, body image becoming unrealistically large when experiencing a depleted or disrupted *self* image.

Powerful emotion can override the usual neuronal configuration to dissolve temporarily the usual sense of self into a *not me/I wasn't myself* reaction. With enough repetition, a state of mind can specifically organize and circumscribe an emotion and its set of experiences. In anger and terror, we all become young.

An important aspect of caregiver function throughout childhood is to receive and accept, to contain and regulate, to modulate and detoxify the child's tension and feelings, especially the more intense and disruptive feelings: to have all aspects of the child's experience visible. The mutuality of interaction requires this regulation of state of mind in order for the child to accept ownership of feelings and, ultimately, to recognize authorship of all internal experience.

The child locates herself in her mother's eyes, movements, gestures, touches, words, and expressions. She may not be able to find herself in the vacant dissociative stare, or she may lose herself in efforts to evoke response from the inattentive parent, absent of empathically resonant words or hugs.

Or, if the child looks to the mother's face and sees a blank stare, this foggy mirror cannot fully reflect back specific experiences to provide needed affirmation. When this inaccurate or unavailable mirroring occurs, the child may forfeit necessary components of emotion and expression, disallowing mind and body connection and continuity.

If aspects of the child are invisible to parents, these unmet basic needs fuel yearnings reactivated throughout life. Desire never evaporates. After childhood and adolescence, unfulfilled needs become wants (and then you can never get enough of what you don't need). Or, an aversion may be constructed to counter intense yearning, for fear that it will not be seen or felt.

If confusion, failure, pain, or trauma become familiar experiences in childhood, an atypical burst of feeling good or of success creates discontinuity, often requiring a return to the familiar.

Failure to integrate body self and psychological self may result in disembodiment, feeling uncontained, without shape, substance, or boundary, a blob, nothing, invisible, or dissolved. Empathic nonattunement to the internal experience in the child's early development fails to establish an internal point of reference for self-reflection and self-attunement.

Action Language

If I could tell you what it meant, there would be no point in dancing it.
—Isadora Duncan

In the absence of accurate empathic attunement by caregivers, feelings continue to be expressed internally as a body state or experience, for example, a churning gut as expression of upset. Later, feelings then register only when embedded within an action sequence, for example, experiencing aliveness only when engaged in a physically stimulating action such as risk or sex.

Endless somatic language often serves as a counterpart to using the body in action sequences, with corresponding action language: heaviness, weighted down, dullness, deadness, lightness, buoyancy, floating, lifted up.

Physical pain becomes a tangible reminder of the control that one has lost and attempts to capture in a body not experienced as one's own. Pain can become an identity crystallized, illness an identity visible.

Some procedural memories not paired with conscious awareness or verbal icon remain as bodily experiences. Limitation to action may occur when the awareness and vocabulary of feelings remain foreign, when feeling has been traumatically infused with action, or when activating a somatic pattern or even a chaotic, disorganized attachment pattern. The body then speaks a literal language, such as purging, pain in the neck, weeping or irritated skin, hyper-tension, dis-ease. The message contains the message. The language of the mind ranges from simple to symbolic as we attempt to conceptualize unformulated experiences, to give specificity to inchoate desires and experiences, and to make the complex as tangible and lucid as possible.

When the body cannot be naturally integrated to become a part of the self, it remains in the foreground, accentuated by asceticism and alienation (such as fasting or self-mutilation), the instrument of action symptoms (such as the addictions), the subject of narcissistic invest-ment and excessive rumination (such as body dysmorphic disorder), or brought into focus unwillingly and unwittingly (such as by pain, physical illness, age, or weight).

Body as Narrator

Some individuals, unattuned to their feeling world and who do not have the full psychological representation of self, make their bodies the narra-tor of what words cannot say, of sensation for which there is no lexicon, and of feelings they cannot bear in their conscious mind. They cannot quite imagine what is absent and use action language to engage its essence by enactment.

How does it feel? may render muteness, while *How does it make you feel like acting?* or *What does it make you want to do?* gleans knowing responses. The one questioned may not know the very experience that is defensively avoided by embedding it in an action sequence. Before registering feeling, he or she may have to speak an action language: *I feel like running/smok-ing/drinking*, or somatic language: *I feel my stomach rumbling.* For some individuals, affect may be both undifferentiated and unformulated, acces-sible only through action and action language. The subsequent awareness and differentiation of feelings is a stepwise process of registering messages from the body's interior, identifying the feeling, translating it into recog-nizable experience, then into shared verbal narrative.

Lacking an ability to distinguish the nuisances of emotions, and without a cohesive body image, these individuals elicit self or body aware-ness as well as regulate affect by the *felt experiences* of their own bodies, such as self-stimulation, compulsive exercise, physical risk-taking, eating disorder, substance abuse, or self-harm. All of these action symptoms are intended as compensatory, as valiant efforts to self-regulate tension, to change the way one feels.

These individuals describe the sense of never having lived in their own bodies, never authentically inhabiting them. Their bodies do not seem their own, remaining unintegrated rather than a seamless aspect of the self. They speak of their bodies as an observer, without a sense of ownership or habitation, of mind and body as separate entities. In some instances, eating, exercise, or other self-stimulating physical activities attempt to create a sensory bridge *in order* to feel and to inhabit their bodies. The body speaks in action experiences, not symbolically encoded and perhaps not subjectively distinguished such that it can be communicated in verbal language.

The Somatic Stage

In addition to expressive and self-regulatory functions, some somatic scenarios may be the enactment of split-off, otherwise disassociated aspects of the self, or of feelings not allowed in the conscious mind. These emotional tallies from inside the cave of the body may be the encryption of a glossary of experiences of an unintegrated mind and body, including body-image disturbances, hypochondriasis, thermal sensitivities, eating disorders, weight regulation, obesity, self-mutilating episodes, and other trance-like states of depersonalization or derealization associated with the body. The body's language has many dialects, many subjective translations of psychic messages into dramas on the somatic stage.

The dilemma for those who have not yet fully integrated body self and psychological self is that they're unaware of what they do not feel and cannot find a way to express not knowing. In this regard, not only is empathy a resonance with another's internal perception and experience, it is also an informed guide to certain experiences as yet inchoate, even unimaginable. To recognize basic sensations and state of mind, and to approximate an experience with words, one must have an internal point of reference. Fundamental sensations and feelings must be identified and differentiated. At certain moments the most important function of a significant other is to register the individual's affective experience and put into words an otherwise unformulated subjective experience. In this regard, empathy at times may be an act of imagination of how someone would feel if they *could* feel, a guide to certain experiences as yet unimaginable by that person.

With failure of this initial embodiment, to not live in and experience one's body as one's own, one of several maneuvers may then be created to augment or supplement this needed developmental experience. Stimulation of the body by such substances as food or alcohol, or such activities as excess exercise or risk-taking, creates awareness of body self experiences in order to anchor, organize, or avoid. The activity, substance, or object may be used to reduce tension and for ersatz nurturing. Repetitive focus on tangible, physical feedback may be necessary to register self-experience, even to feel real. Psychosomatic symptoms may create the affirming validation by way of pain or feedback of the reality of the body. An individual may turn to his or her own body to create such satisfaction in various ways to self-stimulate, even to self-harm. Various symptoms of self-harm use the lexicon of the body in action language to articulate experiences inchoate and unformulated.

With physical and emotional intrusiveness and overstimulation by caregivers, primitive protective measures mobilize to develop a higher threshold to stimuli, a tuning-out, or a withdrawal. The threshold to register experience is then raised, requiring a more intense or extreme experience. Remedies crafted include anorexia nervosa to differentiate and control the body, excessive exercise to establish distinctness and physical mastery, compulsive weightlifting to establish a firm body outline, or various actions that force recognition, such as exhibitionism.

Future Self

> *I am the interpretation I project onto reality.*
> —June Aspell, *Seed* magazine

Several thousand people were asked in a study to predict how much their values would change in the next ten years, and how much their values had changed in the last ten years. At every age, people vastly underestimated how much change they would experience over the next decade. Most of us can remember who we were ten years ago but may find it hard to envision who we are going to be.

Time is a powerful force that transforms our preferences and reshapes our values. We are always making decisions that profoundly influence our future selves. We know our genes do not necessarily define who we are, or who we become. We come closest to understanding the self—who we are—through the narratives we weave about our lives.

Our brains are wired to the present, alert to pleasure and immediate threat. We are pulled to quick gratification and have trouble visualizing our future selves. We engage mental time travel to plan activities, to rehearse situations, to prepare for contingencies.

This sense of ourselves persisting across time results both in our ability to re-experience as well as pre-experience events. Pre-experiencing involves our imaging what an activity might feel like in the future. It is a type of prospective memory, a future thinking in which we can picture ourselves doing certain actions, being with friends, traveling to specific places. This future thinking allows us to project ourselves forward in time to imagine an actual experience. Different from active planning, it distinguishes us from other animals (we think).

Our vision of the future amalgamates relevant memories and experiences to imagine a future context and its possibilities. This active construction previewing future events relies on our repository of memories to combine reconstruction and imagination. Remembering the past and imaging the future involve remarkably similar neural signatures.

We differ in the degree to which we focus on our past, present, or future. While people who live in the present enjoy spontaneity and freedom of in-the-moment styles, those who are present-oriented are at times more likely to engage in risky behavior.

People who are able to envision their future selves save an average of two to three times as much for their retirement years. Those who can best visualize and most identify with their future selves plan their lives with longer-term payoffs in mind. In addition to saving more money, they engage in healthier nutrition and exercise practices. Envisioning our future selves, the essence of feeling connected with the future self—of who we will become—can guide our behaviors in the present to create longer-term rewards economically, physically, and spiritually.

We retain a constant optimism about our future selves. For example, most people up to the age of 75 believe that their future will be better than their past. Emotions are usually stronger when imagining the future than in recalling the past. We have an optimism that we will have more time in the future, so we readily postpone a task until later. We imagine that a year from now we will have an ordered life and have time to fit in extra activities. But to consider the same for next week, we wouldn't possibly take anything else on. Optimism about free time in the future can potentially lead to procrastination.

The Wise Self

> *Health is the ability to stand in the spaces between realities without losing any*
> *of them. This is what I believe self-acceptance means and what creativity is*
> *really all about—the ability to feel like oneself while being many.*
> —Phillip Bromberg, *Standing in the Spaces*

Lynda is a well-known, multiple-bestseller author who initiated a Mentor Coaching session by presenting two exciting, though quite different possible courses of action. Both were great opportunities for her: one, a series of retreats in a Caribbean resort, and the other a sequence of speaking engagements arranged by her agent. The retreats were a particular love of hers, an extension and application of ones that she had done throughout North America. The speaking engagements required a good deal of travel, but would expand her reach and sales to still newer audiences. They involved essentially the same time period, and both required energy and travel that took away from her primary love of writing at her office, a seaside cottage an easy walk from her home.

Both choices—retreats and speaking engagements—appealed to her sense of adventure, and both were especially lucrative, offering several times what her writing would bring. She recognized that she did not need to make more money, but both the retreats and presentations enticed her. She had worked very hard and very successfully to have such elite choices. She, and then we, had examined all of the benefits and drawbacks of her various options, and she was very clear about what they entailed. She was drawn to the significant money she would make, yet something still felt unsettling to her, as she acknowledged that she did not really need the money.

We had worked earlier on preserving and protecting the essence of her energy, such as at times when she appeared publicly and would inevitably be recognized and people would want to talk with her, want her autograph, and want to engage in conversations and take pictures with her. Even something as simple as a shopping excursion brought some depletion of her energy, taking a toll on her creative endeavors so that she needed to recharge when she returned home. So even routine matters had to be strategically planned.

I recommended for her current decision that she plan and schedule a self-reflective exercise. For this scheduled appointment with herself, I suggested that she begin with a progressive relaxation exercise. Once she was totally relaxed, I suggested she not focus on anything other than her relaxation and her body, to move beyond the competing voices of the options, exciting opportunities, enjoyment of fame, desire for solitude. To move *underneath* her conscious role, identity, and successes to resonate with her true self, emotions, and needs. To listen to the loving, caring essence and to the deep, intuitive wisdom of her Wise Self.

Lynda reported at our next session that she found the exercise revealing. She found the experience of accessing her Wise Self to closely parallel the state of mind and reverie of her writing.

She recognized that her great desire was the creative engagement of the next writing project she had already outlined, and the demiurgic energy that she experienced in her primary love.

She knew that she needed to say *no* to both the retreat and speaking projects, and to engage the writing project that was her deepest desire. As she embraced this decision, her dilemma melted away, and she experienced her authentic enthusiasm and creative excitement.

When not blocked by emotional neglect, the Wise Self is essentially a state of mind of compassionate reflection and progressive mindfulness. Access to this state allows awareness of all other states of mind, a gift of pure, present reflection for future reference.

The Wise Self can be accessed and developed through practices of self-awareness, self-reflection, and self-compassion through enhanced empathy with one's self. These mindfulness practices enhance the functioning of the prefrontal cortex to develop this sense of a Wise Self that can then serve as guide.

The Wise Self is an imaginary, yet very real, guide embodying balance, wisdom, resilience, even patience. Like a vision of success that one lives into, this Wise Self can house ultimate aspirations to serve as guide to achieve them. A mentor as well as beacon, it embodies internal ideals and external models. From this position, one can shift focus among different states of mind throughout the day. States of mind can be recognized, assessed for authenticity and utility, and best fit for a particular task.

The Wise Self is an internal guide, an advocate with a perspective of wisdom that transcends impulses, imperatives, and usual logic. The Wise Self can understand both desire and motivation, and advocate decisions in one's best interest that align with the true self. The Wise Self has the deepest internal reference point possible, the antithesis of fitting into what others want, or the imperative of what one "should" do.

An internal force, a state of mind transcendent of other states, it is able to take a superordinate focus and perspective. The act of refocusing with the Wise Self in mind strengthens the resonance and belief in the true self.

Questions can be posed to this Wise Self and then listen intuitively for answers.

This ultimate mindfulness and empathic resonance with one's self can become the highest order of reflective wisdom, of understanding and resolving complimentary and collaborative paradigms.

The Wise Self will even give direct messages and communicate reciprocally. Perhaps even give you her name.

Feelings

The Truth Takes Flesh

The truth takes flesh in the forms that can express it.
—Emerson

Feelings reside in the details, in the tiny cracks and crevices of each moment. Rather than the wide-angle observations and abstractions, it's the intricate and exquisite close-up focus on specific matters that reveals one's affective, nuanced soul and character. Feelings not understood are like the horse leading the rider, sometimes at a gallop, sometimes at a very slow walk, but always the dominant force. Other intense, unintegrated feelings create pain at that raw, rubbing border of mind and body.

Feelings, the subjective experience of emotions, must eventually translate into the language of the mind. They must originally be empathically recognized and resonated with by caretakers in order for a child to have emotional registry and understanding. When a feeling has not been identified or coupled with a descriptive language, it remains encrypted in the body. Feeling organizes, encodes, and files memory. Feeling and its resonance retrieve specific and nearby memories.

Feelings are ultimately the perception of a particular state of the body coupled with certain thoughts or language to represent them. A feeling experience, such as sadness, is experienced in the body alongside the mental representation of loss. Pleasure, perceived by sensory maps of the body traveling predetermined neural pathways, associates with mental images specifically connected with particular enjoyment. Certain emotions, especially shame, have a value coding of unacceptable or unwelcome, so they are camouflaged and rendered invisible to perception.

Our connection to the past is unidirectional. Incidents and experiences from the past come into the present sometimes to an extent that makes the present and past indistinguishable. Yet we can never reenter the past. The illusion of returning across that threshold to redo the unsatisfied or rectify the unrequited may be enticing, but it is perpetually deceiving: forever in pursuit, yet uncertain what exactly is being sought. The barrier of that passageway into the past is invisible, yet very real. The most intense suffering is not in remembering past traumas, but in limitations of this present moment. To be able to remember the past, rather than to perpetually relive it, we must distinguish the boundary between past and present.

When a feeling is abandoned by defense or disconnection, the space created where the feeling would have continued instantly fills with memory of action, thought, experiences, or expectations from the past. The occupant of this space left vacant in *stopping present experience* is then perceived to *cause* the subsequent experience; rather, it is the *effect* of the stopping. Only when we stop our present experience does the past inhabit the space created. With a signal of discomfort or pain, movement to another software program (state of mind), complete with its own set of beliefs and assumptions, instantly occurs.

The Residence of Feelings

> *Everything that is important is invisible to the eye.*
> —Antoine de Saint-Exupéry, *The Little Prince*

Inside each of us feelings have their own place of residence, each dwelling in a room with close, sometimes odd neighbors. Passion may reside very close to sexual excitement, though with space for future expansion. Love visits but does not live with either of these two, and even though nearby, it is always superordinate. Power and attachment both adjoin sexuality, in a fourplex arrangement with tenderness, sharing a common wall for those unafraid of intimacy and juxtaposition of powerful feelings and vulnerability. Fear and its cognitive agent, restraint, block access to passion. Playfulness inhabits a place a little further away, somewhat closer to the top, in a room with brilliant colors, on the same floor as anger.

Rage and sorrow are deeper, in the basement, while shame is boxed in solitary confinement underground, below the basement. In an internal landscape, some other feelings may not seem to reside in the mind at all, but exist in the churning orbit of the gut, painfully housed in the aching head (rather than the mind), in the eyelid's spasm, the weeping rash, the allergic response. Some states have color and brilliance, others have blackness, with an even blacker hole at the center.

Emotional traumas, if unresolved, have feelings residing in a reservoir of unfinished business. These feelings associated with trauma are walled off, like the body walling off an abscess to prevent contamination of the rest of the body. The abscess is active yet segregated, relegated to the hinterland of dissociation so the remainder of the system, uncontaminated, is protected. So it is with events that resonate emotionally with those walled-off injuries, to signal a warning pain with any touch too close to the lesion. Viewed differently, this awareness announces a need to resolve the residual conflict in order to discontinue the waste of energy in masking awareness. Even when that mask is whimsical, it is dead weight, like an anchor that can't be pulled up when we want to move ahead.

Registering Feeling

Everything in our brain is looking for the cause and effect relationship of something we've previously experienced.
—Jon Ba

An invisible maze of connections exists as a blueprint in the profound darkness of the limbic brain. Receptors await, specialized portals of the feeling system, ready to fit inside and outside into an interconnected whole. Feeling chemicals ignite new neurons, span synapses, cross paths and relay stations to form new patterns of meaning. We only vaguely understand how we assemble that storehouse of meaning into words that match external shapes. We understand less still of the lurking paradoxes crossing in the invisible neural pathways.

Some people may not be able to respond to the question, *How do you feel?* First, one has to take an internal point of reference and *recognize* the inner origin of experience. This internal focus is difficult when the usual point of reference is external, to be affirmed or validated by others. Then, from this internal perspective, the experience itself must *register* as emotion (the whole mind-brain awareness of affect). Focus on the body self and immediate sensory experience may be necessary as prerequisite to awareness of feeling. Feeling, the subjective awareness of emotion, must then be *differentiated*, *indexed* with a descriptive word, and finally *communicated* in understandable language.

Moving from a tangible, specific focus to an internal, intangible scrutiny of experience and feelings is a process. In a relationship, one has to be free to speak of feelings in action language without committing the action, and to have the play/work space in which to do it. As one person aptly observed, *Sounding wild and out of control is the antithesis of being wild and out of control.* Or as Nietzche noted, *The thought of suicide is a powerful solace; it enables a man to get through many a bad night.* For someone who is accustomed to action as a way to register experience, as well as to relieve tension, a contemplative pause and reflection are a challenging anathema, outside usual identity.

Like true feeling, every note in music has a center where the tone rests purely and fully. Those few individuals who have perfect pitch know innately where to go. Everything around the center of the note is still the note, but it is not the best of the note, the richness of the center, the place where great musicians know to go, the sweet spot. To go outside that particular spot is to approximate but not to completely reside inside. Mathematical geniuses are often good at the violin, to successively approximate the note, to feel their way into it. The journey to the specific note by working within an abstract musical structure is mathematical genius applied.

In talking about feelings, and feeling about thinking, words may get in the way. And sometimes words aren't specific enough. Or important enough.

Some disclaimed action, attributed to insignificance or "just happening," makes the author seem like the passive recipient rather than the creator. *The thought came to my mind. My mind refused to think about it. My mind played tricks on me. I couldn't help being late.* These locutions disclaim one's self as agent, as creator of thoughts, feelings, and experiences. Other disclaimers include a slip of the tongue (sometimes attributed to Freud), being late, or various accidents not viewed as motivated, meaningful, and/or intended. Thoughts and feelings do not "occur" to us, nor are we the victim of thoughts or feelings that we create.

Feelings never lie. The body cannot deceive, though it may speak in enigmatic code. Internal positions often polarize around active or passive. Indications of the passive position reveal themselves in language of being the subject of one's decision or feelings: *This just happens to me. My anger got the best of me. My anxiety stopped me.* This language positions the speaker to be the victim of the feelings that he or she generates. A feeling is a verb. For example, anger is not a noun, a reservoir of emotion to be expressed like an abscess for healing to occur; rather, it is a verb, there when it is created. Each of us is the author of our story, of each feeling, and of all that we think, say, and do.

Accustomed experiences and feelings travel along well-established neuronal connections with their predictable neural networks. A neural network contains the template of a particular style of relating, habitual ways of response to certain stimuli in the environment, and specific expression of attachment patterns.

As we acknowledge and own everything about ourselves, and listen carefully and explicitly to all the messages from the interior, we can take ownership of our whole truth.

Feelings Come First

We have so many words for states of mind, and so few for states of the body.
—Jeanne Moreau

We enter and exit states of mind fluidly and invisibly, like the precision baton passage between relay team members. Our familiar repertoire ranges from creative energization and quiet happiness, perhaps through anxiety or boredom, to relaxation. More extreme, reluctantly inhabited states exist: depression, nothingness, deadness, emptiness, overwhelm, and confusion. Feelings, the subjective experience of distinct emotions, are a component of each state of mind.

Feelings always come first and trigger state change. A new experience may feel different, a state of mind that has no history and, as yet, no associations. A changed landscape. For some, relaxation or contentment may not be a place previously inhabited, thus lacking continuity with the past, the known. All the usual states with their familiar content at times may not be accessible.

A state of mind is a psychophysiological state, an internally organized software program of expectations, attitudes, meanings, and feelings. Each state of mind has its own developmental history, its own set of experiences to filter and organize perception. Like each specific software program, a state of mind is a model that determines perception and processing, emotional tone and regulation, access to memory, and behavioral response patterns. The unique software package of each state of mind determines what data are relevant, and once input, how processing occurs.

The regulation of feelings and states of mind involves the understanding and mastery of access to a particular state of mind without altering consciousness to do so (i.e., while "staying present"). Perhaps nowhere is this more poignant than the regulation of mind artists and writers employ to enter a creative state. For example, Dame Edith Sitwell would lie in the stale solitude of an open coffin as a prelude to enter the mindset she needed to write her macabre literature. Other writers create states of mind to fit their intended work: Dr. Samuel Johnson and the poet W.H. Auden stayed in a stimulated state with continuous consumption of tea when they wrote; Willa Cather read the Bible to set the right tone prior to writing; George Sand went immediately from lovemaking to writing; Voltaire used his lover's back for a writing desk; Benjamin Franklin wrote while soaking in a bathtub to focus his thought process; Coleridge used opium before each stint of writing. The painter Turner liked to be lashed to the mast of a ship and taken for sail during a violent storm so he could later recreate this experience on canvas. Some authors play a piece of music repetitively during the course of writing to create an emotional framework to house their evolving story.

The corresponding state of mind of the reader often matches with that of the author, in which the author guides the reader to a particular state through the senses: the music and voice of the words, the texture of imagery, the rhythm of feelings.

Each of us has a continuum of states, with some awareness of what state works best for what endeavor, even of how to enter and exit different states. We become more or less cognizant of which state to enter for a creative endeavor, which state to enter for conceptual planning, and what state of attention and concentration works best for each task from the alertness of a business presentation to relaxation for sleep.

Perhaps the most natural method of regulating state change is distraction, such as jangling car keys to shift the crying infant to a calmer state. One may learn an internal distraction so fluidly that it may appear as an attention deficit problem. Likewise, an individual discerns various ways to reconnect the mind and body, such as by distraction, or building a somatic bridge to engage the senses, such as exercise, a warm bath, or breathing exercises.

Action symptoms of stimulation of the body, such as use of alcohol or drugs, or inflicting self-harm, attempt engagement of the body as foundation of emotional experience and organization. Physical reconnection by these action symptoms establishes only a temporary balance.

How can symbolic language and speech fully describe nonverbal phenomena? Much occurs before a child's verbal abilities appear. Some experiences may be difficult because there has never been reason, occasion, or perhaps an empathically attuned and trusted other with whom to create verbal expression of certain experiences. We are unaware of what we do not feel, and cannot find a way to express not knowing. Certain experiences are not organized enough to retrieve as explicit memory in order to verbally organize them. A procedural memory may not be consciously known, and may be denied or inaccessible simply because it has not existed in a symbolic realm. It is, then, simply beyond description.

And sometimes, despite highly evolved intellect, there may not be the words to say it. Some of life's experiences, such as preverbal life, the spiritual or mystical, or disorganizing trauma, cannot be named and explained. Sometimes a cohesive narrative is insufficient, even when it is possible to explain the complex variations and multilevel impact.

Words are inadequate vessels for some of life, especially for that which should never have been, such as trauma. And words are not enough for that which never was, such as unrequited love.

Mastery

The Story of Effectiveness

Seeds of Mastery

A man should learn to detect and watch that gleam of light which flashes across his mind from within, more than the luster of the firmament of bards and sages. Yet he dismisses without notice his thought, because it is his. In every work of genius we recognize our own reflected thoughts; they come back to us with a certain alienated majesty.
—Ralph Waldo Emerson

Our uniqueness is a seed planted at birth that seeks growth, transformation, and flowering to its full potential. This innate force, an intrinsic motivation to be effective, is the bedrock of our driving force as humans.

I have observed videos of direct infant observation studies by psychoanalysts and developmental psychologists showing that infants as young as three months old have an intrinsic desire to be effective in their environment. When they do, they experience pleasure at mastery. This fundamental motivation permeates everything we do and extends for a lifetime.

Einstein gave us, among many innovations, an understanding of the unified field theory: that each of us is a bundle of energy that interacts with another person's energy field, and with the composite energy field of a group of people.

When Albert Einstein was five years old, his father gave him a compass as a present. Its needle, changing directions as he moved the compass about, instantly transfixed him. The idea of an invisible magnetic force touched him to his core. He would later wonder about other forces in the world, similarly invisible and equally powerful. This simple question of hidden forces and fields became his life's work. He acknowledged often thinking back to the compass that sparked his initial fascination.

Ingmar Bergman was nine years old when his parents gave his brother a cinematograph—a moving-picture machine with strips of film. Ingmar traded his own toys to be able to use it. He took it to a large closet and watched the flickering images that it projected on the wall. Something magically came to life each time he turned it on. His lifelong obsession became the desire to master and produce such magic. The sensation of creating an animated reality became an invisible force in his life.

John Coltrane experienced spiritual and emotional longings that he did not know how to verbalize. As he drifted into music as a hobby, he played saxophone with his high-school band. When he later heard the great jazz saxophonist Charlie "Bird" Parker perform live, the sounds he heard touched Coltrane's primal core. Coltrane desired to find a way to effectively express his uniqueness to give voice to these deep emotions. As he focused on this form of expression, his personal mastery was to become one of the greatest jazz artists of his era, and of all time.

James Hillman speaks of these kinds of discoveries in *The Soul's Code* as the spark that ignites a life calling.

At times we may disregard or lose touch with these signals from our central core. When we connect with this essence, the visceral reaction resonates with our authentic self. Perhaps even a life's purpose.

One of the common features of those who have become true masters is the awareness of experiencing the world differently from others and finding a way to express that uniqueness.

The Evolution of Mastery

> *One can have no smaller or greater mastery than mastery of oneself.*
> —Leonardo da Vinci

For effectiveness to evolve into true mastery, we must submit to a period of self-directed apprenticeship. This practical education and time of developing new effectiveness in mastery occurs each time we acquire new skills, every time we change careers, each entry into a new phase of life. The experiences are cumulative, however, since we don't have to start over entirely each time to build a new application and extension of skills. The challenge is to not succumb to old stories, insecurities, or beliefs that would ghostwrite a limited story. We must create a new story, which requires discipline and transformation of independent thinking to traverse creative challenges.

Choices of this transition include the challenge to not play it safe, to not reenter the old story, to not resort to old narratives and solutions. The challenge is also to continue acquiring knowledge, readying oneself with new information. We must proceed organically by taking a chance, self-correcting, and continuing forward movement rather than reengaging the familiar. Danger and difficulties are ways of measuring progress in a planned, strategic apprenticeship in the journey of transformation, with decisions informed by multiple perspectives and information.

Any change and transition involves an apprenticeship, a period, and practice of acquiring new skills.

It is this apprenticeship that is depicted as the 10,000 hours required to become a true master at anything: an elite athlete, executive, master criminal, chess player, writer. This initial stage includes an essential rewiring of the brain. When something is repeated often enough, it becomes hardwired and automatic, a skill's set of neural pathways. This neural network is developed to remember even single tasks, accounting for why we can still ride a bicycle years after we first learned.

This process of hardwiring requires dedicated focus and repetition. Neuroscientists emphasize that it is more effective to dedicate a brief period of time to a skill, even two hours of intensive focus, than ten hours of diffuse concentration. This power of focus, a present and centered state of mind, is like recording a program on a particular channel to consistently etch the experience. An acquired skill moves from a challenge to mastery to ultimately become the default mode. When our brains create new neurons and networks to make the skill an automatic response, far less energy is required. It becomes a habit.

Sustained focus reaches a point of total absorption in the practice or task, a flow in an immersed state of mind, blocking out anything else. The experience is transformative and embeds a mastery that transcends words and description. Pleasure becomes redefined. Challenges then dissolve much as your lap does when you get up to walk. The phase of apprenticeship moves to a sense of autonomy, an expansion of mastery that then becomes second nature.

Many who succeed remarkably in various endeavors had the experience in their youth of having mastered a particular skill, whether it was a sport, a musical instrument, a foreign language, or an academic pursuit. Having this experience as a behavioral pattern to engage and master becomes a powerful template—an embedded model—buried in their minds to inform current engagements and an expectation of success. This template can be formed at any age. The experience of overcoming frustration to enter a cycle of celebrated achievements evolves from this lived experience. At times of doubt, the procedural memory of mastery resonates to inform sustained engagement. This belief in one's self sustains efforts.

The mastery of a skill or a process is transferable to other endeavors; scrutiny and insight can make it more conscious and accessible. To recall a time of mastery at a task, however small or seemingly insignificant, can fuel faith to transcend frustration, insecurity, and boredom in order to master a current task. The Mentor Coaching principles of shrinking the change and laddering success with specific, measurable step-wise goals strategically further this process. Doubt and insecurity can be transformed into a sense of effectiveness with each step.

Beginner's Mind

The problem is never how to get new, innovative thoughts into your mind, but how to get old ones out. Every mind is a building filled with archaic furniture. Clean out a corner of your mind and creativity will instantly fill it.
—Dee Hock

Remember recent experiences of excitement and childlike joy with new experiences, such as with nature, traveling to a new country, or engaging a new idea?

Mastery retains the spirit of a beginner's mind, as we experience things in childhood with an openness, a first-time freshness without preconceived ideas and developed notions influenced by others, when we were totally receptive to new information. The beginner's mind does not have to think outside the box because it is, by definition, without a constructed box. Rather than feeling nostalgia for this intensity with which we experienced the world, we can reengage that beginner's mind. This requires reopening our awareness and experience that has been diminished in intensity because of constraint, invalidation, defensiveness, or attack of our beliefs and assumptions. The *beginner's mind* challenges the *conventional mind* as we actively address our own narrative and story.

Generating a new story reengages that beginner's mind. We do that by remaining open, asking questions, embracing childlike excitement and playful approaches, and thinking beyond words and limitations. This creative reverie accesses preverbal and unconscious forms of mental activity that generate surprising ideas. We must sustain the risk of failing and the anticipation of being criticized in order to expand beyond the familiar and habitual way of thinking.

A powerful sense of purpose and passion can overcome setbacks and failures. A deep-rooted interest sustains the rigors of hard work to get to creative action, surpassing doubters, critics, and nonbelievers.

Brainstorming to allow imagination to soar catalyzes creativity and intuition. Deduction and logical thought are components of a different mindset, however, not to be interspersed with this creative time. Each is valuable, yet each is a different state of mind, much like the difference in creative writing and editing.

The creative process is elusive, one for which we receive no specific training. Most of our creative endeavors are highly personal, often idiosyncratic, and likely guided by individual spirit and passion, rather than by logic foreclosing freedom.

The creative process of a beginner's mind requires an initial period of open-endedness, a contemplative space to free associate, fantasize, dream, and engage emotions. This generative state of mind needs its own dedicated time and space, plus a framework of support that prevents interruption. Structure provides freedom.

The neocortex of our brain has approximately 300 million pattern recognizers, which, having recognized and defined a pattern, then give it a name. That symbol becomes part of another pattern, ultimately housed as a metaphor. The forebrain is a metaphor machine, which accounts for ours being a uniquely creative species. The challenge is to allow and create new recognition and new patterns, rather than automatically perceiving what we do as fitting into an already existing sequence. Quite often people come up with creative, even genius, ideas but fail to put them into action.

The creative stimulation of new ideas activates both dopamine and adrenalin. Putting something into action requires not the *sprint* chemicals of dopamine and adrenalin, but the *marathon* mediator of norepinephrine, replacing the exciting creative stimulation with long-term hard work. At times it is difficult to sustain the less exciting work of development and completion, when the preference is to reengage the excitement of another new beginning.

It is also essential to embrace uniqueness, in that creative efforts cannot be in comparison or in competition with anyone else. Creativity is each person's developmental process, timetable, and endeavor, an evolving story that does not reference anyone else. This patience allows a full immersion of engagement to slow-cook ideas and grow them organically. We can always know the difference between procrastination versus dosing, timing, and titrating. Likewise, the dyad of avoidance and unnaturally drawing out a process has to be distinguished from the patience required to allow the project to take on a life of its own, absorb mental energies, and become its own rich engagement.

Many years from now, as we look back, we will see the product of our creative mastery, not whether it was completed two or three months sooner or later.

Transferring Models of Mastery

All truths are easy to understand once they are discovered.
The point is to discover them.
—Galileo

In discerning the function of mirror neurons, neuroscientists discovered another component of effectiveness: that we can place ourselves inside the minds of another and experience our own version of what that individual may be thinking and feeling.

This unique capacity of mirror neurons in the brain helps us understand the ability to *think inside* things around us. It is how animals learn. Modeling through mirror neurons can pass on certain highly developed skills. Mastery at this level of developing particular skills allows rapid and effective decisions, a learning without words or language. It helps us understand how preverbal patterns and learning can occur in infants. In this way, we can learn from the cumulative knowledge and experience of millennia. We can also reverse present ineffective habits in a matter of a day, and hardwire a new story in a matter of weeks.

A mother rat can build a nest for her young, a spider can spin a web, and a beaver can build a dam even if no contemporary ever showed them how to accomplish these complex tasks. Although these are not directly learned behaviors, they are learned over thousands of lifetimes by DNA encoding.

Recent discoveries in neuroscience have also overturned the long-held belief that the brain is genetically hardwired. We now know how plastic our brains are, how our thoughts determine our mental landscape and generate the neuronal highways to the villages of our neural networks. Our minds shape our brains, and both affect our health and functionality. Our internal storyteller generates our entire experience, from what we create to what we perceive and process from external events. We create our own stories, our own world.

No matter how much we desire to experience what others experience, and develop intuitive and precise empathy, we always remain on the outside looking in. Though we have mirror neurons and empathic desire to place ourselves inside the experience of another and imagine their experience, we must develop the ability to think outside our own system and ourselves. If we study another person, even another culture, to the point of developing empathic powers, we achieve significant insights. Empathy calls for entering the belief and value systems of another, their particular myths and ways of seeing the world.

Components of Mastery

> *Become who you are by learning who you are.*
> —The Greek poet Pindar, more than 2,600 years ago

We usually equate thinking and intellectual powers with success and achievement. However, what distinguishes those who truly master a field from those who do their jobs is often an emotional quality. Beyond reasoning and intellectual ability, the factors that play a larger role in success most often include desire, persistence, patience, and confidence. Motivation and energy can overcome most challenges and obstacles.

When we lack a sense of purpose and thus feel bored, this state of mind tends to close off pursuit and introduce passivity. Likewise, when we feel overwhelmed, we often retreat into a form of passivity. With overwhelm, too many choices, or lack of clarity and specificity of how to proceed, we revert to our comfort zone of inactivity, or at least to our routine, habitual response. By limiting the circle of action to familiar habits, we create the illusion of control. Repetition and its predictability masquerade as effectiveness. And the less we attempt, the fewer will be our chances of failing. The more we perceive passivity and inactivity as inevitable, the more palatable it becomes.

Whatever remains unconscious will inevitably be attributed to fate.

We become attracted to certain narratives that fit our individual stories: the beliefs and assumptions that we hold both consciously and unconsciously.

Our minds affect our health and functionality; our willpower becomes our physiology. We *create* the patterns of our lives, rather than *responding to* the patterns of our lives. Through our own mental operations we are essentially responsible for so much of what seems to just happen to us.

As we proceed with creating a new story, the old ideas, beliefs, and perspectives become inactive as new powers of mastery unleash new potential. *The experience of effectiveness and mastery guides us through this transformative process.*

That means not only that everything that seems to happen to us is created by us, it is also a form of instruction that we can pay attention to, learn from, and use as guide for change and transformation.

Intuition Initiating Mastery

The intuitive mind is a sacred gift and the rational mind is a faithful servant.
We have created a society that honors the servant and has forgotten the gift.
—Albert Einstein

Those who achieve mastery immerse themselves in a total absorption in a field over a period of time to acquire information and expertise, and achieve an intuitive feel for the whole. I heard Jane Goodall describe her experience of living with chimpanzees in the wilds of East Africa; she began to think and feel as one with the chimpanzees. She could then see elements of their social life that no other scientist had ever discerned. This dynamic and intuitive grasp of a whole is in part a function of time, in that the brain is actually altered after repeated experiences.

At a high level of mastery, intuition and rationality paradoxically combine to shape new creative experiences and products.

Various people who achieve mastery describe sensations of suddenly possessing a heightened intellectual power after years of immersion in a field. Albert Einstein realized not just the answer to a problem, but an entire new way of viewing the universe through an intuitive visual image. Chess master Bobby Fischer spoke of thinking beyond various moves of his pieces on the chessboard, that after a time he could see "fields of forces" to allow him to anticipate an entire direction of a match. Pianist Glenn Gould ceased to focus on notes or components of the music he played but instead saw an entire architecture of the piece to be able to express it. Thomas Edison had a vision to illuminate an entire city with electrical light, an intuitive blink he had through a single image.

Each of these masters described an experience of intuition allowing them to encompass a greater perspective.

This experience of *seeing more* transcends rational and logical thought and intelligence and involves a different part of the brain from the one that performs rational, logical processes.

Time, intuitive feel, and experience become foundation for internalization, to make it our own, a story told in our own voice. Learning from our mistakes and never stopping at the first right answer are all components of a growth mindset, catalyst to mastery.

Intuitive awareness helps us process complex layers of information not even accessible to the conscious, logical mind, to gain an understanding, a sense of the whole. Today this level of thinking is even more critical than ever before.

Looking ahead and conceptual planning is a benefit; looking too far ahead may be detrimental. At times managing anxiety and uncertainty means simply to discern the next best action, the next step.

True mastery with the development of high-level intuitive power makes us become younger in mind and spirit. More than a function of only innate genius or talent, mastery also involves time, immersion, and intense study applied to a particular field of knowledge. Achievement of mastery comes with development of a strong internal guiding system and a high level of self-awareness. Sensitive observation is neither distracted by technology nor enamored by it.

There are many paths to mastery. A key component is to know our mental and psychological strengths, and to dedicate focus and practice to capitalize on them. In any endeavor, when we learn a complex skill so that it becomes automatic, we free our minds to focus on the next higher level. Once fundamental skills and knowledge are learned and assimilated as information, they are internalized and become part of our neural system.

We're able to think in a different way with mind and body integrated, reason and instinct co-mingled and transformed. The key is having the patience to absorb the discipline and the fine points that are intrinsically part of the creative building blocks.

I recall experiencing a particular kind of energy in being in the room at Château du Clos Lucé in France where Leonardo da Vinci sketched many of his scientific inventions. Seeing the desk where he sat to make those drawings and sensing his creative spirit was magical. His mastery that produced *Mona Lisa* came from the same energy field that went into inventions he sketched at that desk, including the forerunner of the modern helicopter, military tank, parachute, calculator, and bicycle.

I recalled the story of how he spent six years working in a studio as Verrocchio's top assistant helping on his large-scale paintings and taking on a responsibility in *The Baptism of Christ*, where he was given the task of painting one of the two angels. This oldest example of his painting revealed the face of an angel that had a quality never seen before, seeming to literally glow from within. The angel's face had an uncanny reality and expressiveness.

Recent x-rays have revealed some of the secrets to Leonardo's early technique. His layers of paint were applied exceptionally thinly, the brush strokes almost invisible. He added multiple layers, each one ever so slightly darker than the last. By operating this way and experimenting with different pigments, he captured the delicate contours of human flesh. Any light hitting the painting seemed to pass through the angel's face and illuminate it from within. These six years of apprenticeship were an immersion in learning various paints and a style of layering for delicate lifelike effects, as well as his background work of studying the composition of human flesh. His endless patience, coupled with a love for detailed work, created this mastery. Painting became for him a quest to access a life force that energizes from within, a work that is both emotional and visceral. He applied the same rigor to capturing images and bodies as he did to applying scientific principles to inventions.

Mastery involves a global perspective, to think beyond the moment, to think more abstractly as well as more specifically, and in greater detail. To look wider and think further ahead, coupled with thinking more concretely and more minutely than ever before.

The Antithesis of Mastery

Genius too does nothing but learn first how to lay bricks then how to build, and continually seek for material and continually form itself around it. Every activity of man is amazingly complicated, not only that of the genius: but none is a 'miracle.'
—Friedrich Nietzsche

The antithesis of the synthesis and creation of mastery is control. To counter a sense of helplessness, control of others or some activity generates a temporary illusion of effectiveness. There is a moment in *Lord of the Flies* when Henry wanders away from the main group of children and the overwhelming struggles they engage in, to go down to the beach and busy himself with the creatures in the sand. As he . . . *tried to control the motions of the scavengers . . . he became absorbed beyond mere happiness as he felt himself exercising control over living things.*

Author William Golding captures the derivative pleasure of being in control of something at a time of otherwise feeling overwhelmed. The children, including Henry, feel out of control without adults and left to their own devices of extracting some small cordoned-off area over which to exert control. The pursuit of happiness for Henry was a cover story for the wish to effectively determine *something* in his world.

The motivation for effectiveness and the experience of mastery constitute an inner force that guides us. To resonate with this innate force we must remain attuned to our primal instincts, intuition, natural inclinations, and curiosity. The antithesis of progress toward mastery is to disregard this innate force, to listen to and fit into the desires of others and of society, to abandon one's self to conform to the wishes and desires of others. The first move toward mastery is always inward: to learn who we really are and reconnect with that innate force with clarity and purpose.

The abandonment of this essential uniqueness in order to please others, fit into a group, or redirect to alternate goals such as comfort or money breaches our contract with destiny. It is never too late to reengage this force. The process is often not a straight line but has twists, turns, successive approximations, and gradual steps.

An equal antithesis of mastery is to consistently oppose positions of authority, to counter convention or rules, which also embodies an external point of reference. Both opposition and conformity occupy the same prison.

One of the ultimate impediments to creativity is when a successful process becomes a paradigm, an established procedure. Subsequently, the paradigm and a lifeless set of techniques are followed that then move from new and vibrant to conformity and rote procedure.

The desire to fit into the needs or wants of others, to accumulate all the voices internalized from others, including parents and significant others, without amalgamating and transforming them into your own voice, creates conformity.

At times, we may be attracted to a false path for the wrong reasons: conforming to directives from parents, social pressures of alignment, focusing on money, attention, or fame. We ultimately experience this as an ersatz effectiveness, a false mastery. Results can include dissatisfaction, burnout, a sense that something is missing, or even a blatant resentment.

A denial of mastery is to believe that it is for the exceptionally talented, that success is for others, for those who are born to succeed, or those who were at the right place at the right time. A *false self* is constructed by consuming what others create, or retreating into limited goals and immediate pleasures, alienating oneself from an innate inclination for effectiveness and mastery. The results are limitation and disappointment.

The desire for mastery is the antithesis of narcissism and selfishness; it is a natural and innate inclination for effectiveness. This fundamental motivation is a natural expression of uniqueness from birth, of following our inclinations enriched with insight, adumbrated by imagination, and consummated by creative discovery.

The *true self* strives for effectiveness and mastery. It is a voice from within, emanating from the spirit deep inside us, below the floor of our unconscious. It is our purpose and life's mission to bring it to fruition. Hindrances to this process include a pressure to produce results, a need to generate profits, or a fear of inadequacy or nonproductivity.

While we work toward and achieve mastery, we have to ladder challenges to sustain the quest and not lose enthusiasm. When we become really good at something, we need to never take it for granted not slur the details, in order to continue the sparkling sensation of new quests.

The Mentor Process and Mastery

A man of talent is not born to be left to himself, but to devote himself to art and good masters who will make something of him.
—Johann Peter Eckermann, *Conversations with Goethe*

Masters throughout the ages have found that a mentor can help focus attention and challenge the one being mentored. The mentor-protégé relationship is an efficient and productive form of learning. The mentor who best fits an individual's needs and connects to that individual's purpose can catalyze remarkable growth.

The reason we need mentors is simple: Life is short; we only have so much time and so much energy; we need help in jumpstarting personal and professional growth. The information in books and courses may not be tailored to circumstances and individuality. We can learn from experiences, but it can take years to fully understand the meanings and nuances of best practices. A self-directed apprenticeship in a field can take many years.

Mentors streamline the process. They invariably have had their own great mentors, giving them a richer and deeper knowledge of their fields and of life. They have learned from ensuing years of experience teaching invaluable lessons and strategies for learning. Their knowledge and experience become ours. They can direct us to avoid unnecessary detours and side paths. They observe our work and provide invaluable feedback for greater efficiency and effectiveness. We participate and internalize their creative spirit to make it our own story. This process simply shortens and enhances a learning curve.

A master mentor is an alchemist who believes in the process of transformation and finds ways to catalyze growth. The best mentors continue to think on a higher level, to synthesize and integrate different forms and fields of knowledge.

Selecting a Mentor

One repays a teacher badly if one remains only a pupil.
—Friedrich Nietzsche

A good mentor will catalyze your own style, then leave when the time is right because the process is internalized, when you will have become your own best mentor. The end in mind from the beginning is for the one being mentored to internalize the process and thus no longer need ongoing external engagement with the mentor.

The mentor you choose should be strategically aligned with your position and your vision. If your path is more innovative, you will want a mentor who is open, progressive, not domineering. If your ideal is more idiosyncratic, you will want a mentor who will make you feel comfortable and help you transform your notions into mastery, instead of trying to shape them. At times mentors show you something you will want to avoid or even oppose, and illuminate beliefs that have been ghostwriting compromised stories.

A mentor who truly has achieved mastery knows deep in his or her bones what is required to reach a creative, productive phase. And beyond. A mentor knows how to supply this form of wisdom and, at times, tough love. Through realistic feedback, a mentor will help the protégé develop a confidence that is substantial and significantly beneficial.

The great inventor Buckminster Fuller consistently generated ideas for inventions and new technology. He recognized that many people have creative ideas but become afraid to put them into action. Instead, they engage in discussions and continuing new ideas, to the detriment of practical application and development of projects. To counter this inclination, his strategy forged what he termed *artifacts*. He would move his creative ideas into application by making models of things he imagined, and then invent prototypes that translated his creative ideas into tangible objects. Creative speculation became a reality of applied, constructed artifacts. In doing so, he could get feedback from others about the practicality of his invention.

Paradigms are accepted ways of explaining a phenomenon—a model of making sense of reality. At times, however, a paradigm can dominate our way of thinking as we look for patterns to confirm what we already believe, and perhaps omit seeing or creating the new and different. Furthermore, the anomalies that do not fit the paradigm tend to be ignored or explained away, when at times they may contain important information.

Stages of Mastery

Whoever in middle age, attempts to realize the wishes and hopes of his early youth invariably deceives himself. Each ten years of a person's life has its own fortunes, its own hopes, its own desires.
—Wolfgang von Goethe

Mastery involves self-awareness along with self-regulation—two key components in emotional intelligence.

A significant aspect of mastery is being in the optimum brain state for a particular task. Examples include being in a creative, expansive state for writing, and in a focused, attentive state for editing. Another example is being in a very positive state of mind for creative problem-solving and mental flexibility, but being in a serious, focused mood to pay greater attention to detail, such as reviewing a contract. An angry mood can mobilize energy and focus attention on blazing through obstacles and fueling competitiveness. A more negative mood gives us a more negative bias toward what we may be considering, put a negative skew on judgments, but be invaluable in considering worst-case scenarios.

We now know that creativity is not just the emotional brain, but a whole brain, right and left, a top and bottom web of connections. To be centered and grounded is to have access to an entire range of states of mind, and thus be in an optimum position to synthesize and integrate information from various sources located in various regions of the brain.

The basis for self-mastery is a combination of awareness and integration of our internal states. A classic model of the *four stages of creative mastery* includes:

- Define and frame the problem. See problems, challenges, and ask questions to find and frame the creative challenge.

- Immersion in the process. A focus to gather ideas and information to put together in new ways.

- Relaxation and centeredness. While seeming counterintuitive, to let go and relax can allow the best ideas to come. The self-mastery is in knowing when to let go, and that we need to let go. Remember that some of our best ideas come while taking a shower, or going on a jog. Trying to force an insight or a completion can stifle creative breakthrough.

- Execution. Implementation requires a purity of immersion, combined with knowing when and how to step into and complete a creative engagement.

Gender

The Either-Or Story

If you look deep enough inside yourself, you'll see everyone else.
—Kinky Friedman

One of the most striking examples of the difference between boys and girls came through my experience in coaching basketball. I coached my son's basketball team for the first three years he played, ages 8–10. The boys were aggressive, competitive, fully focused on basketball during the workouts. Every Saturday before a game, we would meet at our home gym to go over plays, and then all pile in my car to drive to the gym where the games were held. During this drive the guys were a raucous group, wanting to listen to songs such as *Eye of the Tiger* to get revved up. This was basketball as I knew it.

After these three years, I coached my daughter's all-girl basketball team as she reached age 8. Again, we began each practice the same way, with a little inspirational talk of teamwork moving directly into basics and then scrimmage. It didn't work. They were distracted, didn't seem to respond, as if they were there for something besides basketball. I was baffled.

As I listened to them and observed them more carefully, I began to sense what I had missed. Basketball was the *content* of the practice, but they were into the *process* of being together and playing together. While I was urging them to concentrate on basketball basics and being competitive, they wanted to enjoy themselves. Soon enough, we began each practice sitting in a circle on the court, just talking. That was their warm-up. It worked. They played better as a team. How strange, yet wonderful, I thought, it must be to be a girl.

During our skull session each Saturday morning before the game, we all talked about such things as hairdos, friends, manicures, and who was "going with" whom at school. Strangely enough, we won most of our games, and they were a tough, dedicated team. We became the first all-girls 10 and under basketball team to play at the Houston Rockets half-time. Still, for players who say, "Excuse me" when they foul an opponent, I suspect that winning was a notion in my mind rather than theirs.

Admittedly, it may be awkward for a dad to share certain experiences with his daughter, because he's never been a little girl. Playing Barbie dolls with my daughter and rearranging furniture in Barbie's Dream House were not places I'd been before. Lauren led me through the shifting alliances of the dolls, moving from room to room in the Dream House, realigning dress configurations and friend allegiances. It seemed more complex than a soap opera, and at first much less exciting than if they were attempting to reach a goal, say sink a basket or make a touchdown. The arms of these beautiful little people didn't even bend, so how could they possibly throw or catch well? The intricate complexities of remembering which of the girl dolls liked which other doll at that moment and who were and were not on speaking terms with each other seemed hopelessly complex.

Eventually I learned it wasn't pointless. It was something girls and women have been trying to teach boys and men for centuries, about affiliation and relationships rather than competition and winning. Still, taking my daughter to work with me, working out at the health club or jogging in the neighborhood with her, even shopping for and preparing a meal together were considerably easier than remembering all the names of the girl dolls and which ones liked which other ones best at that moment, and why.

And just to be sure I'm engaged in sufficient continuing education, she has provided me with four granddaughters.

Men and women are simply wired differently. Brain mapping shows a striking contrast in neural circuitry. Male brains were found to have more connections from front to back within a hemisphere, making them optimized for coordinating perceptions with action, such as learning a new task or following directions to a location (assuming that they actually ask for directions). Female brains have more connections between the left and right hemispheres, which enables them to integrate emotion, reason, and social cues in responding to situations. While these differences are not absolute, social conditioning also shapes the connection pathways. Each of us has part of both gender characteristics in our brains.

The Gendered Self

I must refuse the compliment that I think like a man. One thinks, or one does not.
—Margaret Mead

A sense of one's gender is a fundamental organizer of body self and psychological self, both subjectively and from responses of significant others. Gender is one of the conventional and unspoken ways in which we order and organize our universe.

The earliest sense of self, including body self, is located in a male or female body, while the characteristics of gender are being defined and formed. Gender identity forms within the first two years of life, and in itself is conflict-free, a foreground issue only in the rare instance of incongruent psychological and body gender. The earliest imprints of gender identification are fashioned by the representations of anatomy and physiology, identification with gender of primary caregivers, and the intersubjective shaping of gender and later sexual role identity characteristics and traits as taught and modeled especially by those caregivers.

Gender is a complex matter, having genetic, physical, and psychological components. Genotypic gender is genetically determined, while phenotypic gender is anchored in the development of internal and external genitalia. Gender identity is the subjective perception of one's gender, of maleness or femaleness, while sexual role identity is composed of all the characteristics of masculinity and femininity. Behavior of males and females differs from just after birth, enhanced by the differing treatment by parents. Gender is used by the child as a way to organize self-cohesion and regulate self-esteem.

Originally, the baby creates the parent, and each mutually influences the other. On my weekend ranch I recently saw the change created by motherhood. A Bantam chicken, skittish and indistinguishable from many others except by her particular color markings, gave me wide berth, and nervously wouldn't let me get within three feet of her. But then, as she sat on her eggs around the clock, she was suddenly transformed. She would calmly look up at me, eye to eye. When her three chicks hatched, she instantly became their protector, constantly aware of keeping them close to her, tucking them under her body each night. The chicks, from embryonic egg, had created a mother, entirely transforming her personality.

In the early, mutually experienced exchanges, the child sees himself or herself in the parent's empathic mirror, locates a self in the reciprocity of eyes, faces, and bodily experience. The resonance of everything that is experienced in feeling and action recognition allows the child to *find* himself or herself in these responses. Or, in their absence, to *lose* himself or herself.

Gender is an important aspect of the experience and internal representation of both body self and psychological self, an aspect of self-experience that is formed in the matrix of interaction with primary caregivers.

Growing up is pervasively gendered. There are constant reminders both in the culture and in the family of the inclusion and exclusion criteria of each gender, especially emphasized around sexual role stereotypes, of what is feminine and unfeminine, masculine and unmasculine. Psychological self becomes shaped by gender, sexual role stereotypes, and perceptions of the body.

The brain does not work logically, but associatively. The meaning we associate to a stimulus determines our behavior. The myriad associations we have to gender become a part of our body self and psychological self-organization.

Our embodied selves are inherently gendered, and we may not even be able to experience ourselves except in the context of gender. For example, we may not be able to imagine experiencing ourselves as ungendered, in any way *not* colored by gender. Our embodied selves make male and female as inseparable as mind and body, as body self and psychological self.

The innate experiences that are gendered become the unspoken, invisible self. When there is uncertainty or conflict about what is within that boundary, the boundaries themselves become rigidly defended, belying their permeability. Various contents become specifically assigned to gender; few, if any, remain ungendered. There are ineluctable differences of gender, such that women nurse babies, as anatomical differences become a correlate of gender.

Gender differentiation and gender identity are so fundamental that the differentness and the overlapping aspects are so often taken for granted. While basic developmental needs are not gender specific, gender perception shapes both the needs as well as their expression. Consider, for example, the gender-specific functions of essential exploratory, assertive, attachment, and adversarial motivations. The earliest sense of the female body and the male body get represented both emotionally and mentally, and are experienced vividly from physical awareness and sensations. The body is fundamentally involved in psychic development; the girl's body is central to her development as the boy's body is to him.

Each developmental juncture combines a unique synthesis of bodily and psychological interplay for both male and female. The specific aspects of each gender at developmental points such as pubescence, adolescence, marriage, pregnancy, menopause, and aging offer additional opportunities to amalgamate and articulate body self and psychological self.

In utero, testosterone floods the male brain, while estrogen bathes the female brain, inhibiting some features and promoting others for each gender. This accounts in part for numerous findings of the initial tendencies of males and females, some of which have a brain basis, and some of which are imprints from parents' expectations and models. These well-known findings of the differences between boys and girls, men and women, give little precedent for understanding how, for example, women tend to worry more about losing attachments, while men more about losing face; how women focus more over emotional infidelity, while men are more jealous over sexual infidelity.

The brain determines behavior, but behavior also determines the brain.

Universal Storylines

Back in October my 7-year-old son broke his arm. When the doctor asked him
what color cast he wanted, my son proudly pointed to the hot pink one. The
doctor was like, are you sure? Pink is a girl color. . . . My little guy looked at
the doctor and said, "There are no girl colors or boy colors. I want a pink cast,
because it's breast cancer month." The doctor turned red. The nurse gave my son
a kiss, and I puffed out like a proud mama bird.
—Tomya K.

Vivian Paley, a MacArthur Foundation Genius Award winner, described
in her book about her decades of experiences as a preschool and kindergarten teacher. *Boys and Girls: Superheroes in the Doll Corner* describes
the clustering of gender-specific behaviors in pretend play as gender roles
coalesced in her classroom. The girls played dolls, pined for their princes,
and rather than run or wrestle or shout, told stories about bunnies and
magical animals. The boys, however, ran, shouted, shot the room full of
imaginary bullet holes, and scorched it with bombs. When toy guns were
confiscated, they were not stopped, as the boys fashioned crayons and
ultimately fingers into guns. When they played pirates or robbers, they
needed, naturally, victims. *Boys and Girls* is mostly about the year she
spent trying to get her children to behave in asexual and unisexual ways.
Of course, it was a spectacular, though amusing, failure.

Paley finally acquiesced to Mother Nature, genes, and social imprints:
Boys choose storylines of adventure, conflict, and daring, while girls
choose ones of affiliation and nurturing connections.

Nalini Ambady demonstrated that even preschool girls at a Harvard
daycare do worse on simple math tests if they are first subtly reminded
of being female. Widely held positive stereotypes can have the opposite
effect. In the same study of preschool girls, Asian-Americans did better
on average if they were reminded of their ethnic background but faltered
if the priming exercise emphasized their gender instead.

Could we ever imagine experiencing ourselves other than through
our gender, informed and organized by it, from within our embodied

(and therefore gendered) selves? The world is gendered, and to encourage someone not to recognize or acknowledge that would be to ignore reality. Mind and body, as well as *doing* and *being* a gender seem inseparable.

Developmental needs and experiences, family context and shaping, as well as the unique subjective experience of the forming self, determine the filter through which gender experiences pass. When caregivers condemn behaviors or qualities as gender-incongruent, shame and self-doubt may be the result. Aspects of self-experience may have to be suppressed or even dissociated developmentally in order to maintain ties with needed important others. The child may then develop gender-incongruent behaviors as an adaptation to failed empathic responses or acceptance by caregivers.

The allowable and the constructed experiences of each gender shape the mental representations of all components, as well as their synthesis.

Unconscious Biases

Whoever won a game of dolls?
—Pat Hein

A Canadian couple made the news when they announced they were keeping the sex of their baby a secret in an attempt to erase sexual stereotypes that society imposes. This is certainly a worthy goal, as girls should be free to play with trucks and boys with dolls. Yet the enigma they created is that while you can keep the sex of a child secret, you paradoxically make it the most important thing possible about the child, not the least. Denial is one of the most powerful forms of engagement.

The writer Jan Morris has spoken of perceived gender differences, including that it matters whether a writer is male or female. She knows both, having been a biological male from childhood into adulthood, then having sex-change surgery to live as a woman. She speaks of many aspects of writing and traveling, of how the female is perceived as not threatening, more vulnerable, more conspicuous, finds fewer doors closed against her, even to the observation that women are kinder to women than men are to men. Having experienced both relationships, she speaks from her controlled study of one.

Archetypes are, by definition, embedded in our psyches as well as in the culture. These unconscious biases become a shadow story of stereotypy that can strongly influence perception and behaviors.

At times we have to distinguish our instinctive thin-slicing of data to quickly come to a conclusion at times from a buried prejudice. Deep within our unconscious we have associations that can only be called biases, even when we consciously abhor them.

Each of us holds a collection of stereotypical beliefs and attitudes about social groups that exist often without our permission or even our awareness. These beliefs color perceptions, expectations, and decisions. The assorted stereotypical notions can be based on gender, race, weight, age, and sexual orientation, among many others. Regardless of our conscious desire to avoid the bias of stereotypy, these connections can shape the contours of our daily decisions.

Social processes and implicit assumptions become familiar through repetition. Ways of thinking and behaving become routinely incorporated in everyday life. Our habituation then fosters a normalizing tendency to take those processes for granted. For example, children who live in a household of violence show aggression and dysregulation that may later contribute to perpetuating the legacy of abuse.

We routinely have normative influences—the unquestioned, established conventions of belief or value—to describe (construct) our realities. Normative statements, usually logically independent and unconsciously downloaded as the fabric of our daily interaction, become an integral part of our lives.

As part of our organizing system, these engrams then exert powerful unconscious impact to determine what we perceive and how we process our perceptions. Normative becomes prescriptive, determining both the value proposition and *the way it ought to be done.*

What's in a name?

We transfer assumptions about females and males even to hurricanes with gender-specific names. We are less frightened by storms bearing female names, leading to less preparedness and ultimately to more fatalities. Between 1950 and 2012, storms with female names caused an average of 45 deaths, compared to 23 deaths from male-named storms. The stereotypic regard of female-named hurricanes is perceived as warmer and less intense than ones with male names.

The meaning that we attach to our perceptions determines its emotional impact. By changing the meaning, we can change the emotional impact. Of all the variables studied to address bias and overcome prejudice, the strongest correlation with overcoming prejudice is a powerful emotional bond. There are many learning laboratories for positive connection, including friends, colleagues, and mentors.

Research suggests, and our experience informs, that we can develop awareness, reshape implicit attitudes and beliefs, and adjust biases. That is, we can develop new life and relationship stories. Authentic bonds with others can stretch our imaginations, invite empathy, and encourage understanding of the full range of human possibility.

An example of a significant gender difference is the finding that organizations with more women in leadership positions make more philanthropic contributions and boost the level of corporate social responsibility. A study by the nonprofit research firm Catalyst found that organizations with three or more women sitting as members of their board of directors made philanthropic contributions *28 times greater* than those of other organizations.

Our unconscious, with its unspoken biases, asserts its presence in every moment of our lives.

My daughter, Dr. Lauren Krueger Weeks (following her earlier basketball career devoted to teaching me about girls), orchestrated a party at her private therapeutic school for one of her professional staff members who was about to have a baby. She asked each of the kindergarten children to contribute to a book of advice to Dr. Pete for his new baby. Her prompt was, *What would you like to tell Dr. Pete about the new baby he is going to have?*

An assortment of the girls' responses:

- Have a beautiful baby shower and be beautiful.
- Smile.
- Don't forget to thank your guests for coming to the shower.
- When your baby cries, pick it up.
- Snuggle with your husband.
- Have fun at your shower.

Responses from the boys:

- Eat your cake.
- Make another baby.
- Open your presents.
- Put your baby upside down, he will laugh.
- Cut up your baby's hot dogs.
- Play with trains with your baby.

She and I were both amused at these stereotypic responses from the children of very well-educated parents in an affluent Boston suburb.

Men still outearn women into the 21st century. New research found that a major factor in the persistent gender pay gap is simply because women do not ask for more money. Men are four times more likely than women to ask for a raise. The failure to negotiate higher pay has accruing effects, resulting in smaller raises and bonuses over the course of a woman's career.

Dead-even power games include playing dolls, house, and makeup. Males tend to engage in games to personally jockey to establish power and pecking order.

We must not forget that men and women share many fundamental similarities, and that people are first and foremost individuals, not types. And where differences do occur, they appear to be shaped more by social and demographic factors such as education, employment status, and financial circumstances than by innate gender characteristics.

The Perception of Gender

> *One can hardly pay greater tribute to the importance of an event*
> *than to proclaim the impossibility of neutrality before it.*
> —Steven Jay Gould

Our initial register of another person is of gender. We first view the geography of the body, and everything else follows. Gender organizes our universe in both conventional and unspoken ways.

Prior to and during conception, gender configures attributions and expectations of the person-in-progress. Birth activates gender-specific attitudes and interactions. The earliest sense of self, including body self, is housed in a male or a female body. The characteristics of gender continue to be defined, formed, and shaped by the conscious and unconscious interchange with the same, as well as opposite-gendered primary caretakers.

The earliest imprints of gender specificity and identification are fashioned only partly by the representations of anatomy and physiology as external emblems in a universe of beliefs. The body conveys gender and registers other disparate notations otherwise unsymbolized. Inexpressive meaning and uncharted feeling may also become crystallized as somatic experiences within a gendered body, to become part of an organizing narrative.

Gender, the perception of innate maleness or femaleness, includes subsequent sexual role identity and characteristics. Behavior of males and females differs from just after birth, enhanced by the differing assumptions and treatment by parents. A large number of observational studies of "normal" families shows that certain gender-aligned tendencies emerged. Both parents emphasized achievement and competitiveness more for sons than for daughters. Both parents tended to encourage their sons, more than their daughters, to be independent, and to assume increasing amounts of personal responsibility. With their sons, fathers were stricter, firmer, more authoritarian, more likely to use physical punishments and more intolerant of behaviors violating the traditional masculine stereotype. With their daughters, fathers showed greater warmth and physical closeness, while expecting gentle behavior and hesitating to use physical punishment. Mothers tended to restrict and supervise their daughters more closely than their sons. Boys were assigned chores that took them away from their mothers and out of the house, while girls were assigned homebound tasks that kept them in close proximity to their mothers.

Though gender is always present, emotion is not inherently gendered. Unless we share that person's gender, we will never know what it is like to *feel like a girl* and *like a boy* because we will never know the experience of the other. An animal raised in captivity does not know freedom. How will we ever know what an opposite gender-related experience is, as compared to experiences of feeling childlike versus adult? Gendered self is defined by certain characteristics, but the concept, seemingly crisp and distinct, is quite blurred, porous, and overlapping. *Doing* and *being* a gender are inseparable.

Could we ever imagine experiencing ourselves other than through our gender, informed and organized by it, from within our embodied (and therefore gendered) selves?

One may not need to be a certain gender, have a certain sexual orientation, or have had certain experiences to work effectively with another person, such as a colleague, in therapy, or mentor coaching, as long as all experiences are welcomed in the exchange, where nothing has to be exiled.

While we are always teaching others how to respond to us, there are, however, aspects of each that have to be specifically recognized. Gender is one. Gender is a kind of transference, the invisible software organizing our perception and processing. Our own experiences from preverbal to present are determined by gender-related interactions and mutual constructions. While gender is never absent, there are many aspects that make it far from the background.

One may not need to be a certain gender or have a certain sexual orientation, or have had certain experiences to relate empathically; when all experiences are welcomed, nothing has to be exiled. If certain desires and feelings are unwelcome and dismissed, unregistered empathically, or categorically collapsed, although gender may be the usual suspect, it may be a spurious culprit.

It is the hope of every individual to be understood by significant others at both a conscious and unconscious level, to innately understand and appreciate the inclusions and exclusions of a gendered and sexual body self. To hope that others will move beyond their own models and biases to stay curious, inquisitive, and open. To sense, as much as possible, what it is like to be inside one's own gendered, sexual body, psychological self, and experience at any moment. To exile nothing based on value or preference, bias or blindness, desire or fear, inchoate or formulated, speakable or unspeakable.

Gender includes the subset of role prescriptions of what we do as a boy or girl, man or woman, of the shape and texture of the expression of developmental needs, of behavior aligned with gender, of how we think about being male or female. It is all of this, yet more, for that is how we internally perceive, organize, and direct what we are doing.

We infer identity by gender; gender is identity. The gender filter through which experiences pass defines congruence and incongruence, identification figures, even heroes. Aspects of gendered self-experience may have to be suppressed or even dissociated developmentally in order to maintain ties with needed others.

The Question of Gender

> *In modern physics, a very different attitude has now developed.*
> *Physicists have come to see that all their theories of natural phenomena,*
> *including the laws they describe, are creations of the human mind.*
> *They are properties of our conceptual map of reality rather than of reality itself.*
> —*The Tao of Physics*

The problem with gender is that there are only two. We reductionistically place a continuum of experiences and characteristics into one category of availability—a procrustean bed holding only one. Gender squeezes everything into male or female, analogous to requiring that every question no matter how complex or multidimensional be answered only and simply as a *yes* or *no*.

Gender is both an idea and a reality. While gender is pervasive and assumed, gender crossings presuppose a gender boundary. The assumption of gender as a given, whether it is doing or being gender, or both and more, has only recently begun to be questioned. Gender may be so fundamental to our concept of self and others that to question gender, as in transsexualism, was considered a sign of psychosis until the last five decades. To attempt to take away manifest gender, to transform it, such as by sex-reassignment surgery, is still rare. Culture defines, constructs, and transmits gender so that we consciously and unconsciously incorporate prescriptions from culture and family in our gendered body.

Boys, perhaps more than girls, must more thoroughly renounce any gender-inconsistent qualities or traits, as boys have to push away from their mothers at pubescence even more emphatically than at the earlier separation-individuation in toddlerhood. At any time of ambivalence, it is less confusing to categorize things as all or nothing, black or white, masculine or feminine, hypertrophying the desired while disavowing the undesired. Testimony to overlapping and interwoven categorical gender assignments includes the need for thorough, mutually exclusive cleansing—a disidentification—to remain agnostic to all gender opposite-related qualities.

As preparation for adolescence, boys dislike and disdain girls and their femininity (thereby their own femininity, projected). Their ritual passage of establishing a male identity distances their own femininity, while often borrowing the peer group identity. Girls entering adolescence become uninvited containers for the projective identification of males' devalued, unwanted, and discarded femininity. At the same time, the boys are curiously attracted to these qualities, as they are to the young women who are their projective containers.

Females embody the femininity split off and expulsed by boys, as females become the repository for sensitivity, passivity, and vulnerability. At this developmental juncture, girls also need to renounce what they see as their own gender-inconsistent traits, those aspects assigned to boys, including aggression and dominance. Phase-specific hypermasculinity and hyperfemininity with corresponding strong same-sex group attachment emerges at the time each gendered person has to confront new further gender elaboration, such as in beginning adolescence/pubescence with masculine/feminine advances of body and psyche.

Masculine and feminine identification, evolving from gender, is so contextualized that it may be impossible to define what *is* and *is not* gender-related or even gender-determined. Sensations, body self-experiences, and emotional responses innate to humans, rather than to a specific gender, are nonetheless invisibly shaped by gender designations, or collapsed into gender assignment.

An individual's gender repertoire and gendered self-concept may affect one's pursuits and restraints in life. While there may be no universal developmental blueprint of gender or sexual identity, consensual narratives of gender and sexual role identity conform roughly with one's body being male or female. As a component of core identity, gender is so fundamental, so much a given, that we do not question it until it developmentally derails.

Any personal exchange has this lesson to teach us about gender and sexual role assignment: Though we are pervasively and inescapably gendered and exist within a perceived sexual role identity, hardly any aspect of being human is categorically restricted to a gender franchise, and the actual experience of gender is elusive and ineffable.

While we can never transcend our gender, we do not have to be bound by its stereotypic constraints.

Anson Dorrance has been the coach of the women's soccer team at the University of North Carolina for more than thirty years. In that time, his team has won 21 national championships. He is the single most successful coach in college history in any sport.

In practice, Dorrance dials the stress way up. He rigorously trains his players to acclimate to specific stresses of high-stakes, high-speed, high-risk soccer. He makes practices harder and more punishing than games, so his team members become more like the professional pilots in the turbulent flight simulator—so used to the stress it no longer overwhelms them.

In games, he dials the stress down. In games, when the stress of competing is all too real, he consciously avoids adding to the women's stress, and maximizes performance by taking stress away.

To teach competitiveness, in every scrimmage Dorrance has players relentlessly play against each other, in one-on-one, head-to-head competitions so they learn the psychological strategies needed to compete. He keeps grades of various components on a 23-factor matrix of every measurable aspect of the game. His teams became known for an aggressive, physical play never seen before in women's sports. He realized that he did not need to yell at the women, because the matrix numbers on the locker-room wall were stress enough.

The best example of how Dorrance coaches women is in his half-time speech. When he previously coached men, his best ever half-time speech, the most motivating one, was when he got so mad he kicked the trash can through the window. In the second half that followed, his team made a total turn-around of energy, tactics, and victory. He reasoned that men need shock at times to wake them up, and for top male athletes accustomed to competition, not even being on the losing end at half-time is shock enough.

But he also recognized the error of treating women that way. His most effective half-time talk for women? He simply came in the locker room and asked, *Well, what do you think?*

When he asked, *Well, what do you think?* he heard a chorus of self-flagellation as every woman in the room took full responsibility for the losing first half. He didn't need to criticize anyone, because they were their own worst critics. And he recognized that his women players were willing to die for him and each other when they felt supported.

That single question from the winningest coach in history—a rabid collector of inspirational quotations, emotional writer of letters—was all he said at half-time to the women. For them, the stress of the game was already sufficient framework. By picking moments *not* to yell at his players, he has won 21 championships.

A research team led by Drs. Nichole Lighthall and Mara Mather at the University of Southern California did a series of experiments to determine how gender differences become more prominent under stress. They first distinguished between physical stress, which is processed in the brain-stem, and psychological stress, which is processed in the limbic system.

Women tend to take less risk and make decisions more slowly after being physically stressed. For men, physical stress improves their performance, and they take more risk and make faster decisions. Brain scans also show these opposite effects of physical stress in males and females.

Under emotional stress, men's brains tune out emotional cues and make them more calculating. For women under stress, their decision-making becomes more entangled with their emotions as activity increases in the emotional regions of the brain. Women under stress seek out the emotional cues.

This means that, to manage stress, women and men need to go about it differently. Things that may help women regulate tension will usually not be noticed by men.

That males spend most of their early lives in groups, while females spend most of their time in pairs, may explain some gender differences in competitiveness. Men who compete more become less concerned about the outcome. Women tend to be hyperrational and want to ensure the win before they compete. Even six-month-old male infants prefer images of groups to images to individuals or pairs; infant girls have no such preference.

Observational studies find that preschool girls are involved in paired activities at least twice as much as boys, who prefer groups. Six-year-old boys spent 74 percent of their time in group activity, while girls played in a group only 16 percent of the time, significantly more in dyads. Boys roughhouse and fight to be best. Girls play games that require taking turns. As children grow into adulthood, this pattern—men socializing in groups and women in pairs—persists.

Expectations and perceptions play a large role in each unique individual psychology. Gender, like desire, shapes what we see, what we want to see, and what we omit from view.

Secrets

The Invisible Story

We keep secrets from lots of people, but most of all we keep them from ourselves.
And we call that forgetting.
—Dr. Elizabeth Lamb in the film, *Trance*

A secret holds onto something, continuously engages by sequestering, reserving its place, frozen in time. The possibility of telling beckons relinquishment of what the secret holds, threatens to unleash what it packages, and adumbrates dissolution of the illusion that is part of the secret. The threat of exposure risks stripping away everything pertaining to the secret, especially its companion—hope. A difficult aspect of telling secrets out loud is bidding farewell to what never was. Hardest perhaps are those secrets shrouded by the silence of shame, the toxic or taboo content cordoned off in the psyche like an abscess by the body.

Originally for a child, a secret keeps an aspect of self distinct from parents, assuring separateness, while the process guarantees connectedness to the one from whom the secret is kept. As children we create a private space within the self, the silent partner of the earlier "no" with its public notice to parents: "This is where you end and I begin; I am not an extension of you. I am me." Telling a secret is both a frightening and an exciting endeavor, of facing fear and possibly shame. Paradoxically, telling a secret restores the privacy intended in creating the secret, for it is the most intimate thing you can do with yourself. The only way you can know all your secrets is to tell them out loud to someone else. Recognition of the existence of a secret initiates its exposure.

In approaching a secret about ourselves we may feel frightened, as part of the unknown associated with the experience that is filed away alongside the secret.

One woman noticed that as she approached her father, certain feelings about her father came up and her throat closed up, which, of course, foreclosed discussion and preserved the secret. She embodied the feeling of wanting to go away and hide, so her throat did the legwork.

Sometimes we can engage something the first time by denying it. The only thing new is to discover what has been forgotten. Secrets speak silent voices, moments stopped in time, essences preserved. Secrets are stored in the place where self resides, necessary originally, yet their abiding presence may rob freedom. Listening to echoes of the spirit, neither the past nor the future seem too far away as secrets are told out loud.

Secrets keep one's needs disenfranchised from the self, as well as from what (or who) could be engaged to meet those needs. To not need secrets is a necessary freedom.

Telling a secret is a relational dress rehearsal for revealing aspects of self in intimacy with another. Such is the act of risk and courage of a little girl to fall in love with her father, not knowing how it will turn out, hopefully never having to consider, worry, or wonder if her intended cuteness would be rejected or humiliated.

Writing in a diary brings a private, internal conversation into view to then hide it. (So that it can be later found?) Something secret may have to be written or spoken to know what it is, just as we may have to lose something to know, by finding it, that we have it.

The greatest vulnerability is daring to expose our best feelings. And only when we feel fully secure can we be aware of how afraid we were. Happy tears come when all the impediments are cleared away, like the joy of reunion.

We regress into our past involuntarily, such as in terror or anger, or voluntarily, such as in love or memory, to find that our earliest passions have receded, though surely not departed. These survivors from an almost forgotten era return as harbingers of secrets buried but not lost. Free associations, stream of consciousness (telling ourselves secrets out loud in the daytime), and dreams (picture-story secrets we tell ourselves in nighttime language) answer necessary, though unformulated, questions.

The answers always give rise to the question, and make its formulation possible. Many times the questions are recognized only after the answers become evident. We have to live the answers first to know the questions. The writer writes, not because of having something to say, but to learn what he or she has to say.

And what remains unconscious will likely be attributed to fate.

Secrets may take the form of unspoken conversations. I recall some time ago how a woman in analysis spoke of the repeated interchanges with me ending in her frustration and disappointment: *When I say really awful things about myself, self-punishing things, I thought you knew that was only one part of the conversation. My silent grandiosity is the other half of the conversation, the part that I counterbalance by labeling it as bad, wrong, or shameful.*

She blanketed her expansiveness and desire to be praised with layers of negativity and self-criticism. She expended great amounts of energy appearing to not need anything or anyone in order to protect her vulnerable self. While critical of herself out loud, she expected me to counter with the notion that she really deserved and could acquire success, her secret that had remained mute for a lifetime. In her unspoken internal conversation, if I didn't respond to negate her self-criticism, I was confirming her assumption of deserving negative judgment. Afraid to say out loud what she wanted, she made sure that her beliefs would be validated. Alongside a hope, always, rides the vulnerability of disappointment. When she crystallized and took ownership of both her surface and shadow stories, she could finally write a new, present story.

People become distraught because they can no longer keep their secrets, and yet they cannot tell their stories to themselves. Instead, they relive their old stories, perhaps writing new endings for them and not realizing that, even with a new or better ending, the old story is frustratingly recreated. By generating a new story, the old story's repetition becomes recognizable, and past and present can be differentiated. The future then has new possibility. One has to have a new story to be in before one can completely give up an old story. The script that disallowed an authentic version of oneself has to be replaced by a new script.

Speaking Secrets Out Loud

Perhaps we can truly speak of pain only when we are no longer enduring it.
—Arthur Golden, *Memoirs of a Geisha*

By speaking secrets of the past out loud (a secret is always about the past, because it exists in a time capsule), form and definition are given to both the void and the repressed. The true texture of the present becomes distinct from the repetition of the past. Telling secrets may be painful, yet the most intense suffering is not to remember past trauma, but to limit present possibilities. We remember in order to forget, to distinguish past and present, to make the past a memory rather than an active, intruding presence. Nothing anchors us to the past more than the present energy it takes to keep secrets.

Several years ago in therapy, a man who abused drugs was puzzled by my question: *If you gave up your symptom, what would you have as a secret?* He didn't know how to answer me. The drug use had been his secret, illicit pleasure. It had been so dominating of his life, so defining of his identity, he would feel lost without it.

A woman writer in psychoanalysis who responded to the same question was frightened to give up the continuity of her restraint. Her mother had taught her that vitality can be used up today, so it should be saved for tomorrow, or else there is no tomorrow. Her mother had saved everything, including herself; then she died. Like her mother, the writer was hiding her sexuality inside her obesity, secure and predictably limiting. She felt vulnerable if she began exposing her secret, to not hold it so tightly and carefully. Her letting go was an anxious separation from the internal bond with her mother. Her weight served as insurance against the expected evocation of the negative, critical comments. Yet she also knew in her evolving writing that when she did not squirrel away her thoughts but instead used all her words (letting her secret self flow onto the page), other words followed exponentially, and she was left full instead of empty.

Within the space of an intimate dyad lies the enigma of how outside becomes inside, and the paradox of reliving that which never was.

How can one reclaim that which was never known, and repeat that which cannot be remembered? The confidante echoes the voice as yet unheard by herself, as well as by her confider. An experience begins to take shape and form. Developmental needs become visible in their actualization, and perhaps enactment, and the people of an individual's internal world become transparent in the characters and dialogues of this relationship. The disavowed versions of a secret self are activated, induced in an intimate interchange, projected into the shared space created by two people.

Although we may be desperate to keep our secrets, the harder we try to bury them, the more they rise to the surface. We are neurologically compelled to confess. There is a war in the brain about secrets. The cingulate cortex desperately wants to tell the truth, but the orbital prefrontal cortex calculates how bad it would be if we talk. If the orbital prefrontal cortex wins, the level of stress hormones goes up. If the cingulate cortex wins, stress level drops.

So it's biologically healthier to confess our secrets. What is it about human nature that makes us fight so hard to keep them hidden?

The Mystical and The Uncanny

If you want to find the secrets of the universe,
think in terms of energy, frequency, and vibration.
—Nikola Tesla

Mystical experiences are revelations within (and perhaps because of) their own state of mind, deeper than the emotional and below the foundation of consciousness. Mystical experiences involve meanings divine or spiritual, beyond human understanding, using another kind of eye (in-sight) into levels of knowledge transcending thoughts, language, or the senses. The mystical, it is said, has no birthday, no native land. William James in 1900 described the related states of consciousness of mystical experiences having the noetic characteristics of ineffability, transiency, and a sense of unity.

Mystical experiences transcend the secrets that reside in the unconscious. The uncanny at times is an experience of memory, the strangeness of the old appearing as the unique, astounding new. The uncanny, a secret that appears unbidden but not forbidden, suddenly comes to light as the strangeness of the familiar. It is more like a memory in which the past and the present seamlessly amalgamate in a novel way. The unexpected, the unbelievable, presents itself unannounced, with uncanny resemblance to the concealed, now illuminated.

Far more specific and unique than simply not knowing, or being surprised, the uncanny is that which is unthinkable, and even if it were, would reside outside words and resist language. Uncanny experiences mix real and unreal, a fantasy animated with dreamlike qualities, like déjà vu. Or an incident that revisits an experience of childhood. The unacceptable, in contrast to the uncanny, simply lies patiently (sometimes, not so patiently) waiting to reveal itself. Its secret peeks around the edge of the forbidden to announce itself in derivative and subtle ways, or even by its reverse image (both the print and its negative are the same image).

Consciously unexpected, logically unbelievable, and unconsciously exhilarating, the uncanny coalesces seemingly unrelated experiences. Such is the case when two in spiritual communion sense each other's thoughts, feelings, or movements.

The experience of the uncanny recognizes a relationship rather than a concurrence, yet as inchoate as it is unfathomable. Whispers of a meaning beyond discernment, knowing that there is no known explanation, begin to explain. Experiences can create their own reasons.

Though engaging the ineffable attempts to know what is not known, to successively approximate elusive meanings, the uncanny cannot be focused in thought any more than the ineffable can be concretely conceptualized. Neighbor to uncanny is incredulous, to discern the existence of *nothing* as a known *something*, to be aware that darkness is actually seeing the dark, rather than not seeing the light.

The Intangible Bond of Secrets

Ignorance of myself is something I must work at;
it is something studied like a dead language.
—Stanley Cavell, *The Claim of Reason*

Someone with a secret is concerned both about holding onto it with the supposed need for it, and at the same time inviting someone else to help get rid of it, to receive it. A secret always involves someone else, someone from whom you specifically keep the secret. Like the worrier, after all, who would he be without his worry (secret)?

Just as worrying implies a future—a conscious conviction that a future exists in which something terrible might happen—a secret is also an ironic form of hope, combined with powerful engagement of those from whom the secret is kept.

For both a secret and a worry, we have to remember. And both the secret and the worry regulate intimacy of its creator: It is threatening to get too close to the object of either, yet both ensure the presence of the bond. (If you didn't have anyone to keep the secret from, what's the point?)

A secret is an obstacle, something you can construct only when it can be tolerated. By recognizing the construction of an obstacle, we can then consider our desire for continuity.

How are secrets (and obstacles) constructed? An obstacle, like a secret, is used to conceal, to pack up an unconscious desire. What is the obstacle (the secret) not letting happen? Adam Phillips spoke of a patient who complained of her toddler son's clinging to her, such that she never had a moment to herself. The son was always in the way, wrapping himself around her legs or her body. Phillips asked where she would be going if her son were not in the way. She responded, *Oh, I wouldn't know where I was.*

Both symptoms and secrets are often constructed as obstacles; obstacles are the unconscious mnemonics of desire. We often nurture our obstacles, or at least ensure their ongoing presence, lest we have to face the feared desire. So, we are always maintaining and indirectly engaging the desire via the necessary obstacle. The death of possibility is both the promise and the threat.

Sometimes we manage a hated aspect of ourselves by making it incarnate in someone else. Provoking anger in someone else continually expels it from oneself, but also keeps it active and close at hand.

Symptoms as Secrets

It is easier to fall ill than learn the truth . . . so take care of your maladies. . .
they always have something to tell you.
—M. Pavic

Every psychological symptom is a secret hiding in the open, in evidence but not in awareness, a way to obscure from the self that which eventually becomes apparent. A symptom houses various enigmas: that every fear was once a wish; that we construct defenses so that we unconsciously sustain contact with what we fear; that we make the object of desire and fear the same so that we can run away from it and engage it at the same time; that fear guides toward, yet masks desire; that the secret (and symptom) encodes the piece of one's life that is not lived, to vividly (and perhaps defiantly) portray that which is unacceptable.

A phobic assignment of danger provides the illusion of safety in its avoidance. The fascination and compelling engagement with the phobic object are coupled with an equally passionate aversion, like the fear and pull of looking over the edge from a great height. A phobia, then, defends against fear by creating a specific and individually tailored apprehension, a designer anxiety.

How surprising, even embarrassing, it is to recognize that a secret has never been secret at all, only an aspect of ourselves from which we have disallowed awareness, that the secret has been ultimately kept only from ourselves. The glass against which our nose is pressed to take in whatever is possible, perhaps even forbidden, becomes a mirror in which we see in ourselves the previously unseen.

We tell ourselves secrets out loud by symptoms, and in other quieter ways in epiphany moments of clarity, synthesis, or oneness with nature. And sometimes by emotion occupying an altered state.

An internal secret may be continuously portrayed on the somatic stage. Freud described emotion converted to physical expression more than a century ago. A *conversion symptom*, a nonorganic dysfunction of a body part or sensory organ, follows an idea rather than an anatomic distribution. An untenable emotion or unbearable thought is converted into bodily expression, usually in a symbolic yet simple way: If one cannot bear to see something, vision may be literally blurred; a white noise may obfuscate harsh, critical words. Or impotence derived from guilt may be the somatic penance for a taboo desire. Aversion may protect from fear of fusion and loss of individual identity.

Every psychological symptom both reveals and conceals, making very obvious to others what we hide from ourselves, continually engaging what we attempt to flee. Symptoms give disguised voice to what we avoid knowing. As sentinel of a process that needs, begs, to be understood, a symptom should be listened to rather than silenced, respected rather than disregarded. A story needing to be heard, it repeats until translated or listened to literally: a pain in the neck, purging something, weeping skin, hyper-tension. People become patients because they can no longer keep their secrets, yet cannot tell their stories to themselves. A symptom is an answer to a question its creator has not dared ask consciously, a story with its own history, dynamics, and motivation.

Symptoms substitute a paradoxical illusion of mastery to cure an absence, to remedy helplessness, to serve as a developmental splint, to defend against emotional pain. Mastery of the original absence or tox-icity is always impossible since it is no longer the past. Symptoms are defensive, a local anesthetic, as well as compensatory, attempting to fill a need. A food binge at an emotionally painful time disconnects from the unwelcome feeling and attempts to fill an emotional hunger. The story of the symptom, including the motivation, begins long before it happens and ends long after it is over.

Symptoms have early beginnings. Every child attempts relentlessly to make his or her parents normal, and becomes symptomatic only to the extent that the parent(s) can't be made normal. If a parent empathically misses, with little register of the child's emotional world, the child then provides the parent with something more tangible and specific, such as a symptom or accident. A symptom states that no matter who you are or how old you are, the child inside will come back and demand any unrequited *need* when awakened by a present *want*.

Professionals often, unfortunately, shift focus to the pathological *result* rather than the developmental *intent*. Clustering the characteristics of a symptom and giving it a name provide the illusion of mastery. In dreams, as with symptoms, cause and effect interchange: The creators of the dreams or the symptoms behave as if what they made is happening to them, as if they are the subject rather than the author. (*My anger took over. My thoughts ran away from me.*)

What does a symptom ask of its creator? The same thing a dream, in its nighttime language, wants: to listen, to hear the message spoken in somatic, action, or symbolic daytime language, to learn from it. To understand empathically the comfort created by the symptom, to appreciate the symptom's immediate power to reduce tension, to recognize the addictive investment in its effectiveness, and perhaps to acknowledge its organizing function to identify and label. (*I'm an alcoholic/bulimic/procrastinator ...*)

The symptom contains the message, yet importantly, it *is* the message. The anorexic by not eating defiantly asserts autonomy from parents and their control, yet ensures attachment because she is dangerously ill. Her painful dependency is in heavy disguise and enigmatic code. (*I don't need you, or anyone; I'm not even dependent on food.*) The visible secret is her emaciated, frail body that screams the need for, and aversion to, help. Control, the antithesis of mastery, hypertrophies as she becomes worse. The process that she began and once controlled now controls her.

Someone who has experienced anxious worry and suffering for a lifetime becomes accustomed to feeling bad. Staying with feeling good is the ultimate challenge. Anxiety has been coupled with danger and trauma. Fear has predicted the future, and the only certainty has been repetition of the past. The pull of the old and the fear of the new inform invisible decisions that become camouflaged in habit, our collection of repetitions.

To feel good, to be inside a new story together in a new relationship, leaves known territory and the pseudo-effectiveness of its repetition. Just to feel good enters new, unfamiliar terrain, with no known landmarks—a separation anxiety from the accustomed. This new anxiety is different. The uncertainty of expansiveness and the awkwardness of feeling good are alongside the familiar restraint and perception of danger. To not construct an obstacle and to not obtrude desire creates its own anxiety. Kierkegaard said almost two centuries ago, "The very possibility of being able creates dizziness." Or, as a man said more explicitly, *Doc, wouldn't it be a drag if I found out what I've been running from all this time was* good *rather than* bad?

In addition to the defensive stopping of a new, uncomfortable experience, at times the neuronal connections just run out, without the synapses organized in a way to sustain the experience along a forward path in an existing neuronal pathway. At these times, the subjective perception about a new experience is that "I just can't keep it going; it fizzles out." This difficulty with sustaining a new experience, even a good one, is analogous to driving down a highway and suddenly coming to the point where the road stops; proceeding is discontinuous, possible yet different, slower, uncertain, along an unpaved route. An individual's experience begins to take a new shape and form, new experiences become transparent in the characters and dialogues of interactions, such as when someone truly falls in love for the first time.

The disavowed and projected versions of one's secret self become activated as a relationship unfolds. The symptoms, those previous ways of avoiding knowing, often begin to disappear as the engagement evolves. The states of mind we call symptoms, such as depression or anger, may become altered states unnecessary to enter.

Symptom as Story

> *No mortal can keep a secret.*
> *If his lips are silent, he chatters with his fingertips.*
> *Betrayal oozes out of every pore.*
> —Sigmund Freud

Nathan was a well-known nonfiction writer, just off a *New York Times* bestseller list. But he was experiencing a writer's block—he had not produced anything for several weeks when he called me for Mentor Coaching.

I asked him to explain his writing process—to walk me through it, step by step, in detail, to describe what he did and what he was experiencing. I also asked to hear his internal dialogue.

He described how, as he sits down to write, *I get nervous and begin doing a lot of different things other than writing. Then I start wondering if I can produce another bestseller, or was it just a one-time happening.*

After exploring the details of this process and his distractions, I could observe, *It sounds like you get really excited—maybe more so than ever—about immersing yourself in the passion you've always wanted to experience.*

When Nathan confirmed this, I continued. *When you read the excitement as anxiety, it puts you in your old story, as if anxiety still equates with danger. In that story, distracting yourself was adaptive—a way of regulating the tension.*

This perception, that coupling of meaning and coping mechanism were part of his old story, now juxtaposed with a newly evolving story. He recognized his current anxiety as feeling different—an excitement—while also an uncertainty about letting go of the familiar.

He reframed his excitement as a validation of being in a new experience, and as a signpost of progress to continue moving ahead in his writing.

The result was that he produced an even bigger bestseller. Nathan's anxiety diminished to become infrequent and mild, more like a souvenir of a place he had been. How else can someone be aware of how far they've come in a developmental journey than to have a fixed point of reference? To validate progress at different junctures? To use the symptom again to experience it as different?

We are never more aware of creating a symptom than when recognizing that we can create both its presence and its absence. It is the enigma of recognizing that we feel most like a child at the very moment we realize we are no longer one.

Ending the relationship with a symptom often feels like an amputation, removing a section of identity, parting with a longstanding loved/hated companion. One cannot just abstain from a symptom. To give up a symptom or a problem, especially those that have been lifetime companions and even woven into identity, is no small matter, no simple *Aha!* recognition and reversal. A psychosomatic pain cannot be stopped logically or consciously: *There must be a new story to be inside before the old story can be relinquished.*

Each psychosomatic symptom is a visible secret bringing together mind and body that have previously existed as a duality. When experienced and expressed directly and fully, feelings unite the mind and body, so that the bridge of a psychosomatic symptom need not be constructed. For example, a woman had intermittent blurry vision. She recalled it first occurring as a girl, when her mother flew into rages and often hit her. She saw the hate in her mother's eyes, and then her vision blurred, protecting her. She needed glasses as a girl, yet never had difficulty seeing clearly in settings with no emotional trauma, such as in her classroom. At other emotionally charged times, she had ringing in her ears, a white noise that would buffer the sharp piercing words of both parents when they were in alcoholic rages. She had been through many medication attempts and changes, none of which seem to work. She thought the ringing in her ears was a side effect of different medications. She now recognized the feelings in her body that she had not allowed in her conscious mind.

Secrets Enacted as Action Symptoms

An action symptom is a secret hiding in the open, embedded in an action sequence.

A freshman in college, Brittany felt depressed and lost. In therapy she stated, *I want an unconditional love that I've never possessed.* Her parents divorced when she was four, and she alternated afterward living with each parent, eventually with grandparents. She described her impulsive use of money as an attempt to possess something tangible, to make herself feel better. *I feel an urge to get something new when there's not enough, and I want more. I never thought I had enough; I never thought I had plenty. I jump up and run to the mall when I have a powerful urge to buy clothes. The urge is like emptiness. I feel frantic, depleted, frenzied. An urge to get something more. I get very anxious. Then I'll go buy some clothes. I feel like I can't leave without something. Even if I don't find what I want, I have to leave with something.*

Spending money as if there were no limit reinforced Brittany's illusion that she could have anything and everything she always wanted: the same momentary feeling she had in the middle of an eating binge. She was inside an impulse: Urge and action were fused.

She would feel good—hopeful—as she bought an outfit. The tag was an indication of the newness, something that no one had seen on her before. Maybe she would be different; maybe the new outfit would change her. She added, *I need something to touch, something tangible. I can hear but not fathom the concept of love.* The good, hopeful feeling would last until she wore the clothes for the first time. As soon as the tags were gone, the hope vaporized.

Brittany attempted to give form and shape to what she wanted, something so vague and formless that she didn't understand what it was. She felt compelled to make it tangible, to convert passive and helpless to active and effective. *That's why I have trouble with and want boundaries. I want to see it and touch it. Whenever I colored in a coloring book as a girl, the first thing I did was to outline the boundaries very specifically.* Brittany favored big, bulky clothes, which stimulated her skin and made her feel *outlined* and thus more real. At times she preferred skintight, Spandex-like clothes to provide a tight, binding container, like being held tightly.

Her urge to shop most often was precipitated by a disruption in her connectedness with someone important to her. Clothes were a concrete way of having the skin stimulation, of being held, just as food was a symbolic nurturing, all representing a valiant effort to regulate her feelings and meet her own needs.

As a girl, whenever Brittany was feeling bad her mother would buy her clothes. In later years, shopping was still the transitional bridge to create a souvenir of her mother. Spending money was a way of giving to herself, of creating an illusion of reconnection with a mother who gave to her a similar manner, who shared the same symbol of love and nurturance. The clothes were a fashionably tailored version of her earlier security blanket, imbued initially with the same magic.

Psychological symptoms involve variations of mental activity, defenses heightened or gone awry, but adaptive in an earlier context. Action symptoms convert any significant emotion or its signal into a specific action scenario. Action engages the body to regulate tension, distract from feeling, change a state of mind, or at the time to attempt to connect mind and body. Action symptoms are unique and addictive, such as the instant change of state with substances or activities. The anorexic, to remedy an anxious helplessness, focuses on a part of her body as *fat* and creates a sense of effectiveness by not eating. Action holds hope of change: One way to temporarily end ambivalence or to seemingly end a conflict is to pick one side and act on it.

Action symptoms involve the symptomatic use of a substance such as food, alcohol, or drugs, or an addictive use of an activity such as spending money, sexual perversions, compulsive exercise, or self-harm. An action symptom may defend against painful feeling by distracting and dissipating it into action. An action symptom's external and tangible focus circumscribes, makes finite and specific, and masters a small portion of the universe to temporarily create a sense of effectiveness. Action symptoms crystallize the elusive into a palpable, predictable hope, to supplement by proxy that which is missing. The very choice of the symptom creates both a tangible effectiveness of relieving tension and an invisible prison; ultimately the mastery reveals itself as an illusion, so the process must be repeated. Once a particular genre of action symptom is chosen, it may become habitual and foreclose other options to grow into a life of its own. This addictive process then eclipses usual pursuits.

Reflective judgment inhabits the potential space between urge and action. This space is where we usually dance with the questions, puzzle about options, and consider consequences. Action forecloses this contemplative space, necessary for feeling and fantasy, and at times ambivalence and confusion. For someone addicted and inside an urge, there is no future, no consideration of what happens after what happens next. All time—past, present, and future—collapses into action. Longer-term purposes neither motivate nor deter at the moment of fused urge and action. The powerful, magnetic pull of an addictive action dissipates anxiety, releases tension, or changes an entire state of mind. If someone is addicted to something, the hardest thing to do is *nothing*. If significant others are unreliable, inconsistent, and disappointing, these substances or activities unfortunately offer predictability.

How someone attempts repair or remedy of a sense of *not good enough* may be to project it onto the body as being *defective* in some way. The body becomes a Rorschach blot, to make tangible and give shape (and thereby, hope) to hungers, taboos, and perceived defectiveness for which there are no words or a language. From a menu of action symptoms can be chosen a way to overcome a perception of defectiveness or inadequacy by exercising or other compulsive activities, losing weight (anorexia nervosa), being more attractive (compulsive shopping), changing the defect (plastic surgery), or imitation (of movie stars or admired others). Other genres of action symptoms include fetishes, in which an object or component of the body is stand-in for a relationship and intimacy, and perversions, an erotic form of hatred.

Money was always intended to be a symbol, so it is a ready stand-in for what we fear is inadequate, undeserved, or unattainable. It serves as the perpetual promise of esteem, value, or power. The individual who compulsively shops and spends to enhance attractiveness and desirability also hopes to address loneliness and emptiness by engaging others to validate worth and desirability. Just the action of shopping, whether in virtual or shopping-mall reality, changes mood. This driven activity often couples with an expansive mood and fantasy that one can have anything and everything wanted. Compulsively buying clothes or jewelry temporarily restores value and affirms attractiveness of one's body.

Relying on other people for their supply of affirmation, enhancement, function, and esteem, these individuals may attempt to find a tangible way to obtain the source or promise of these emotional goods, countering the anguish of boredom, emptiness, or deadness. The compulsive shopper's new clothes concretize the promise of attractiveness, to garner responses and perhaps reestablish a ruptured bond. Shopping and spending change a state of mind, and organize efforts of validation and affirmation of her body, as if establishing contact with a secret part of the self not in evidence. For some individuals, the most salient aspect of the shopping and spending is the engagement with the sales clerk. The exclusive attention and empathic perceptiveness to the wishes of the shopper create a temporary replacement for the disrupted bond precipitating the shopping excursion. Credit cards and the internet offer further detachment into virtual money and space, providing an addictive magnet of distraction into the abstract.

Action symptoms may seem to be the best or at times the only way to register an experience, regulate tension, or even predictably evoke responses from others. Action symptoms may become an identity, such as alcoholic, bulimic, impulsive. When one feels lost or disorganized, directing focus on the body's action attempts cohesion. The inchoate transforms to the specific, tangible action. At times of insult, trauma, or perceived empathic disruption, these individuals may engage in action sequences that in some way stimulate the body, such as pain, gorging, starvation, overexertion, risk-taking, compulsive sex, wrist-cutting, body mutilation, drug or alcohol use and abuse. Though the action symptom is driven, automatic, obligatory, it subjectively creates an effective sensorimotor experience of the body self. If viewed as a *disease*, it may be a life sentence, for a disease is something you can't control. And you never have to separate from a disease.

The entire scenario in which the action symptom is embedded contains the developmental quest to regulate tension, restore esteem, or fill emptiness. As proxy for the real thing, it has to be repeated. The neural networks and neuronal pathways become automatic and well grooved, the default mode.

An action symptom has an immediate and magnetic power of tension reduction. The effectiveness of the action symptom makes it difficult to relinquish, because as it can instantly change the way one feels. The challenge of separation from this loved/hated yet predictable companion requires understanding the story of the symptom, the motivation, the specific and detailed enactment, and the experience before, during, and after the symptomatic act itself.

For those who select from the menu of action symptoms—who speak in such action language as food to fill an emptiness, or money to denote power or worth—internal experience may not have evolved to metaphor and symbol (though the action chosen may be quite symbolic). For someone so accustomed to action as an instant relief of tension, contemplative pause and reflection are anathema. (And, of course, there is no pill to deal with the problem of wanting to take pills.)

Rather than attempting to remove a symptom that may be its creator's loved and hated best friend as predictable comfort, relief, and loyalty (such as food, smoking, or the idea of death), the relationship with the symptom must be understood and respected. Empathic listening and collaboration may reveal the use and purpose of the symptom as it undergoes developmental change. (You don't have to search for a magic bullet once you recognize you've created an illusory enemy.)

A symptom can serve the function of a placebo. The placebo pill is a symbol of a medicine with an attached story of expectation. The process of its effect validates the power of the mind. A placebo is a white lie, a fiction that creates a truth. This created truth emerges from the story and belief surrounding the inert placebo, a truth so powerful that it can also exactly reverse the pharmacological effect of a particular medication. An experience is created by anticipating it. We see what we believe, and we judge before it happens. To someone consumed by an addictive process, the idea of the food, drink, or drug changes the state of mind before the substance is actually ingested.

A final farewell to a symptom may be to try on its clothes one more time to be sure they no longer fit: that the old fears and negative thoughts no longer feel the same, that the once-familiar symptom doesn't work any more. How better to know how far you've traveled than to have a fixed point of reference, to engage the symptom one more time, just to be sure, like viewing the real body at a funeral. We are most aware of what was missed in the past when creating it in the present. It is most difficult to give up what has already been taken away, to let go of what is already gone. Often loss of the illusion is more difficult than the loss of the real thing.

Sometimes the most paralyzing experience is to fully recognize freedom.

Attachment

The Systems of Relationship Stories

All happiness or unhappiness solely depends upon
the quality of the object to which we are attached by love.
—Baruch Spinoza, 17th-century philosopher

In a TV reality show focused on couples who race against each other around the world and perform challenging tasks, Tim and Karen were the show's dream couple: smart, successful, beautiful people. As they encountered various challenges, details about their relationship emerged. Karen wanted to get married. Tim was reluctant. He valued his independence; she wanted to get closer. At pressured and intense moments during the race, and often after an argument, Karen wanted Tim to hold her hand. He was reluctant to do so, as it felt too close, and he did not want to succumb to her every whim.

In the final show of the season, Tim and Karen were ahead and close to winning the big prize. But at the finish line they were beaten. After the season finale, during the interview, they were asked in retrospect if they would do anything differently. Tim responded,

> *The race in no way resembled real life. It was the most intense experience I have ever had. During the race we didn't even have time to be angry with each other. We just dashed from one task to the next.*

Karen responded in a different way.

> *I think we lost because I was too needy. Looking back, I see that my behavior was a bit much. Many times I needed Tim to hold my hand during the race. I don't know why it was so important to me. But I've learned a lesson from that, and I've decided that I don't*

need to be that way anymore. Why did I need to hold his hand so much? That was silly. I should have just kept my cool without needing this gesture from him.

Karen's basic assumption was that she should control her emotional needs and regulate herself in the face of stress. She assumed the problem was that she was too needy. However, attachment studies show that our brains become wired to seek the support of a partner by ensuring the partner's psychological and physical proximity. If that partner fails to respond or reciprocate, we are programmed to continue our attempts to achieve reciprocity until the partner responds. If Tim and Karen understood this, she would not feel ashamed of wanting to hold his hand during particular stress. And Tim would have known that the simple gesture of responding to Karen by holding her hand could give them an extra edge they needed to win. Had he known that by responding to her need early on, he wouldn't have had to devote time later to crisis management caused by her compounded distress. He might have been simply inclined to hold her hand when he noticed that she was starting to get anxious, instead of waiting until she demanded it.

Additionally, and very importantly, if Tim were able to accept Karen's support more readily, he would have engaged in the bungee-jump challenge which he initially refused to do, walking away after taking off his gear. Ultimately, he mustered the courage to take the challenge, but because of his hesitation they lost their lead.

Attachment principles inform us that *people are only as needy as their unmet needs.* When emotional needs are not met, behavior focuses on trying to engage others, to be effective in getting them to respond to meet needs. The paradox is that the more effective people can be in depending on one another, the more independent and daring they become. Tim and Karen were simply unaware of how best to use their emotional bond to their advantage to win the race.

Karen's and Tim's unawareness of their respective attachment roles is understandable in light of parallel social attitudes, especially among males, to scorn basic needs for closeness and interdependency, to idealize independence. The erroneous belief that people should be emotionally self-sufficient is ubiquitous.

The ideal of 20th-century parenting and 21st-century business leadership is that of an autonomous, self-reliant, fearless, adaptive, problem-solving person who is absorbed in work and play, with no particular attachment needs to any place or person. This model has been disproven time and again, as we now know how important intersubjectivity and connection with others become in optimum performance from infancy throughout adulthood.

The Attachment Behavior System

It has often been assumed that animals were in the first place rendered social, and that they feel as a consequence uncomfortable when separated from each other, and comfortable whilst together; but it is a more probable view that these separations were first developed, in order that those animals which would profit by living in society, should be induced to live together... for which those animals which were benefited by living in close association, the individuals which took the greatest pleasure in society would best escape various dangers, whilst those that cared least for their comrades and lived solitary, would perish in greatest numbers.
—Charles Darwin, 1871

We now have ways of mapping the shores and landscapes of the brain to capture the snapshot of a mood, to locate on the brain's map the specific centers of pain, pleasure, disgust, and even satisfaction at the downfall of the rich and famous who commit atrocities and indiscretions. We can track a tumor and trail a stroke, measure blood flow and hunger for glucose, quantify the quest for oxygen and locate a specific gene, but remain puzzled about how to authentically connect with another person.

The attachment system is an internal organizational scheme of relating to important others. The downloaded programs that guide interactions become a template for future relationships. The fundamental style determines an unconscious expectation or belief system of the possibility of how nurturing, intimate, and reciprocal relationships will be experienced. The more important the relationship, emotionally, intimately, or functionally, the greater is the likelihood that the individual's fundamental pattern will appear.

Darwin spoke, perhaps earlier than anyone, on attachment patterns and their impact. His focus on *society* and on *comrades* adumbrated the significance of the application of attachment patterns to optimize performance and enhance social and emotional intelligence. The first researcher in attachment theory, John Bowlby, beginning more than five decades ago, was, in fact, a Darwin biographer.

Attachment styles are consistent over a large range of cultures and countries and can predict to a significant extent how each person will respond in important relationships. Originally, each attachment pattern reflects a different strategy of an adaptive engagement—what it takes to effectively maintain a necessary bond with a primary caregiver.

Psychologist Mary Ainsworth observed distinct patterns of child behavior upon reunion with a primary caretaker and developed a theory of psychological attachment in relationships. The baby's behavior seemed an expression of the child's anticipation of the quality of comfort evoked by the caretaker's responses toward the child's distress. The child who was accustomed to being comforted would expect the caretaker to respond in an available and effective way at a distressing time. Conversely, the child who had learned through repeated experiences not to expect reassuring actions would not be soothed by the caretaker's reappearance.

The kind of implicit questions asked of an attachment system include:

Is my mom close by?

Is she available to me?

Will she comfort me?

Attachment failures can occur when:

- A caregiver is willing to be available but is not empathically attuned.

- The caretaker wants to be available but is absent at a crucial time of need or crisis.

- The caretaker is there, but instead of providing a safe haven, is insensitive, off-putting, or shaming towards the child.

- The caregiver is there, but smothers and overdoes functioning for the child, not allowing self-expression and the development of self-regulation and confidence.

Attachment behavior is any behavior with the intent of effectively getting a response from the caretaker. That is, attachment *behavior* is the breakdown product, the evidence of something not working right, and the attempt to reinstate the connection and the security of attachment. This *protest* is designed to reengage the caretaker.

The attachment system is a mental model, a set of basic assumptions or beliefs about one's self and the world. The repeated responses of the particular attachment style of the caretaker form a *self-dimension* centering around closure questions: *Am I worthy of being loved?* and *Am I competent to get the love I need?* Another set of beliefs forms an *other-dimension*, centering around two other important questions: *Are others reliable and trustworthy?* and *Are others accessible and willing to respond to me when I need them to be?*

These combined experiences and subsequent beliefs about *self* and *other* shape expectations about future relationships, forming basic *attachment styles*.

Primary Attachment Styles

The original development of an attachment system is based on one fundamental question: *Is the attachment figure accessible, attentive, and responsive?* If the child perceives the answer to this question to be *yes*, he or she feels effective, loved, and confident. This security produces a behavior of greater exploration of the environment, playing with others, and social interactions. If the child perceives the answer to be *no* or *maybe*, he or she experiences anxiety and is likely to exhibit behaviors to enhance the engagement of the caregiver, or to simply withdraw and give up. Those who give up— the avoidant style—appear not to be particularly distressed by the lack of connection and retreat to their own devices of self-regulation.

Early experiments gave rise to developmental trajectories of how long-term relationship patterns are impacted by fundamental style. The caretaker-infant attachment pattern is one the caretaker originally experienced himself or herself, and one the infant will download as an operating system to propagate in his or her children and colleagues.

The particular type of attachment relationship with primary caregivers determines the individual's resultant sense of security, agency, organization, and self-regulation. This fundamental pattern then informs the type of interaction that individuals will have with others throughout life. Each attachment pattern reflects a different strategy to attempt an adaptive solution to a challenge presented by different kinds of environments and caregivers.

Certainly other influences impact individual development throughout childhood, adolescence, and adulthood, but more than five decades of research shows evidence of the lasting impact of this fundamental attachment style from earliest life. Each person extrapolates basic relationship patterns, not only of parenting, but of other important relationships as well.

The Secure Response

Securely attached children, when upset emotionally, seek comfort and closeness from their caretakers, using them as a secure base. Then, once calmed, they can expand, explore, and play. The secure child, upset when a caretaker departs, will reunite with the caretaker eagerly and openly. He or she is comforted, and distress melts away. The child's *self*-definition establishes a pattern of effectively seeking comfort and reassurance. Its *other* dimension assumes the caretaker's availability and willingness to comfort emotional upset. These experiences establish a pattern of future expectation and the use of others to be comforting, the anlage of collaboration.

For example, someone more secure in their developmental relationships will more likely be emotionally and socially intelligent, more responsive to the needs of others, and engage in mutually focused strategies of collaboration and conflict resolution. These people tend to cope with stress more successfully and will more likely establish a close interpersonal relationship with others. The relationships of secure attachments tend to be more satisfying and long lasting.

The Anxious/Ambivalent Response

The child showing an ambivalent attachment, who is also upset when away from a caretaker, becomes more upset than the secure child, even angry. When the caretaker returns, the child also goes straight to that person, but all is not well as with a child in the secure group. The caretaker is not able to comfort the child. The result is a pattern of inability to regulate discomfort with another person and ultimately with one's self, and the expectation that others are not capable of giving comfort and protection. More extreme behavior—a tantrum or crisis—is needed in order to effectively elicit responses from the caretaker.

Those with insecure attachments—whether manifesting in avoidant patterns (dismissive, distancing of oneself from others) or anxious (distressed, seeing others as uncaring)—will have less satisfying and less successful relationships.

The Avoidant Response

In the same situation of separation and reunion, the child who consistently experiences disappointment in and lack of emotional comfort and confidence from the caretaker suppresses feelings and simply avoids contact with the caretaker. This look of indifference appears as self-sufficiency, yet it masks significant anxiety and distress.

Someone in an avoidant retreat may then use other more predictable substitutes to provide ersatz nurturing. Food and, later, money may be stand-ins to function in this way. An attachment pattern can then be established early in life with objects to substitute for the less predictable people.

The Disorganized Response

When caretakers are inconsistent, the result can be a combination of secure, ambivalent, and avoidant responses. The caretaker is responsive and attuned to the child's needs at times, but then becomes distant and aloof, or even exceedingly intrusive and interfering. This unpredictability leads a child to experience ineffectiveness.

With a disorganized attachment style, children question their sense of self and others and lack confidence in their abilities to predictably get their caretaker's attention. They subsequently do not regard others as trustworthy or accessible, much like the avoidant group.

The Science of Adult Attachment

Even into adulthood, our strongest emotional experiences, and thus our most evident attachment pattern activations, are tied to our closest relationships.

Adults show patterns of attachment to their romantic and work partners similar to their patterns of attachment as children with parents. The attachment process, initially describing how infants relate to an older, wiser caregiver, has significant application in the interaction of protégé and mentor, and in leadership styles in an organization.

Attachment—the characteristic manner in which we perceive and respond in relationships with important others, whether romantic or collegial—determines a foundation of working alliance. Each of the styles differs in the ways of perceiving connection, dealing with conflict, and in communicating wishes, needs, and expectations in a relationship.

Those with a *secure* style feel comfortable with close relationships and foster warm collaborative reciprocity. *Anxious* style people desire connection and intimacy, but are often preoccupied with their relationships and tend to worry about a partner's ability to reciprocate. *Avoidant* style people equate intimacy with a loss of independence and consistently attempt to minimize closeness and commitment. *Disorganized* style people show an inconsistent response to others, with a mix of secure, anxious, and avoidant responses.

Without insight or understanding, we operate in a preprogrammed, essentially unconscious manner. Attachment patterns of behaviors and emotions to generate connection, safety, and protection are embedded in our genes. Throughout evolution, genetic selection favors those who become attached, as it enhances survival. The brain is a biological mechanism specifically focused on creating and regulating our connection with attachment figures.

Analogous to the child engaging a frantic search coupled with protest behavior to reestablish contact and attention when parted from a primary caretaker, we still experience aspects of this in adulthood with separation, crisis, or uncertainty with an important other.

Adult Attachment Pattern Characteristics

Attachment Patterns to Objects

J. K. Rowling was a single mother living on welfare in the early 1990s in the Scottish city of Edinburgh. She had moved there following the breakdown of her marriage to a Portuguese journalist. As the *Daily Mail (U.K)* reported her recollections,

> *I was as poor as it's possible to be in this country. I remembered 20 years ago not eating so my daughter could eat.*

Then she got an advance for the first *Harry Potter* book, which began a different trajectory for her.

> We stopped renting and I could buy a house. Next it wasn't just advances, it was royalties coming in. Then you need advice on not blowing it. I was terrified of pressing the wrong button and losing everything and having to look my daughter in the face and say, "We briefly had a house, and now through a stupid error . . ."

Today, as the world's only author who has become a billionaire through her work, she still has significant residue of her old money story—her lifelong attachment pattern of her relationship with money.

When she met TV host Oprah Winfrey, Oprah asked, *Have you accepted now that you'll always be rich?*

Rowling said, *No, I don't know that. It bears no relation to what is in your bank account, it is purely emotional.*

Some evidence suggests that adults end up in relationships with partners who confirm their existing beliefs about attachment expectations. Attachment researchers from John Bowlby to Mary Main, including more recently Cindy Hazan and Phillip Shaver, have contributed to the understanding of the basic attachment styles.

Knowledge of attachment patterns can be applied to enhance adult collaborative relationships and inform successful leadership interactions. The working model of expectations, beliefs, and behavior patterns can be transformed.

Secure Attachment Style

Feeling warm and connected to important others comes naturally, with enjoyment of an intimate attachment without being overly worried about relationships. Effective communication of needs and feelings enables accurate reading of emotional cues from others and responding to them. Successes and problems can be shared openly, with reciprocal availability of sharing.

Secure adults are more satisfied in relationships than insecure adults; in them, they experience greater longevity, commitment, trust, and interdependence. This secure style has much to teach in generating more effective interactions. Security and secure-based behavior in adults is promoted by seeking support from a partner or significant other when distressed, providing support for the distressed person, and showing empathic concern to alleviate distress and insecurity during relational conflicts.

Sensitive attunement and responsiveness to another combines with an openness to share ideas, questions, discoveries, self-reflection, and self-expression. Greater delay of gratification and enhanced self-regulation are the result. These people also tend to both seek and attract similar secure type people for personal and professional relationships.

I find it relatively easy to get close to others and am comfortable depending on them and having them depend on me.

I don't often worry about being abandoned or about someone getting too close to me.

Anxious (Ambivalent) Attachment Style

This group, while they desire to be close and connected with a capacity for intimacy, harbor a fear that the significant person does not wish to be as close or interactive as they would like him or her to be. For this reason, relationships can consume a good deal of emotional energy, with sensitive fluctuation in a partner's moods and actions. A tendency to take a partner's behavior personally often leads to upset and negative perceptions. Preoccupation with the bond can, however, be minimized if the other person provides a good deal of security and a sense of connection.

If those with an anxious attachment style wait longer to gather more information before reacting, they can make use of their uncanny ability to decipher situations as well as to read others to their advantage.

I find that others are reluctant to get as close as I would like.

I often worry that my partner doesn't really love me or won't want to stay with me.

I want to merge completely with another person, and this desire sometimes scares people away.

Avoidant Attachment Style

With this group, maintaining independence and self-sufficiency assumes primary importance, with a preference for autonomy over intimacy. While perhaps desiring to be close to others, they feel discomfort with too much closeness, tending to keep a partner at a distance. In important relationships, an individual is often alert for any signs of control or encroachment on personal territory. Others perceive in them an emotional aloofness and distance.

I am somewhat uncomfortable being close to others.

I find it difficult to trust someone completely.

I value my autonomy over anything in a relationship.

Partners want me to be more intimate than I feel comfortable being.

However, when an empathic, nonjudgmental, empathic alliance is established, even the avoidant person may dare to interact in a more engaged way.

Disorganized Attachment Style

This attachment style is characterized by having no consistent style of response to attachment figures. These individuals show a combination of responses of both anxious and avoidant types, sometimes secure, but in an unpredictable, inconsistent way. They act from a basic disbelief in the trustworthiness and predictability of others.

A pattern may be repeated in which someone fosters helplessness or dependency in another by functioning for that person more than is needed. While the intent is to be helpful or compassionate, the result is creation of codependency with another.

This compulsive caregiving continues as a way of operating in personal and professional life. Originally it interferes with a child's autonomy and exploration, discouraging independent thinking and action. In an adult collegial relationship, it has the same consequence. The adult will express doubt about the ability to function autonomously, even though the patterns are not in conscious awareness or intention.

In a mentor-protégé relationship, the mentor needs to be aware of an inclination to repeat these same characteristics of functioning for the protégé; instead, the task is to instill a process of autonomy and self-functioning.

I can't seem to stop mothering my adult child/functioning for my partner.

You can never tell exactly how someone will respond.

It's too easy for me to slip into codependency in a relationship.

The attachment system is a mechanism in our brain to track and monitor the safety and availability of our attachment figures. Each system becomes activated when someone is engaged in a close, connected relationship. Otherwise, it lies dormant. For example, when a relationship evolves to intimacy or colleagiality, those with an anxious attachment style have a system that becomes activated to become more vigilant to changes in emotional expression, and have an acute sensitivity to cues from others. However, they often jump to conclusions quickly and tend to misinterpret emotional cues.

Understanding the attachment system is more crucial for people with anxious and avoidant attachment styles. This recognition allows one to not take various actions personally, to not misread cues, and instead to establish strategies for realignment of a relationship. An important insight for anyone in a relationship is to recognize that if there is any unsettling or derailment, all that is usually required is a minimum reassurance from a partner to get back on track. Without that reassurance, worries will multiply. So the more attuned each is to the other's needs, the less energy it will take for repairs.

Studies in attachment science have looked at the question of whether we are attracted to people based on their attachment style or ours. Some research suggests that avoidant individuals prefer anxiously attached people, and vice versa. This becomes true in a complimentary way, as both reaffirm the other's beliefs about themselves and about the relationships. The defensive self-perception of the avoidant style is to be independent and strong, and this is confirmed by the belief that others want to pull them into more closeness than they are comfortable with. The anxious attachment style perceives wanting more intimacy than a partner can provide and uses this information to confirm both a basic belief and the anticipation of being let down by significant others.

Without awareness, each style is drawn to repeatedly reenact a familiar script. An activated attachment system can masquerade as true love or, in a business setting, as dedicated collegiality. If you date someone and feel anxious, insecure, even obsessive, only to feel elated occasionally, this can feel like true love, with the hope of the elation expanding and being more central than it is. This activated attachment system generates energy but is the antithesis of true love, which, in the evolutionary sense, means peace of mind.

The Dependency Paradox

Once a partnership is established, interdependency always exists. It is not a *functioning for* the other, as in codependency, but a *connection with*—an intersubjective awareness of understanding, empathy, and reciprocity.

The paradox is that the ability to function autonomously—whether in childhood or adulthood—stems from the knowledge and trust that someone is beside us whom we can count on. The dependency paradox allows us to act more independently by being interconnected (rather than the misnomer of dependency) with an important partner. The paradox is that the best way to independence and autonomy is to have a connection with someone you can trust and with whom you share a bond of loyalty.

Dr. Brian Baker, psychiatrist and researcher at the University of Toronto, found that with a satisfying relationship, spending time in the presence of your partner can lower blood pressure to healthy levels. On the other hand, with dissatisfaction in a relationship, contact with the partner will raise blood pressure, which will remain elevated as long as physical proximity to that person persists. What we learn from this is that when our partner—life, marital, or business—is unable to reciprocate basic attachment needs, we experience a sense of disquiet and tension that can leave us more exposed to different elements. Emotional and physical wellbeing are both in the balance.

Consistent research shows that the partners we choose can influence not only how we *feel* about ourselves, but also the degree to which we *believe* in ourselves in attempting to achieve hopes and dreams. A partner who fulfills intrinsic attachment needs, with whom a secure base develops, can provide the context for emotional and physical health as well as for achievement. An inconsistent or unavailable partner does the opposite.

Part of the task, then, is how to go about finding that partner, co-creating a secure base, as well as becoming that kind of partner to reciprocate in a relationship and create more effective attachment patterns.

Those tasks include identifying our own attachment characteristics, the attachment styles of those around us, and co-creating a secure base for optimum performance and achievement individually and collectively, whether in a marriage or a business.

Evolving Attachment Systems

At a retreat to help an organization develop its own internal mentoring program, I did a demonstration Mentor Coaching with one of the mentors. I asked her initially what she wanted to focus on in our session. I then asked what she wanted to take away from the coaching session. She was vague, speaking in generalities about mentoring sessions with one of her protégés with whom she had significant challenges. She could not get beyond vague generalities. She indicated that she could not get him to focus on specifics.

After unsuccessful efforts to get her to focus with me on what she wanted specifically to get out of the session, I paused and asked if I could share a hunch with her. I wondered if she was experiencing the same reluctance as her client to share a meaningful exchange, preferring instead to stay at a distance, even though feeling stuck.

She confirmed that this was true and said how embarrassed and reluctant she felt to share any of her struggles in front of her peers. She had never before participated in a demonstration coaching, or had witnesses for a mentoring session. I told her that I understood entirely, and that it wasn't easy to share intimate details about an experience in front of someone else, and especially a number of peers.

I suggested that her experience was an *exact read* of her protégé, an accurate and sensitive barometer of the protégé's experience. I posited that the reluctance that she was experiencing with me and showing me through her embarrassment was *exactly* what her protégé was trying to tell *her*, though in the process of the attachment, rather than consciously and with words.

She immediately understood what I was saying and recognized that was precisely what was happening. She then began to open herself to discuss aspects of the engagement that were challenging but accessible to her and collaborated with me on strategies and ways to address this issue with herself as a prerequisite to addressing it with her protégé. Immersed in her own discomfort, she was unaware of the unfolding interactive attachment pattern and its parallel between herself and her protégé.

We came to see that when she felt confident about herself as a mentor, and about sharing her story, that she could be totally present with me. She then knew that she could help her protégé evolve his story and dare to risk some of his experiences with her. Her parallel with both the process and the attachment pattern in the engagement with me allowed both of us to see how her protégé was teaching her exactly what it was like to be him.

An attachment style usually becomes activated when strong emotion becomes involved, whether to do with a person or object, such as money or food. For example, we are more likely to develop emotional attachments to brand and particular products when we are alone and afraid.

It is not only the broad systems of *secure*, *anxious*, and *avoidant* that characterize attachment. Each individual creates numerous nuanced and individual attachment patterns, subtle or overt, adaptive or not. The styles will be consistent over time and manifest in a similar way in various relationships. It is when the attachment pattern recreates itself in the relationship with the Mentor Coach that significant understanding and leverage for strategic change can occur.

The key factors in studies showing transformation in attachment style involve a knowledgeable mentor as catalyst to provide a secure base for reflection and insight into both the content and process of the attachment interaction. The major factors in providing a secure base include empathic understanding and noninterfering support.

The perspective of the style of attachment can inform inquiry into what goes right in relationships as well as what goes wrong. Identifying the attachment style is not about labeling behaviors as healthy or unhealthy, right or wrong, or more or less developmentally evolved.

It's about the need to recognize a style in order to initiate evolution to a more effective pattern. Knowing which behaviors are effective and worthwhile becomes important. For example, those with a secure attachment style know how to communicate their own expectations and respond to another's needs effectively without having to exaggerate or resort to protest behavior.

The transference process is a simple concept, but elusive to recognize. The attachment pattern is a basic template for activation of the process of transference. Transference, the perception of a current situation in terms of the past, uses old software that may need updating. Someone will be the same person with the Mentor Coach as in any other aspect and every other relationship of his or her life. Those who create conflict and collect injustices have the same software informing perception and behavior in a new relationship to recreate a similar narrative and process. The basic attachment pattern will be recreated in the process. People always show us exactly what it is like to be them while they tell us about other people and situations in their lives. These self-statements recreate aspects of the attachment process in each new relationship and fall under the shadow of that narrative arc. With a foundation of trust and a working alliance, it can evolve to a new story.

The ways in which basic attachment styles interact in everyday situations hold information about more effective engagement. Adult attachment patterns can be put to powerful use in many situations to guide people to more effective relationship and leadership experiences. For example, creating a secure base with no crisis or drama in a relationship can allow the focus to move to significant accomplishments of collaboration. A colleague or partner may have a different attachment style from yours, and the challenge is not converting that person to your style or fitting into another's style, but gaining insight about creating common ground to develop strategies that improve satisfaction and effectiveness in the relationship.

While it is certainly possible for someone to change his or her attachment style, the prerequisite for change is awareness of a fundamental style, with a strategic approach and a systematic way to create a new story.

So, how to promote security and secure-based behaviors in an adult personal or professional relationship? The answer: provide mutual support and empathic resonance, collaborative support in addressing distress or problems, and mutual concern about resolving conflict to develop satisfying and enhancing strategies.

Our brains can be rewired. Existing models, including the quality of relationship patterns, can be revised, updated, and replaced by new experiences. Older representations, even though fundamental, can be overwritten—a new attachment story can be created, to influence relationships with important others for the remainder of adulthood.

Since attachment styles are a product of life experience, beginning with our interaction with our parents during infancy, this means that those styles can evolve, change, and adapt to more evolved forms. Just as someone can be coached to enhance social and emotional intelligence, more adaptive and secure attachment patterns can be formed.

The Neuroscience of Conversation and Collaboration: Toward Secure Attachment

Think about someone you know who is secure: how they behave in relationships, the way they interact in the world. For this role model, notice how they act and speak in different situations, what they ignore and what they respond to, and especially how they respond to colleagues. In their book *Attached*, Amir Levine and Rachel Heller give an example. *Once when I disagreed with my manager, I came out very strongly against him. He showed a genuine interest in what I had to say and created a dialogue with me instead of a dueling match.*

Another model is the relationship with your pet. Despite the various things that pet does, including waking you up at night, destroying your valuables, demanding your undivided attention, you probably overlook those behaviors and feel positively toward that pet. The connection with your pet is a good example of a secure presence in your life. You don't assume that your pet is doing things purposefully to hurt you, don't hold grudges even when the pet eats something of yours that is valuable, and still greet it warmly when you come home. You stick with your pet no matter what, as the pet does with you. This is a quintessential secure relationship model.

One of the tools most frequently used by people with a secure attachment style is effective communication. When two people connect empathically, they mirror each other's posture, gestures, movements, and tone of voice. When engaged in a connected, empathic exchange, one's emotional state will become socially contagious, affecting one other, or a whole group.

The most effective communicators keep the burden of clarity themselves, through brevity, clarity, and simplicity. Because working memory only selects two or three chunks of data at a time, we know that the listener can only focus on two to three tiny chunks of information for a brief period of time. Because of how the brain processes language and communication, brevity and clarity significantly enhance receptivity.

Internal strategies of connection and collaboration include a conscious focus on relaxation, staying present, cultivating inner silence, increasing positivity, and remaining resonant with deepest ideals. Resonance with the other person's experience and state of mind always comes first. Greater receptivity occurs when one speaks slowly, briefly, showing appreciation of communication, remaining positive, and listening deeply. To get inside the experience and story of the other person is quintessential for empathic connection and significant attachment with that person.

A secure attachment with another is predicated on creating the experience of security and confidence first in yourself. Your experience is then most likely to create connection to the other person. When you feel secure, the other person will gradually become more secure as a result of being with you. By being centered and grounded consistently, you are able to use more of your empathic ability to sense what the other person needs and experiences. Someone can become more secure as a result of being with a secure person. Those who are secure quite often have an innate and intuitive ability to soothe and reassure their partners.

For example, during the shift into parenthood, anxiously attached women were found to be more likely to embrace security in their

interactions with their partners if they perceived that partner as support-
ive, available, and accepting during pregnancy. This security can create a
shift in a partner's attachment style. It has also been found that people
with a secure attachment style are more likely than others to forgive their
partner for wrongdoing.

An important caveat is that people with secure attachment style need
to rely on their instincts, and by doing so can discern early in a relationship when someone is not cut out to partner in a working relationship.
So it is important to recognize this rather than to feel responsible for
the partner's happiness and persist in the effort despite instincts saying
to end the relationship. Likewise, in a healthy relationship it's important
to remember that just because you *can* get along with someone, doesn't
mean you *have* to or *should*.

Regardless of the particular style and nuance of an attachment system, the greatest satisfaction occurs when fundamental needs are met
and reciprocal understanding is enacted.

An understanding of fundamental style is hugely important, because
people under stress resort to their fundamental style. Those with an anxious attachment style cope with stress in a relationship by activating their
attachment system to try to get close to their partner. People who are
avoidant have the opposite reaction and cope with threats by distancing
themselves from their partners and turning off their attachment system.
The closer the anxious partner tries to get, the more distant the avoidant partner becomes. So one partner's activation further reinforces the
other's deactivation, creating a cycle with destabilizing results. For each
to move toward more security, both need to find a way to feel less threat-
ened in order to create a common ground for understanding.

And attachment issues can spill into more areas of life to significantly
affect the essence of a working relationship. The gap can widen if conflict
is unresolved, and challenges become greater.

Attachment research shows that basic styles are stable but plastic.
While they tend to stay consistent over time, nevertheless, they can change.

The key factors in understanding that working model include to
recognize and own that each of us is the author of our own attachment

story, to assess what works and what does not, and then to decide what to change, keep, enhance, and let go. Then with this awareness we can take the final steps to map changes, create them, and evolve identity to incorporate the changes. Addressing greater cohesion and positivity to develop adaptive strategies can inform us how to better enhance conflict resolution, increase satisfaction in working relationships, and optimize interpersonal effectiveness for increased performance and productivity.

This relationship inventory of the attachment bond with a significant other can be crucial in evolving the working model to be effective and efficient. Understanding the basic workings of attachment can prevent conflict before it happens.

The hormone of connection and bonding, oxytocin, plays a major role in attachment processes and strengthens attachment by creating social cohesion to enhance trust and cooperation. Enhanced connection increases oxytocin production, which then can serve to immunize a relationship against conflict.

The essential message is that relationships should not be left to chance, as understanding attachment patterns can provide a foundation for effective, masterful connections with others. The science of attachment can significantly enhance effective working partnerships and collaborations.

An abiding principle is that we can remain true to our authentic selves and address our attachment patterns to important others in significant ways.

Empathy

The Bridge to Common Ground

Could a greater miracle take place than for us
to look through each other's eyes for an instant?
—Henry David Thoreau

Empathy is to place ourselves in the inner world of another person without getting lost there. Empathy describes a listening perspective positioned inside the experience of another, to resonate with and understand his or her subjective reality. Empathy neither infers nor extrudes kindness, sympathy, consolation, gratification, or commiseration. Empathy describes a point of reference, a particular attunement to another individual's internal experience that permits appreciation from the vantage point of that person's own framework of thinking, feeling, and meaning. It is a scientific way of listening. Empathy positions one foot in the shoe of another's subjectivity and resonates with that experience and point of view.

To lose oneself in another is the antithesis of empathy. For example, codependency obfuscates empathy, as it requires not seeing all of someone. Being in love with who someone could be, rather than who they are, is one of many ways we project an aspect of ourselves onto another.

Listening from the inside includes awareness of another's internal and perceived external systems and of their model to perceive and process. This mode of human relatedness, understanding, and responding is described by psychoanalyst Evelyne Schwaber as *an early and ubiquitous human nutrient.* Contrast the early description by Freud of the analyst being an inscrutable mirror, a surgeon operating in a surgical field of the patient's mind, to the version depicted by Dr. Susan Vaughan in *The Talking Cure,* in which she indicates that in psychoanalysis her patient must . . . *let me become a character on the set of his internal drama, let me get inside his head and help him rearrange the furniture.*

Accurate empathy, to be attuned to the entire subjective reality of another individual, even requires attunement to what that person is omitting, to stick up for an aspect of someone not given sufficient oxygen for awareness or activation, to see beyond the problem, and to focus on what to look for and toward. An empathic model may guide both participants in an interchange to register perception and inform intuition.

Empathy strives to be equidistant between components of a conflict, a neutrality that does not know what the answer will be, does not need for it to go one way or another, and knows that there are many truths to tell without having an investment in which one is most important at this moment.

Empathic listening hears the surface story as well as the shadow story not given conscious recognition or words: the one that may be going in the opposite direction from the surface story. To align only with someone's wish colludes to avoid focus on the fear. Empathy allows understanding of both sides of a conflict or internal dichotomy in order to fully appreciate both components, such as wishing and fearing, wanting and not wanting the same thing. Each side of a conflict has its own motivation. To choose one side of a conflict and act on it creates the illusion of resolution. Fear is guide to desire, and both must be understood. It is quite compelling to align with one aspect of another's conflict, such as wanting him or her to get better, or admonishing an adolescent just to do something the way the parent wants. In doing so we forfeit empathy's attunement to the other side, the resistance to change, and the security of repetition.

Empathy is, among other things, simply a way to join someone in listening. When we identify with our child, we imagine her strengths and vulnerability and join her in resonating with her effectiveness, rather than separating her out by disidentifying with her. A small boy who zooms into the room as a superhero receives an empathic comment about how this is an amazing thing to be, rather than dousing the state of mind by reminding him that he's actually a little boy. When he falls over something, we feel it in our own bodies. Empathy assumes a sameness with someone else rather than highlighting the difference.

Repeating back to another person what is said is imitation, only approximating identification and understanding. Essential in the empathic interchange is resonance with another's experience. This is to select what seems a central, salient aspect of experience or feeling, to process its meaning, to reflect its essence in the interchange, and to listen for what is conveyed and the response it evokes, for further calibration.

Types of Empathy

> *If the historian will submit himself to his material*
> *instead of trying to impose himself on his material,*
> *then the material will ultimately speak to him and supply the answers.*
> —Barbara Tuchman, *In Search of History*

Each of these three forms of empathy has an upside and a downside, and together they form an empathic spectrum.

Cognitive Empathy

Cognitive empathy is to know the perspective of another person, of what that person might be thinking. This attunement can help in negotiation, finding a way to motivate people, and in performance enhancement. A study at the University of Birmingham found that managers who were good at taking another's perspective were able to help workers achieve their best efforts.

The downside: Cognitive empathy can lead to cold calculation—understanding another's point of view without taking emotions into account. This is informed detachment. Con artists are particularly adept at reading how their victims think.

Emotional Empathy

Emotional empathy is when we can sense what other people experience, as though their emotions were contagious. This emotional contagion occurs largely because of mirror neurons in the brain, a complex set of neural response patterns that fire when we resonate with another's emotional state. We sense the echo of another's experience in our own minds and bodies.

The downside: With emotional empathy, some may have difficulty managing their own emotions if they are powerful and sufficiently distressing. With the openness and capacity for emotional empathy, one may need to protect from depletion and contamination. Too little involvement, on the other hand, is indifference. The balance is informed caring that doesn't get in the way of someone having all his or her experience and working with it.

Compassionate Empathy

Resonance with another can produce the experience and knowledge that we are all connected. An example of a balance is staying cool in a crisis, yet sometimes allowing oneself to regulate emotion and state of mind enough to respond appropriately. A judgment call in compassionate empathy recognizes where we can and can't be effective in doing something in order to put full energy into what can be determined.

The downside of compassionate empathy is loss of objectivity, especially if it involves counter-identification with others. An example is my own experience during Hurricane Katrina. I witnessed high-level leaders being curiously detached, despite abundant evidence that they needed to take action. I saw on television the suffering and misery that people in New Orleans experienced. My own response, since I did some of my medical training in New Orleans, was, *I know those people. I treated some of them. That guy wading through the water carrying his baby—I could have delivered him when he was born.*

Empathy is not an end in itself, but a means to a better end. When someone carefully crafts a speech or tells a story, the art is to allow the emotional response to reside in the listeners or readers, rather than expressing it for them, or suggesting how they should feel. We can learn from the poets, who give it to the readers or listeners to experience themselves.

Empathic Derailment

No, Krueger, first you have to be with me before I can go someplace new with you.
—A psychoanalytic patient accurately confronting me with moving too
quickly into a dynamic interpretation before establishing empathic
resonance to communicate understanding

In any relationship, despite dedicated empathy, we invariably have an error of parallax: that difference between looking at the speedometer from the passenger's side and the driver who reads it dead-on. We can approximate another individual's subjective experience and reality, but we can never *be* that individual. One's own model or system is not a belief, but an individual reality, "just the way things are," including and explaining everything that validates, invalidating anything that disproves.

In every relationship, each participant must be an eager student to learn what it is like to be the other, to appreciate the delicacy of an internal balance, to know that certain words can soothe while others bite, to recognize that the tone transporting the words can stimulate or stymie conveyance of message and meaning. It is only an illusion that real feelings disappear when occluded by denial or dissociation. Each person has different states of mind and he or she may not know what might flip the switch throughout the day to another state of mind, or become the emotional tripwire that detonates the unseen land mine.

At times, when empathy fails miserably, a noble yet misguided effort at repairing the rupture with another may be to induce a parallel experience that masquerades as empathy. For example, the adolescent, angry and frustrated at parents, wants *to show them how it feels* and acts in a way to evoke similar anger and frustration in the parents. This attempt to induce empathy paradoxically results in distancing. The child wants to induce empathy, to have the parent understand vicariously by suffering, as he or she does, to convert the trauma of helplessness to the triumph of effectiveness.

These are inevitable blind or blurry spots in our empathic view because, despite dedicated and sincere attempts, we cannot escape our own psychologies and systems. Our own unique experiences both inform and skew our perceptions.

There are continued occurrences and boundary skirmishes at the interface of the differently organized subjective worlds of two people. Remarkable similarities of background, style, or mental model of two people may appear as attunement, and the overlap of parallel experience and assumption may masquerade as empathy, yet actually preclude it. Likewise, significant differences of background, culture, or psychic models of assimilating and registering experiences may require focused attention to construct an empathic bridge to a common ground of understanding. In either case of exceptional similarity or disparity, unspoken assumptions may create bias or blindness. Any categorical assignment (the essence of racism) subjugates the other real person to a projection of one's own assumptions.

The Power of Empathy

> *You saw me not as black or white, but clear, to see the person I am so I can feel more real. I've never been seen before beyond my skin.*
> —A heartwarming comment by a black woman
> from rural Louisiana at the conclusion of her therapy

Empathy hinges on our ability to initially reflect on our own experiences, to be aware of our subjectivity. This allows us both to predict how our words and actions will influence others and be able to move beyond our own subjective awareness, to enter the subjectivity of another, and create a common ground for sharing the experiences and resonances with another.

All signifiers of personal meaning and construction (reality, relationship, experience, perception) carry the unspoken foundation question: *From whose point of view?* This is what empathy is primarily about: to really *get* another's point of view and convey it while not abandoning our own point of view, to help another see and know an experience more clearly, and to see beyond. *Beyond* may be the previously unrecognized, disregarded, unacknowledged, or taboo. Salient experiences may be bypassed through empathy to reflect back feelings, following someone's point of view to validate feelings and logic. It is the responsibility of true empathy to use the vantage point of the listener to be in the moment with the speaker, *and* to use the listener's point of view to move together to a new place of reflection, understanding, or meaning. Two divergent pathways meet, as L. W. Sander has described in infant research, and both are changed.

All the present moments of lived experiences, sewn together, create an evolving pattern of meaning and relating, the basis for new implicit and explicit learning. Any new experience has an unknown future. Only repetition of the past, which by definition preempts the future, can be predicted with assurance. A new experience moving forward is both unfamiliar and uncertain.

To be empathic with another, we must move beyond our own position to inhabit the experience of another, to know how the person feels, senses, perceives, and processes subjective and intersubjective experience moment by moment, frame by frame. It takes two for someone to be empathic: one to be attuned, the other to be open to allow that empathic connection. At times, empathy infers what another individual would feel if he or she *could* feel, to shine light into a dormant portion of the interior landscape. One analytic patient put it most succinctly: *I want you not just to empathize with me, but to stick up for that part of me that's not coming through yet.*

Ultimately (lastly for some) is empathy for one's self, an internal attunement that may seem elusive and ethereal. This intimacy with one's self precedes and makes possible true intimacy with another. The greatest thing in the world, it has been said, is to know how to belong to yourself.

Psychoanalysis

A Retrospective View*

My ideal doctor. . . I can imagine entering my condition, looking around it from the inside like a kind landlord, with a tenant, trying to see how he could make the premises more livable. He would look around, holding me by the hand, and he would figure out what it is like to be me. Then he would try to find certain advantages in the situation. He can turn disadvantages into advantages. He would see the genius of my illness. He would mingle his daemon with mine. We would wrestle with my fate together, like Rupert and Birkin in the library in D. H. Lawrence's Women in Love. *I would also like a doctor who enjoyed me. I want to be a good story for him, to give him some of my art in exchange for his.*

—Anatole Broyard, *Intoxicated by My Illness*

The Basic Model

Psychoanalysts often focus on scary fantasies, cold mothers, dead people, and bad dreams, and perhaps in the process lose happiness, creativity, hope, love, humor, inspiration, and other positive transformations. Psychoanalysis has not found a celebration of nearly enough passions. The biggest challenge for someone who has consistently felt bad is to stay with feeling good. The analyst who is enticed to further analyze the origins and dynamics of the bad feeling colludes to stay in the old story

---

*Over a decade ago I retired from the practice and teaching of psychoanalysis and have since engaged in Executive Mentor Coaching. Psychoanalysis, psychology, and neuroscience research have remained areas I integrate into the dynamic model of strategic coaching that I practice and teach. This has provided a rich perspective to address mind, brain, and behavior change that has evolved over time, and one I hope is useful to you, the reader, as well.

rather than co-create a new one. A well-analyzed old story is still an old story. The ultimate truth of the reason for misery is often mistaken as the ultimate remedy for creating happiness. Too many theories are built around past deprivation and deficit, current problem and conflict, and not enough around present possibilities of joy, success, achievement, and transformation.

In dealing with human suffering in his time, Freud was always interested in both what medicine, religion, and science could *not* do, and what psychoanalysis *could* do. Perhaps where psychoanalysis later became waylaid is that it focused too exclusively on cures instead of new ways of living. This may be precisely the place that Mentor Coaching has taken over—where psychoanalysis left off.

Freud demonstrated how ingenious we are at not knowing ourselves. His recognition of the importance of the unconscious processes in the daily operations of our minds has been validated, even enhanced, by neuroscience research, with findings that 90–95 percent of our operating systems is unconscious. Our self-knowledge can be inaccurate, with a large portion of our minds inaccessible to consciousness. We suffer, as Freud pointed out, from the ways we use to avoid our presumed suffering. Psychoanalysis became a different way of listening to the stories of our lives by telling them in a different way. And how the conscious surface story is ghostwritten by the unconscious shadow story.

Psychoanalysis became a new language and a new story in itself, a scientific study of reflecting on our own thoughts to discern the hidden forces guiding our behaviors that bring our true beliefs into conscious light.

Psychoanalysis is undergoing its own necessary evolution from Freud's brilliant creation, now a Model T compared to the current vehicles of developmental research and neurosciences. While most psychoanalysts idealize Freud too liberally, nonanalysts denigrate him too excessively. That Freud said something doesn't make it automatically wrong. Though he may not have been right about everything (women, childhood abuse, and the death wish, among others), Freud has affected our daily lives by illuminating the unconscious, demonstrating the presence of conflict within each mind, highlighting the default decisions masquerading as habit called personality, and adumbrating current neuroscience. Yet Freud should be saved, with respect and honor, to see how far we've come.

There is ample anecdotal evidence that Freud was not a Freudian. During my residency I had the honor and opportunity to learn from René Spitz, M.D., the first official psychoanalyst who had a training analysis with Freud. He was professor emeritus at my residency program and in his mid-80s when I knew him. A group of fellow residents and I took him to see *Wild Child* by Truffaut and to dinner afterward. In our discussion with him, he told stories about his analysis with Freud and reminisced openly about how much he enjoyed it. He mentioned that his analytic hour on a Thursday was just after lunch. But once he came in early, on a Wednesday, and after lying down on the couch, spoke his first thought: *My great desire is a cigarette.*

Freud responded: *Then have a cigarette.*

Spitz said, *But Dr. Freud, what about the rule of abstinence, that I'm not supposed to be gratified in any way by you?*

Freud said, *What the hell. If you want a cigarette, have a cigarette.*

Spitz said that the next day when he came in for his appointment, Freud had a tin of cigarettes sitting on the table beside the analytic couch.

Freud, simply making it up as he went, as a true inquisitive scientist, had not yet formalized his theory into doctrine from which no one could stray (only his followers did that). It was up to subsequent analysts to describe the provenance of nomadic thoughts, as ones that deviated from *the psychoanalytic posture*. In fact, Freud gave birth to psychoanalysis trying to help those who were confined by their own narrow-mindedness. The treatment of people's clichés gradually moved toward becoming one itself.

The very essence of psychoanalysis, of free association, a free flow of consciousness not inhibited by usual conscious restraints, is to allow oneself, willingly, to lose the plot. To depart from usual inhibitions and restraints. The process, as it were, became the essence of the cure.

The official position was to develop self-examination, self-reflection, and self-questioning: To allow self-doubt and to not have to think about things beforehand to make them come out just right.

There's a point where the analysis of the past reverses forward progress, where stopping to understand is just another way of stopping. To effectively analyze is not to return to the past to rework it, but to reconsider and reframe from a present perspective.

The Basic Model

After psychoanalysis all our narratives of the past—indeed, all our coherence and plausibility—are suspect. They hide more than they seek.
—Adam Phillips, *Becoming Freud: The Making of A Psychoanalyst*

Psychoanalysis still has a *bactericidal* model, believing that developmental growth will occur by seeking psychopathology, overcoming resistance to examining it, and ultimately eradicating it. Much energy is expended in search of defenses and psychopathology, to get the patient to admit something by continuously illuminating it. This bactericidal model brings the old story alive in full flourish to be understood insightfully and to resolve. But ending misery doesn't create happiness. A man indicated of his former analyst, *He would remain silent and anonymous, then wonder why I felt lonely and like I was the only person in the room.*

A newly emerging *bacterostatic* model looks at the healthy, the adaptive thrust of mastery, and holds normal developmental stages and their facilitation as a model. The activation of renewed growth and development of the self in foreground and focus give meaning and contrast to still-active impediments and interferences.

A new story must engage innate capacities, facilitate developmental growth of the entire self, and enlist potentials and possibilities. The clinical exchange, rather than the patient projecting onto the blank screen of the analyst, is a partnership, a mutual and collaborative co-creation. The present moment expands a here-and-now experience to create and conceptualize within a present context new emotional couplings and a revised current model in order to reactivate emotional development. The analyst must become expert on the unknown, master of scarcity, creator of new metaphors, all the while moving toward the fundamental, the everyday simple.

Psychoanalysis involves the art of seeing the contradictions and conflicts inherent in one's mind, the unconscious organizing assumptions ghostwriting a life narrative, and the compromised potential speaking in derivative voice hoping to be heard. Reality is the same truth coming to rest in different places; truth is contoured by the surface on which it rests. While the Catholic Church offers confession to align falling with salvation, psychoanalysis inverted the paradigm to reframe sin as unconscious desire.

People come to psychoanalysis because they can neither keep their secrets from themselves nor tell them to themselves. They come when they are unhappy, because in some way they are unable to be as kind as they want to be, *especially to themselves.* They are remembering in a way that does not allow them to forget.

Symptoms are a disguised, involuntary memory. Symptoms are reminders that desire is unforgettable, and repression is a way of retaining things by supposedly getting rid of them. We are reminded of our disowned counterparts in symptoms, dreams, slips of the tongue, and memories. Repetition is a refusal to remember.

Psychoanalytic interpretation allows the patient to resume contact with that which he has never actually lost, but simply hidden away.

I have known those who, in keeping with Rainer Maria Rilke's famous remark, would never have psychoanalysis because, "If my devils are to leave me, I am afraid my angels will take flight as well."

Some things, like the pre-Columbian figures in my library, were protected for centuries by being buried and forgotten. Other things may be destroyed by being dug up and remembered.

As with other things in life, we see only derivatives, only icons of a process. These icons—the tangible referents—are too often mistaken for the real thing, as the cause of the effect, rather than simply as markers of the process.

This is where Freud had wisdom but was waylaid in his understanding of it. He recognized that something had gone wrong with someone's feeling for themselves and others, and he saw sexuality as the icon of this disruption. *Tell me how someone makes love and I will tell you everything about their character*, he was reputed to have said to Hungarian psycho-analyst Sandor Ferenczi.

Freud had one thing significantly backwards: that the abnormal was the key to understanding the normal. Later, after Freud and after two world wars, the blueprint of human bonds as between primary caretaker and child was recognized by those studying normal development and attachment patterns, and it continues to be studied.

Psychoanalysis has evolved, since Freud's time of thinking of basic human motivation as sexual and aggressive drives, to considering how we desire intimacy and relationships as part of a developing sense of self. That over a lifetime we want effectiveness, mastery, and good company more than good sex. Of course, there are still a few strict Freudians who have not parted from the original theory. Many psychoanalysts have evolved, however, to incorporate the mind and brain sciences.

An individual will always indicate what is most important, what is therapeutic and what is not, what needs are still unanswered. Each of my former analytic patients taught me what it is like to be him or her. Not always, however, in logical, conscious, daytime language, but at times in somatic language, or in enactments designed to demonstrate an internal experience. These behavioral and attachment patterns occur in the shadow traffic of transferences and in the interchange, in which the analyst plays a part, the patient plays a part, and then both talk about it. And nothing ever seems symbolic at the time it is being experienced.

As both patient and analyst experience the rich, archaic layers of the psyche, all displayed in the current relationship, each is *in* that present moment, more profoundly and simply, than ever before. This necessary enigma allows the patient's earlier life experiences to become transferentially activated in the present, to move from vague, formless, controlling procedural memory to juxtaposition with the new and different story. As the old story and the new story are both vividly alive and intermingled, the past can be interpretatively cleaved from the present. A new mutually formulated developmental model for current experiences contains and integrates evolving meaning. This dyadically evolving story, more than solely insight and understanding, awakens hope. Truths are both discovered and created.

With immersion in new experiences, present and past can be discerned and dissected. New lived experiences crystallize a mourning of the past, including the old model. One is never more aware of what was missed in the past than when having it now. These new experiences alter neuronal connections in the midbrain where emotions and meanings are synthesized. New couplings are created. For example, a patient's mother asking *Why?* may typically trigger an emotional reaction to evoke a state of mind characteristic of an earlier age, containing the perception of negative judgment and criticism. The age of that dialogue is from a much earlier time. However, in the present moment and not taking it personally, *Why?* may simply be seen as the mother's style, perhaps her own uncertainty, and her way of maintaining a bond with a now adult son or daughter.

A patient must live the experience of the old story within the container of the new story in order to tell the difference between the two, and ultimately to convert the old story into memory. We remember in order to forget. And, at times, experiences create their own reasons.

Psychoanalysis is the study of the ways in which we deceive ourselves. One's own model or system is not a belief, but that individual's reality, "just the way things are," as we tell ourselves, including and explaining everything that validates, invalidating everything that may disprove. Psychoanalysis has no franchise on understanding and is only one of many types of catalyst for change. It is simply one fictive method to know nonfictive truths, a subspecialty of helping individuals change their minds.

The Basic Rule

Psychoanalysis, which started as an improvisation in medical treatment, became at once, if not a new language, a new story about these fundamental things, and a new story about stories.
—Adam Phillips, *Becoming Freud: The Making of a Psychoanalyst*

Freud proposed the "basic rule" in psychoanalysis as free association, to allow what was unconscious to emerge without censorship.

Free association offers the possibility of a present experience of spontaneity and access to emotion and its expression and, on a broader venue, the emergence of patterns and metaphors that link past and present. Free association is ultimately a paradox, because if a patient could freely associate, an analysis would not be needed. And by the time the patient can associate freely, analysis is over.

For those who need to develop a more cohesive narrative, who need to focus more specifically on specific experiences and ultimately develop internal organization, saying everything that comes to mind and free association (Freud's injunction) can be qualitatively different. Saying everything about an internal experience is to more fully explore in detail the awareness and meaning of this moment's emotion, its developmental history, the dynamic scenario of its current foreground position, perhaps the interdigitation of procedural memory (transference) with new relational meaning (the new story). Saying everything is necessary for both patient and analyst to empathically immerse themselves together, allowing patients, perhaps for the first time in their lives, to be empathic with themselves, to create an intimacy internally shepherded by the analyst. In this mutual involvement, the analyst is witness / observer / interpreter / collaborator / co-author.

The analyst's neutrality is to remain equidistant between each side of the patient's conflict, the internal push-pull. This position, neither disinterest nor passivity, entails not knowing what the answer will be, not having a need for it to go one direction or another, and knowing that there are many truths to tell with no investment in which is most salient at this moment. The patient needs to have no one ghostwriting his or her story.

The new biological model has shown that every psychic event, whether implicit or explicit, is determined by some emotional precedent that activates a neural network—the brain location of experiences and meanings. Psychological events such as free association, dreams, and slips of the tongue all relate to preceding emotional events and resonate with internal experiences, with the relevance and meaning to be understood.

There are also, paradoxically, individuals for whom free association is the antithesis of what is needed for expansion and change. Those who are already loosely organized and tend to ramble need help to contract, focus, organize, and conceptualize their experience. Rather than passively free-associating, they may need to focus more actively on self-regulation and organization, or on a specific aspect in which feeling resides in the detail rather than in the broad brushstrokes. For a dissociative patient, what may appear as free association may actually be state changes or a distraction to move away from a feeling. The attention-deficit individual, already wired for stream of consciousness, needs also focus and structure.

Those who are more detached may need to create intensity and emotional relevance, rather than continuing to say everything that comes to mind. The obsessive who needs the release of free association to allow what is internal to emerge can also use free association as a defense, spinning away from an affect in order to elaborate further associations, all the while avoiding intensity and specificity of feeling.

Many years ago I heard the well-known psychoanalyst Ralph Greenson speak of asking a patient his middle name, to which the patient responded, *Raskolnikov*. Rather than explore the meaning of this antihero of Fyodor Dostoevsky's *Crime and Punishment*, Greeson said, *What are you talking about? That's not your middle initial.* The patient announced, *No, but I free-associated to the question.*

Another perspective on the basic rule was offered by a senior psychoanalyst involved in my original training. Known to be both crusty and terse, he said, *There's only one basic rule in psychoanalysis. And that's that the patient pays you. Everything else is a recommendation.*

Transferences

You tricked me out of feeling solitary by being others for me.
—Clive Wilbur

The activation of existing neural networks and pathways linking implicit processes and explicit memories is the old story. Understanding this old story that psychoanalysts call transference is so much more than pattern matching (e.g., of an old relationship with a current one) or symbolism (of perceiving or acting as if the analyst were like one's mother or father). Transference is the active process of perceiving, processing, organizing, and attaching meaning in present time. Transference is a verb, the activation of neural networks that link explicit memory (facts), implicit memory (procedural and associative memory), affects, and motives. Unconscious and conscious conflicts come alive vividly for both patient and analyst. No archeological dig to the depths of the psyche is required, no safari to the distant past is necessary, as any unresolved or unfinished business from the past will inevitably intrude into the present, collapsing the necessary space between past and present. A patient will have many kinds of transference reaction over the course of an analysis reflecting the entirety of developmental processes and contents, the activation of implicit memories of experiences and processes, as well as activation of what never was, of needs not met. Past experiences, beliefs, composite attributions, and assumptions project onto the present to create a continuity of self over time.

Undisturbed, our sense of self continues in a default mode. We see what we believe, providing both validation and continuity.

Developmental arrest prematurely forecloses aspects of one's emotional system. Analysis perturbates that process to reopen consideration, and the attuned analyst becomes a transference projection screen, developmental guide, and co-author of retranscription. The nuances of an individual's unique system of software programs (states of mind) must be appreciated as they become more evident in order to undergo revision. Models of relationships and attachment patterns get established very early in life and become the software through which subsequent relationships are perceived, organized, and processed. This software is viewed by an individual, not as one way of looking at things, but as the reality, as the way things are. A fish cannot describe water; it can't get outside the system in order to do so.

Unconscious mental processes provide the explanation for psychic determinism, the notion that everything in one's psychic life is no accident. A related contribution of psychoanalysis is that of multideterminism—that we are continually making alternative lives, that we are in a world and have a psyche of multiple plots. Although it may not be that all accidents are meaningful, meaning can be made of accidents. Freud, who used psychoanalytic theory to turn accidents into significant intentions, would later have slips of the tongue named after him. Accidents become disowned intentions. Accidents become the best way, at times the only way, to do certain things that are disowned. Freud simply took the luck out of accidents and made them nonmystical sources of meaning. All sorts of things, including accidents, remind us of who we are.

The accident can be considered a counter-intention, an insufficiently repressed desire, a piece of personal history wanting to be lived out, even if in disguised and disavowed form. Coincidence simply means that two things happen together.

Interpretation

Those times of depression tell you that it is either time
to get out of the story you are in and move on to a new story,
or that you are in the right story
but there is some piece of it you are not living out.
—Carol S. Pearson

Insight and understanding are not enough to replace old lived experiences. A new lived experience is required, one that creates new neuronal pathways and networks, the building of new highways and villages in the brain. When new brain circuits are etched with the impressions of new beliefs and experiences, some gene expression is altered by producing different cellular protein, as was revealed in remarkable research initiated by Eric Kandel. The continuity of new experiences, such as the immersion in the new story in psychoanalysis, forms different synapses in new neural circuitry as well as revising mind software. With charged emotional cues or particular stress, the newer experience may be disrupted with a return to the default route, the old story. Some present experience can seem magnified because of its resonance with the past. The new choreography in the ballet at the synaptic cleft alters structure along with function. When we change our minds, we change our brains.

Creating new lived experiences and thereby new procedural memories is the most meaningful aspect of a therapeutic relationship. This relational process is not primarily a product of insight. The patient needs to sense the analyst's belief in him or her to make the next step into new territory, to plunge ahead into an unknown experience, to allow an uncharted feeling, or to seize the moment in a fully affective, authentic way. This implicit relational experience becomes a new procedural memory.

Interpretation is the co-constructed generation of new meaning. Since Freud's time, interpretation (originally, making conscious what is unconscious) is still as important as it is overrated. The emotional state of mind of the patient and foreground dimension of the transference determine the patient's receptivity to collaboration. A new model must be formulated to understand and incorporate new experiences, or else the new story will seem an accident, lucky, or "only a matter of time" until "reality" (the old story) returns. The creation of a new model, this revised plot, becomes hope personified.

An interpretation is an attempt to find the words to say what the patient can't quite say, of giving meaning to what has been elusive, of giving shape to what hasn't been fully felt. Equal to the vertical movement of unconscious to conscious, the horizontal cleavage of present from past illuminates assumptions, defenses, and meanings that are no longer adaptive. The past and present are never more distinguishable than at the moment of juxtaposition.

Cezanne used a related interpretation for his art: *I don't paint things; I paint the difference between things.* To distinguish current experience from past procedural and associative memory is a part of the process of coming to the end of the past, to make the past a memory rather than an active, intrusive, repeating presence.

The feelings, meanings, actions, and assumptions of a patient are subject to scrutiny only to the extent that the patient can actually experience them. This emotional engagement supersedes exploration of defenses, abstract mental mechanisms, and mechanics. An intellectual bypass may inoculate against necessary feelings and place the analyst in a position of authority, as the arbiter of truth eclipsing the patient's potential to become his or her own authority.

The Working Alliance

I was reflecting on the previous attempts I had made over the last two decades to engage therapists and analysts. My initial typical attempt at engagement would be some variation of this exchange and internal dialogue: I am seated in the chair across from this person I have never before met. I know I have so much terrain to cover before there is any possibility of understanding. I am looked at blankly. This blankness is raising questions in me: "Am I boring her?" "Am I shocking her?" "Am I confusing her?" I am in need, and my need is making me feel insecure, adding to what I already bring. I am in need and sitting here, or else I would be at the beach. I wonder if this person before me has gotten together with other persons like her to decide which behaviors to be, which are accepted. The blankness she has in her face raises questions on top of what drove me to arrive here: "What is this person across from me thinking?" "What is she feeling?" "How is she reacting to what I am saying?" "Am I too much?" "Am I too little?" I'm burdened by this person because of her blankness. It is upsetting my insecurity more. The experience of never knowing is in addition to this flurry of what she thinks, of the many, "Does she think I am (fill in the blank)?" And the (blanks) are mostly negative, such as stupid, ignorant, naïve. Her silence is unnerving. Too many of my experiences have been intolerable alone. I haven't known the questions to ask myself. It is very emotionally expensive to be in her presence. My feeling upon leaving was often as though an unloving parent had scolded me. Yet I kept going back. What would have been beneficial would have been to break through the glazed, hazy wall I erected unknowingly, and if she could have said, "This is all really going to be okay." It would have only taken something simple, but it was like she could never break character in the play being enacted, the role decided when the professionals got together and decided which ways to be with a patient. Those were the experiences I brought when I came to see you for the first time. Only now, after all this time, a time

when we are almost done with our analytic work can I finally tell you. And I
can tell you because with you I could experience all of me for the first time.
—A former patient

Most often, failed treatments terminate not because of incorrect technique or unaccepted interpretations, but because of the unrealized
opportunity for a meaningful, emotional connection between two real
people working together. Patients often recall these moments of authentic connection with particular clarity as a nodal or pivotal event in the
analysis, representing so much more of the process than could be ver-
balized or symbolized. The process is what happens while we are talking
about something else. It is the *something more* that is the magical ingredi-
ent. It is what occurs between two partners in a creative pairing; it is the
relationship that produces change.

At the very beginning of my residency training in psychiatry, an internationally known psychoanalyst, one of those people for whom the word
"brilliant" must have been coined, spoke to my assembled colleagues in
simple ways that captured our attention. He told us about a woman whose
psychoanalytic work with him was nearing its completion after three
years. Together they looked back in her analysis to what they had learned
together. He asked her if there were any issues or moments in the analysis
that had been particularly important to her as turning points. As he asked,
he was thinking of the many insights, key interpretations, and nodal discoveries that had been part of their mutual work, wondering which of these
for her was a particular watershed. Without hesitation, she said, *The time
you handed me a Kleenex.* This moving moment spoke of her coming to
the end of her experience of barrenness since childhood, and the renewed
emotional growth through empathic understanding. It was an incident that
served as organizing metaphor for an entire process.

Suffering can be transformed by words.

So often in creating a new story together, the patient presents something quite new, intriguing, or different, defying or transcending all catego-
ries of analytic responses, and requiring an innovative collaboration. Truth
always conspires to assemble itself before us, and truth is stranger than

fiction because fiction has to make sense. If indeed the patient is to develop a new signature, both the patient and analyst are in a unique, authentic, mutual creation that is different from anything the patient has known. And each analysis should be different from any other for the analyst, highly specific to this patient, the process not technical, habitual, routine, or rote, not the voice of silence or sterile interpretation, but a unique, collaborative, co-authored experience.

Corresponding to the patient who has been trading freedom for safety, aliveness for certainty, and creativity for repetition may be the analyst's trading innovation for ideology, and subjugating uniqueness to theory. Insight and understanding are no more magical than couch and theory. It is the relationship that cures, the shared moments of new implicit learning that create new procedural memory and explicit meaning. The analyst must speak with his or her own voice, not a borrowed voice from prepackaged theory of formulaic thought and dead language. The freedom to create one's own voice from an internal point of reference, enhanced yet unencumbered by history of how the voice developed, is prerequisite to a creative and collaborative process of constructing a new analytic story with the patient. Aspects of this new story ideally incorporate a plurality of theories and ideas to inform rather than to direct, to create rather than conform. An individual becomes his or her own authority, not living a life ghostwritten by inflexible predetermination or invisible presupposition. When both patient and analyst each have their own voice in this newly minted joint story, the analysis will have its own rhythm, personality, and plot.

At best, what the analyst does with each patient is not about being right, having pristine theory and technique, or idealizing insight and understanding. The bottom line: *Does it work?* Meaning and hope may not lie preformed and awaiting discovery in the patient but have to be generated by catalyzing personal growth and expansion. For the analyst, hope often takes the form of a positive engagement with both the analytic process and the passion and richness of engagement with life.

As anyone attempts to study someone else's mind, both become part of the field of study. Whether tracking bodily, affectively, relationally, dynamically, developmentally, or systemically, three subjectivities are at play: the patient, the analyst, and the intersubjective third of the new relationship story.

No analyst (or anyone else) can tell individuals how they feel, what they think, or how they are motivated. Life cannot be encapsulated into a concept or collapsed into an identity. All we can ever offer another individual is to share our experience of him or her, to make a self-statement about another. However informed, however much one knows about the other, it is still, only and simply, a self-statement. Recognizing the reciprocal of that principle, that someone else's comments about us, however pointed, personal, factual, and authoritatively spoken are only their self-statement, may allow us to not take it personally. (Things, of course, are never as simple in reality as in theory.)

The New Story

The real journey of discovery consists not in seeing new landscapes
but in having new eyes.
—Marcel Proust

Psychoanalysis regularly traffics in enigmas, such as the psychoanalyst reflecting back to the patient inchoate experiences for which there may be no words or language. The analyst must listen carefully, simply, literally; deepest truths are clothed in the simplest of garments. He or she must believe what is said the first time, before other words get in the way; the slip of tongue is like the adolescent sneaking out an upstairs window late at night yearning consciously for adventure, yet unconsciously needing to be contained. There are signs: the twinkle of an eye from the little girl hiding deeply within the older woman, the rumbling stomach shouting swallowed pain, the second *no* that always means *yes* (or one would have been sufficient). Listening from inside another is that most uncommon of bonds, because the more we learn, the more simply we can speak. Sometimes words are not important enough, yet for many things they are sufficient. An internal domain is entered into which patients have perhaps never before allowed anyone, even and especially themselves.

An unconscious organizing position may be that one's life has already been predesigned, meaning preconstrained. Attempting to break free of those constraints engages both the obstacle and the desire. True freedom arises from not creating the obstacles. We always come back to what we run away from and engage it more powerfully with each return. Sometimes we engage something initially by denying it: the vividness of its reverse image in direct proportion to its importance.

One patient indicated at the end of our work, *The most important thing you ever said to me was in the beginning when you said, "I'll believe in you until both of us can." Now I do, too.* I responded, *When I said that, I knew that you'd be able to teach both of us why.* The most important process in any relationship in which growth is central is to know that the other person believes in you. This belief is invisibly reflected and nonverbally communicated by the parent to the child, or the analyst to the patient, so that ultimately one can come to believe in oneself.

The shared analytic relationship is never symmetrical, for the focus is on the patient, yet it is quite real, not solely reducible to the traditional notion of transference-countertransference, or any composite of metapsychological terms. So many of the patient's needs to attach and ally, to explore and assert, are fundamental and essential developmental needs that can now, finally, be fully experienced. These basic needs may have been disallowed until this current holding environment exists, with evolving trust and security. The simple, here-and-now content is never to be disregarded, as the message contains the message: What someone actually expresses needs to be fully explored before the venue is changed to the symbolic or unconscious. But this is true in any relationship.

Psychoanalysis is the art of seeing the contradiction and conflicts inherent inside someone's mind, the obfuscated assumptions, the unquestioned reality, the invisible decisions camouflaged in pattern, the developmental needs given muted or distorted pleading voice. The noble intent is often shrouded behind a destructive or compromised result. We suffer, as Freud indicated, not from conflict, but from bearing it too little and too unconsciously. The journey to resolution and growth, rather than to retreat or repeat, begins with moving the drama to the center stage of awareness to recognize and own. Above all else, psychoanalysis should have the purpose, not only of help for the patient to gain insight and understanding about how his or her mind works, but also to help evolve within this new story, to be more fully real and human.

The urges within, pressing for recognition, perhaps find their voice in accidents, dreams, or slips of the tongue. These reminders of unfinished business, voices of the past and present coalesced, occur daily to remind us of who, unedited, we are. The past, rather than in prepackaged form seeking attention and disclosure, lies quietly waiting for reassemblage, reconstruction, and reworking of understanding into a new and present shape.

The psychoanalytic experience is a unique, partially altered state entered by both parties in order to create a new story. Psychoanalysis is, among other things, a story about how we are making up our lives. This process activates the old story that is not yet the old story but is still *reality,* "just the way things are." Suspension of usual action and social imperatives, the immersion in the process of one's experience, and the mutual and reciprocal interaction all foster entry into a state of reverie individually and collaboratively. To enter this suspended state and create a new story, the synthesis of a new life narrative can occur, to make sense of the old while at the same time transforming/creating a cohesive new plot. The old plot may be well entrenched and consistent, as in the experience of victimhood from a traumatic past. A life story may have seemed so opaque simply because there was no end point, no internal ideal of *good enough* to create effectiveness. Without this internal ideal, nothing is ever good enough, and the abiding quest is for *more,* yet more is never enough. You can never get enough of what you don't need.

How the state of mind of one individual affects the state of the other in a relationship, the matching, resonance, and coinciding of states, become crucial nonverbal components. For example, the analyst's somatic responses of sleepiness, arousal, restlessness, tenseness, or speechlessness can be a sensitive barometer to the patient's state of mind. These experiences may be particularly difficult to understand if only a linear, dynamic model of the mind is considered, rather than the mind and the self as a system with changing states of mind.

How do you find a way to talk about experiences as yet without conscious icon or verbal narrative? For those individuals who have not had sufficient emotional attunement in early childhood to differentiate feelings, or even to desomaticize emotion, communicating aspects of internal experience and affect by symbolic language is a challenge. These individuals maintain an external, action-oriented focus, regulate tension by physical discharge, and are vulnerable to action symptoms, such as addiction or impulsivity. They may feel lost and vague, unable to describe their feelings, which the analyst may read as resistance and interpret as a defense against feeling. The patient then feels criticized, furthering alienation and isolation. The patient experiencing restlessness, ineffectiveness, and boredom often induces resonant experiences in the analyst, allowing accurate awareness of aspects of the patient's internal world.

Just as gender automatically shapes attributions and assumptions from an initial encounter, an individual's bodily presence nonverbally shapes an interchange. Expression through the body offers a rich mélange of communication. The body language of movement, the boundary of skin, and the gut of private self all underlie the verbal offerings of the individual, of a self that is always and ultimately embodied. Psychoanalysis has unfortunately favored the intellectual aspects of the clinical exchange more than the experiential, and has historically valued the word and intellect in ways that have at times maintained the gap between mind and body.

Verbal interchange is only one of the ways that meanings are communicated. Nonverbal communications include body postures, facial expressions, voluntary and involuntary movements, position and position changes, looking and not looking, motor sequences of body alignment, alignment within space, and facial mirroring, to name only a few. For some individuals, attunement to both body self and psychological self may register only in action sequences or action symptoms that involve the body, such as tension, pain, self-harm, compulsive activities using the body, or substances taken into the body. Tiny demeanors and impalpable dispatches, as well as the theme and grand gesture, all portray implicit somatic memory for the blended music in the dance of the analytic work. Dimensions of any interaction include implicit memories and nonverbal sequences from the simple and literal to the abstract and symbolic.

The previously untreatable patient may be one whose symptoms have not been listened to as his or her own story, whose noble attempt at adaptation has been viewed as pathology, or whose attempt to *focus internally* is elusive and undeveloped. To have anger, or the defense against it, interpreted as a basic aggressive drive may only validate and enhance its expression. Consider the different impact by, first, viewing anger as active and immediate counter to hurt or helplessness, to protect bruised self-esteem, or alternatively, viewing it as expression of basic aggression, validating a motivation of both aggression and destruction.

Psychoanalysis is not the observation of a dance, but a partner dance, the co-mingling of two real people respecting the old story and its past adaptiveness, while honoring the newly evolving story. We gently accept patients handing us their soul, their best feelings, and hope that we will give it back, enhanced. To hope that they can give us, as well, the white-heat rage and shattered hope spawned from the fires of helplessness and fashioned into a transferential arrow pointed directly at us, and know that we will neither retreat at its firing nor flinch at its impact. To hope that we will see the genius of their symptoms, those secrets hiding in the open, and mingle our creative passion with theirs to understand the adaptive intent imbedded in the pathological result. To be perhaps the first person in their life who has totally believed in them, so that they can ultimately believe in themselves; to know that you have to be in a new story before you can give up an old story; that for a long transferential winter the old and new stories are so intermingled they don't feel different; that the hopelessness of the present is procedural memory of the past, activated now so we together can distinguish past from present, never losing the scent to the trail of renewed development.

Unlived

The Uninhabited Story

And yet the ways we miss our lives are life.
—Randall Jarrell

At a recent retreat for executives and professionals transitioning from retirement into a next contribution or career, I asked them to write down the first response that came to mind for a question. The notion of immediately writing something ensures an emotional response, a right-brain reaction, before being processed by the left, logical, reasoning brain.

I asked, *What is your unlived life?*

Every one of these accomplished people, paragons of success in the world's eyes, was astonished to recognize that they had an unlived aspect of their lives that was either unrecognized or, at most, only residing in their peripheral vision.

These parallel lives include the conscious life that we live and the unlived life, the one that we might yet have or feel that we should or could have. This unlived life may be an elegy of unrequited desires, unmet needs, or sacrificed goals.

Although perhaps unspoken, unlived aspects of life occupy a portion of our attention. These fantasies and longings may be for the people, experiences, or things that are absent, what we feel we're missing out on, what we could be doing, or should be doing but for some reason are not.

In the film *Sliding Doors,* the protagonist boards a train, barely making it before the door closes. But then an alternative story unfolds, in which she is one second too late, the door closes, and she misses the train. From that point on, parallel stories portray alternative realities for a lifetime.

We may live somewhere between the life we have and the life we would have had. Each of these dual stories constructed by us has its own story arc, its own drama, its own dynamics.

The road not taken may hold the myth of our potential, the shadow inevitably bumping up against the recognition of what might have been. We may then regret and resent, grieve and let go, fantasize and remain hopeful, or plan and realize. Or all of the above.

What Might Have Been

> *History is not merely what happened;*
> *it is what happened in the context of what might have happened.*
> —Hugh Trevor-Roper

Some aspects of our lives are defined by what might have been, of things never experienced or pursued. How do we know whether we have realized our potential? The unlived life may be of achievement idealized, of perpetually engaging a potential that never could be.

Darwin believed he demonstrated that everything in life is vulnerable, ephemeral, without design, and lacking God-given purpose. The antithesis, a belief in infinite talents, untapped ambitions, and limitless potentials, can be an abiding quest, a perpetual optimistic pursuit.

Yet has anyone, really, ever had the adolescence he or she should have had? Or taken enough chances? Or had enough chances to take?

Are our unlived lives, our fantasized, wished-for lives more important to us than our actual lived experiences? Aren't we always, at every juncture, making our lives more pleasurable, or at least more bearable, by picturing what might be? Almost inevitably in our imagined, unlived lives, we are more special. As such, we're obligated to reflect on whether the need to be special obfuscates a realistic view of ourselves. We may become obsessed about what is missing in our lives, about the potentials we are not fulfilling, about the pleasures that elude us.

We deceive ourselves at times by internal bargaining. Rather than admitting, *I'm never going to write my novel,* it's *I'm going to start next month.*

Our solutions illuminate our perceived problems. This means that our fantasy lives, rather than being a refuge from real life or an alternative to it, become an essential component of our real lives.

Both our lived and our unlived lives make us who we are.

To give up what might have been is the most difficult thing to mourn, as we have to say goodbye to what never was, as well as to the hope of getting what we wanted in the way we wanted it. This goodbye is the final step into the present and may involve significant emotional work. And lead to significant freedom.

Surface and Shadow Stories

> *I am both of your directions, life.*
> —Marilyn Monroe's journal

Our surface and shadow stories are dualities of the lived life. The surface story is what we consciously focus on, our known and lived experiences. The shadow story, the beliefs that ghostwrite behaviors, the unconscious models and attachment patterns downloaded beginning early in our lives, also manifest in real ways, often outside awareness.

The *surface story* that we use to run our lives with conscious intentions and aspirations may be *I want to generate more income and create wealth.* Yet the *shadow story* can silently oppose the conscious intent, through such messages, as *Money is unspiritual.* Or, *Some people were not born to have money.* Or even, *I don't have what it takes to make significant money.*

We are often clear about what we want, but uncertain about what we need. The unlived story resides alongside the surface and shadow stories, in yet another dimension. We may be quite conscious of the unlived story, as it evolves a life of its own and goes through developmental stages along with us.

One unlived story for me involved the decision to leave academic psychiatry and engage in a full-time clinical practice of psychotherapy and psychoanalysis. Although I was still teaching on medical school and psychoanalytic institute faculties, it was a significant transition, particularly after it meant passing up the opportunity to head the Department of Psychiatry where I had attended medical school. Afterward, at each meeting of an The American College of Psychiatrists, an honorary professional society comprising department chairs and serious academics, I would briefly revisit my decision and silently bid another farewell to the academic career I could have had at that point, had I continued in it.

Frustration Outlines the Unlived

> *Nothing I know matters more than what never happened.*
> —John Burnside, *Hearsay*

Our frustrations may be the last thing that we want to know, just as the last thing we want to do is look at ourselves in the mirror when we're angry. Frustration implies that there is a potential satisfaction, as yet still elusive. Frustration reassures, suggesting a promise of a different future. Of course, only the impossible is addictive, a promise never kept. An addiction is an unformulated frustration, a behavior that becomes a central organizer in one's life.

Frustrations that are difficult to construe introduce the possibility of misunderstanding the nature of satisfaction. We know, unequivocally, that if someone can satisfy us, they can also frustrate us. In fact, only someone who can give us satisfaction can give us more than temporary frustration. We know that someone matters the most to us when they profoundly frustrate us.

Isn't falling in love the reminder of a frustration we didn't know we had? Someone we did not know (so could not know we wanted) suddenly has the capacity to make us feel either better or worse than we ever imagined. Or both. It's as if we had been waiting for someone we never knew until that person arrived. We were not aware we were missing someone until that person appeared to fill a desire. Their presence is required in order to make their absence felt. A love relationship intensifies satisfaction as well as introduces the possibility of frustration. Fantasies originate from a compilation of prior experiences, both real and wished for. When we finally connect with someone, we will then start missing them. It is the paradox of feeling we've known someone forever when we have just met.

In this way we may be always trying to find what is missing, what we feel we lack, without knowing it until it's found.

Unconscious Contracts

The way through the world is more difficult to find than the way beyond it.
—Wallace Stevens

People engage in unconscious contracts with each other—the unspoken small print of expectations and assumed contingencies that we have with another person. These agreements are without the other's conscious participation, a contract with a single signator. We don't even apprise ourselves of these contracts. How can we, if they're unconscious and we are, by definition, unaware? So we can never quite know exactly what we are agreeing to—even with ourselves. Attachment patterns are forms of unconscious contracts. The patterns of emotional and behavioral responses beginning originally in the caretaker and infant are referred to as the *attachment system.*

This system of experiences, emotions, and memory processes of the attachment bond to originally important others is later generalized to interactional patterns and relationships throughout adulthood. The expectations and experiences from that early attachment style are downloaded unconsciously as the fundamental template of relationship and behavior patterns.

These unconscious contracts, the models of attachment based on procedural memory, govern how we approach subsequent relationships. Just as the attachment archetype with the primary caregiver forms the first template of interaction, the configuration is mutually determined. The way the infant behaves toward the primary caretaker exerts a powerful influence on the caretaker's behavior. The baby creates the parent. The subsequent interactions are also co-created.

The unconscious contract is inevitably formed by what we sense it will take to be effective in engaging the other person. The contract becomes like an emotional spell cast over a relationship in order to effect some particular outcome.

We may begin our lives with unchosen families, generate unchosen desires, and engage in unchosen wars. Our unconscious intentions, sometimes coming to the surface in the form of accidents, can appear paradoxical.

The Freudian slip is an accident meant to happen, just as someone may allow certain desires to only be expressed as obstacles.

Accidents become disowned intentions, camouflaged aspects of the unlived life that speak through supposed mistakes. The accident gives us access to an unavailable desire, only to disown it once it is made known. An accident is a meaningful production of what may be forbidden—an intended, even motivated error with built-in deniability. The paraparaxis of a self-inflicted accident is to acknowledge a forbidden desire, perhaps to recover the past, even to link us to our history.

A desire, of course, does not seek decoding, but wants satisfaction. This version of the self, of an unconscious contract, is what psychoanalysts refer to as unconscious desire, and to opposing surface and shadow stories as conflict.

There are those for whom being successful has not been a success. This is often because the model that is used to fashion life choices doesn't really work in the world. Examples include codependency, regulation of mind states with substances, writing one's own rules, and disregard for others.

A parent's job is to establish models in the home of what works in the real world. If it doesn't work in the real world, then it shouldn't work at home. In this way parents teach their children how to get along in the real world .

Heroes

It is sometimes more difficult to sustain good fortune than to overcome bad.
—Benjamin Disraeli, Earl of Beaconsfield

In childhood, we lived vicariously through our heroes. My heroes ranged from Mighty Mouse when I was a very small child (though limited to thirty minutes on Saturday morning minus commercials), to Superman, to Mickey Mantle, and later to my favorite athletic coach who, while leading us to championships, inspired me to seek my career calling when he repeated often, *The mind is the most powerful thing in the world.*

We revere our heroes in childhood because they hold some of our unlived, even unlivable, possibilities. A continuum of heroes exists in various forms: from older siblings and smart classmates to athletes and celebrities.

Our projections onto our heroes can serve to pull us further along, into greater achievements. Eventually we claim our own potentials to realize them rather than to continue to project them. This projected identification involves some form of effectiveness, a mastery of borrowed power. When the models are impactful in another direction, such as with gangs, the identification has a negative result.

We suffer when what we do departs from our ideals. Ideals, the preferred version of ourselves, of who we are and what we live up to, when fulfilled, registers as self-esteem. The effectiveness and mastery of living up to an attainable internal ideal serve as a powerful force throughout life.

Romance and the Unlived Life

Zarathustra goes to the grave with the unfulfilled dreams of his youth. He speaks to them as if they were ghosts who had betrayed him bitterly. They struck up a dance and then spoiled the music. Did the past make his path so weighty? Did his unlived life impede him and consign him to a life that seems not to pass?
—Friedrich Nietzsche

We attempt to capture, especially in adolescence, part of our unlived life, a completion of ourselves, in a romantic partner. The qualities we most seek in a partner are the unlived potentials ready for emergence and development in ourselves. In fact, we often see what we need to do next by recognizing it first in another. That hidden part of ourselves emerging by way of its travel to a partner then comes back to us. We projectively identify in another what we are most ready to experience, and then perhaps become consumed with that person in whom we have deposited a part of ourselves.

The vulnerable reliance on the romantic partner is that they must respond exactly as we want them to, to reflect back precisely that unlived and previously unrecognized part of ourselves. Then, ideally, by recognizing and owning what we attribute to the other person, we see our unlived potential with a new depth and meaning.

At that point we ultimately withdraw our projections to relate to the real person in a real way. To cling to the projections would be to still be in love with who the other might be, who we want them to be, a form of codependency. If our illusions do not become metabolized into growth of our own potential, if we do not grow our own missing pieces to become essentially whole, we continue an unlived life.

A measure of the unlived life: Does it fit with *needs* and *ideals*? What to do if an unlived aspect clashes with our ideals, our ethics, our moral imperatives?

Jungian analyst Robert A. Johnson tells a story of an aging Don Juan who pursued sex with women compulsively and relentlessly. Although he actually found no satisfaction in it, he felt driven to do so. He lived on a trust fund and had total freedom to pursue his quests. He was not at all free as he perceived himself to be, because he was constantly in the grip of his compulsion.

Doctor Johnson asked him, *How can you express this energy without literally doing it?* He pursued with this man how he could honor his creative urge while simultaneously not enacting it, for doing so had not enhanced his life but only drained his energy. Although this man resisted addressing the question, Dr. Johnson kept asking him, *How can you do it while not doing it?*

Eventually this man came back bringing a notebook with a series of pen-and-ink drawings of erotic subjects executed with remarkable skill.

He had a hidden, undeveloped talent as an artist. Beginning with a few sketches, these evolved into portraits, then still-life drawings, and ultimately paintings of people and animals.

Today this man is quite successful as a professional artist, selling art at a number of galleries and teaching art. His creative productivity and contribution redeemed his unlived life from compulsive enactment.

Reclaiming Ourselves

There are two kinds of people . . . One kind, you can tell just by looking at them at what point they congealed into their final selves. It might be a very nice self, but you know you can expect no more surprises from it. Whereas, the other kind keeps moving, changing. With these people, you can never say, "X stops here," or "Now I know all there is to know about Y." That doesn't mean they're unstable. Ah, no, far from it. They are fluid. They keep moving forward and making new trysts with life, and the motion of it keeps them young. In my opinion, they're the only people who are still alive.
—Gail Goodwin, *The Finishing School*

Decisions are usually made by unconscious processes seconds before we are consciously aware of them. Almost a century ago, Jung identified these internal operating systems as *complexes*. The developmental psychologist Jean Piaget later called them *schemas*. Neuroscientists currently describe these phenomena as *neuronal networks*.

When we create an experience, neurons that fire together form configurations that are more likely to fire together again. This means that what we take in from the environment is influenced by the cumulative experiences we've already had, as well as the emotional response of the moment. So what we have seen and felt dictates what we now see and feel.

Responses tailored to past situations, ones that were adaptive in the past, provide reference points for organizing experience. Yesterday's solution can, however, be today's problem. We often have an abiding wish for life to be stable and unchanging. We seek form, structure, and meaning, yet then we can become limited by it.

Unlived aspects of our lives will be projected onto others to the extent that we are unaware of or do not recognize them. Every statement we make is a self-statement. Anything that we devalue in another is what we devalue and attempt to reject in ourselves. What we fear in ourselves we will flee or fight in others. What we perceive to be lacking in ourselves we maneuver to get others to function in that way for us.

Insight into how we were raised, the attachment and behavior patterns we engage, and precisely who we fall in love with, can all provide insight into what is unlived in us. In this understanding, the unlived and deferred lives of our parents had a significant influence. We also recognize unlived aspects of our own lives in the people we admire and seek for mentors.

The Next Right Thing

If you could live one day over and over again, would it be a birthday, or your wedding day, or would it be a day that you haven't yet lived? A day full of quiet moments and endless smiles, where you laugh and play and feel like a kid again? And are simply alive?
—Ad for the state of Colorado

Jean-Paul Sartre tells a story about a young married couple who have breakfast together each morning. After breakfast, the wife kisses her husband goodbye and sits by the window all day to cry until he returns. When he does, she perks up. The psychologically minded might see this young woman as suffering from separation anxiety. Consider that she actually suffers from a fear of freedom. As soon as her husband leaves, she is free to live her unlived life, but this freedom terrifies and paralyzes her.

People are often experts about what is missing in their lives, about experiences they haven't had, and what their lives would be like if they were to have them. Yet they also have a very limited repertoire of possibilities of how their lives would be better if these missing things were actually brought about.

Alfred Adler, one of Freud's earlier followers, told a story of an initial interview with a patient. He carried out a comprehensive evaluation, then took a detailed family history and an elaborate account of what the man was suffering from. At the end of the consultation, Adler asked the man, *What would you do if you were cured?* The man answered him.

Adler replied, *Well, go and do it then.*

That was the treatment: to go and live his unlived life. This man did not need psychoanalytic interpretation, to mourn missed opportunities, or to understand the dynamics of uncompleted action. His problem was initiating action, and when he did that, he had no more problems.

All we have to do in life is the next right thing. At times, it may not be clear what the next right thing is, but we can almost always know what it *isn't*.

A crucial turning point in our own individual history is that we must learn to live the unlived life, to find a conscious place and current form for what has been underdeveloped, forgotten, or abandoned. There is much to be learned from what is missing. And there is no single recipe for finding our unity and fulfillment.

We inevitably and always must come to terms with where we are, not with where we were, or where we should have been.

We must learn to live our own unlived life, not that of anyone else, not even that of an earlier self. The initial awareness includes recognizing and owning a story in order to assess it, then deciding what needs to change. Additional aspects include mapping changes, authoring the changes, and programming new and evolving identity to incorporate those changes.

Each phase of life brings challenges. As we enter the late afternoon and evening of our lives, it takes more work to remain young. Bodily functions become a focus of new daily routines. Do we engage this process and align ourselves to enhance practices of exercise, nutrition, and healthy habits? This is itself an awakening and a recognition of changes necessary now that earlier we considered only peripherally.

The qualities that are underdeveloped or unlived in ourselves may be the very qualities we seek and respond to in others. Rather than enacting the pursuit of someone who represents these qualities, we may first need to find a way to relate to and develop these qualities in ourselves. To pursue them with the wrong person or at the wrong time may lead to tragedy and pain. To recognize the qualities that shine in others, and perhaps attract us to another, can provide insight into our own potentials ripe for development. We may then need to look for ways to honor and nurture these aspects of our unlived lives in real rather than symbolic ways.

Frequently, prominent, wealthy, famous, or professional people who feel that they must appear as *all good* may be tempted to enact their *unlived* side in a conscious or unconscious manner. If you're drawn to a *bad boy* or a *bad girl*, it may be a sign that you're too dutiful and diligent in your own life, trying too hard to be good without listening to the other side that needs to be heard so you can balance your life in ways more fulfilling and fitting with your ideals, rather than enacting an unexpressed taboo.

How to listen to these desires and needs in ourselves without crossing boundaries and doing something destructive? How to nurture these qualities and needs within our own ideals, to express what is unlived in satisfying and ethical ways? To fill in missing pieces of an unlived life so that we can feel fulfilled and whole?

The shadow self, all that is unconscious, with perhaps some unlived aspects, can be incorporated into a conscious surface story. Consider engaging these qualities and energies in a lived story, to transmute them into actual existence in your everyday life. An unlived life will find its expression in unconscious acts, projections on others, psychological disturbances, somatic illness, or indiscreet enactments such as rage or love affairs. The wisdom to transmute these needs (as distinct from wants) and ideals into ongoing expression will generate life-story changes.

What Ought To Be

> *Succumbing to an influence they never realised,*
> *they were merely dupes of the instinct that possessed them,*
> *and life slipped through their fingers unlived.*
> —W. Somerset Maugham, *Of Human Bondage*

Thomas Aquinas said that evil is the absence of good.

A wise old monk added, *Don't forget the rest of the sentence.* There was more to that sentence, as the monk noted. The missing part of the sentence: *that ought to be there.* So the correct statement is: *Evil is the absence of good that ought to be there.*

This completion emphasizes that what is unlived needs to make its way to consciousness and not be ignored. The absence of what ought to be there, of what needs to be ready for consciousness that is denied or repressed, is powerfully important.

Aspects of the unlived life excluded from consciousness are the ones that create compromise: symptoms, accidents, denied needs, refuted ideas. If something crucial to our fulfillment has been deleted or disregarded, some part of ourselves will begin to speak to us: headache, hyper-tension, pain, churning gut, sore back, and tiredness. Or perhaps a disturbing and repetitive dream. A symptom is a story that the body suggests, demands that we listen to. When we listen to whispers, no one needs to shout.

A man in his late 80s put it very wisely and simply:

> *In the twilight of life I choose the learning way, which is not one of guilt or regret, but more an awakening and appreciation of the courage and receptivity that I have witnessed through the years by others who were ageing.*

This is a lesson and insight that we do not have to wait until old age to acquire. We learn from the cumulative wisdom of those who have gone before us, of the unlived lives we see and hear reflected on, as well as our own. To make conscious our view of time is a step toward enlightenment.

Imagine

Live in the service of something higher and more enduring,
so that when the tragic transience of life at last breaks in upon you,
you can feel that the thing for which you have lived does not die.
—Gilbert Murray

Consider one or more of these ways of accessing aspects of your experience as a portal to the unlived: prayer, meditation, imagination, self-reflection. This homework can access and reclaim unlived aspects of ourselves. This is essentially an immersion, a solitary occupation requiring discipline and engagement without interruption. A mind state that you enter and respect, to keep an appointment with yourself just as you would any important appointment in your life. To engage in this process regularly can bring together aspects that have been undeveloped, fragmented, undiscovered, unlived.

It may take courage to look with an open mind at aspects that have been repressed or suppressed, to find how they may be given expression. It is natural to ask these questions in midlife, and again at an older age in a time of transition from a lifetime career.

In the beginner's mind there are many possibilities, but in the expert's mind there are only a few. Perhaps there is just one. At times we have to engage the distinct art of using a beginner's mind, to open an approach to transcend, as much as possible, the biases of our knowledge, the inclination to confirm what we already know, and to seek only what our radar has been coded for.

The power of symbolic experience in the human psyche is just as great as physical experience. With visualization, the same changes occur in the brain as when input is actually received through the optic nerve. Imagination can realign attitudes, change behavior patterns, and create meaningful, nurturing experiences. Imagination allows the recruitment of aspects of ourselves not consciously considered, of realities deeper than the events of our daily lives.

We talk to ourselves all the time. These internal conversations not only remain passive but replay old tapes and repeat the same cognitive patterns without actively engaging them. Consider allowing imaginal dialogues to flourish in your daily life alongside abstract thought and socially directed communication. The real and the imagined are not antithetical. Sufis call this state *gana*, the annihilation of individual selfhood so that the spirit of play can show through. Spiritual traditions have ways and procedures for achieving such states of receptiveness and creativity. Meditation slows the body and quiets the mind as one way of achieving this.

As you begin to look at your unlived life, you may find a multitude of aspects and characteristics that seek expression, all of which are an authentic part of yourself. Each of these potentials is valuable to consider *if* and *how* to express. This draws on everything available to you, from the inside out.

Desires cordoned off and denied do not go away, but generate more power because of the continuing engagement to repress them. What is deleted and disregarded exerts its power in derivative forms.

Not all of these discoveries and aspects of ourselves may be for public consumption or polite society. Some of our best human qualities and our noblest energies of love, generosity, tenderness, and connectedness may be as difficult to express openly and genuinely as some of the other attributes. In fact, imagination may be the most useful way to cope with the difficult and embarrassing aspects of the seven sins that we all have in some form in our personality: greed, cruelty, rage, envy, jealousy, lust, and avarice. Engaging in these aspects through imagination and a private dialogue can address the unlived without violating any of the cultural and social rules of our lives.

An Unlived Quiz

There is no greater agony than bearing an untold story within you.
—Maya Angelou

Imagine the end of your life.

List the important items that you would regret not accomplishing or experiencing.

- A passion that you did not follow or explore.
- List the people you envy. Underneath each person envied, write the latent, unlived aspect of yourself that person represents.
- What would it be like to not look to anything external to validate yourself: wealth, power, social position, beauty, influence, prestige?
- What are the unlived aspects in your life that you have not expressed?
- The unlived qualities that you have not given full expression?
- What ritual or symbolic act can you create, as the frustrated Don Juan did with his sketches initially, to give expression to an unlived aspect?
- Ask yourself, as the Don Juan artist ultimately did: *How can I do this while simultaneously not doing it*? This opens yourself to your symbolic life.
- How can you allow a beginner's mind, rather than being bound to usual ways of being and thinking?
- What is necessary for you to undertake the next stage of your journey?
- Can you give yourself permission to explore new paths?
- Does fear keep you in a reactive, protective stance, perhaps bound to outmoded patterns or ways of being?
- Are you ready to grow into new ways of feeling and thinking?
- Will you marshal the courage and energy to realize your unlived possibilities?

Living your unlived life can begin today, right now.

Joy

The Story Beyond Words

Do not the most moving moments of our lives find us all without words?
—Marcel Marceau

Joy, generated and perceived from within, is perhaps the least studied of all human emotions. Excitement, happiness, and pleasure all activate; joy soothes. Our bodies discern certain feelings by whether they stimulate or calm. Excitement, risk, sexuality, happiness, winning, and flirtation stimulate. Contentment, relaxation, joy, nurturance, and a smile calm the heart and mind.

Happiness links with specific experiences, excitement with action, anticipation with events. Joy's quiet, soft, internal glow is as inexplicable as it is peaceful. We don't have to have a reason to feel joy.

Joy is spiritual. It is about love and birth, reunion and unity, contentment and connection with one's self and another. Happiness, however, as a state of being, evolves from doing and becoming, the resolution of problems, the mastery of situations with delightful competence. Esteem, neighbor to both joy and happiness, results from the meeting of internal ideals and goals. And bliss usually requires the active presence of another imparting a pleasurable experience. When someone praying or meditating alone has a unitive mystical experience, that person may also experience bliss, as it seemed St. Teresa of Avila did.

While joy is more contented than excitement or happiness, tears of joy spring forth with the clearing of impediments, the happy/sad moments in which we now have what never before could have been, while saying goodbye to what never again can be. Profound sadness at the mourning of a faded necessary illusion (such as the wish that someone will meet all your needs and wants) must dance at times with the joy of creating now what is presently necessary.

Joy is the emotion that its creator, whether artist, inventor, writer, parent, or entrepreneur, experiences at the moment of creation. Joy accompanies a transcendent state in which we experience something greater than ourselves, when we bring something new into being. It represents an aspect of a heightened awareness to realize our potential, to intuitively pursue an experience.

Hopeful expectancy must surely be a distinct psychological state. This openness to something beyond ourselves may fuel the exploration and creativity to learn something new. This receptive state of mind can initiate an intuitive journey to the *something greater.*

In joy, there are no moments, no clock or calendar. Joy lives in, yet transcends, the present moment. It sees beyond, even over, the horizon. Sorrow and grief certainly occupy another dimension unmeasured in time.

The oceanic feeling of connection becomes joy personified, the antithesis of alienation and abandonment. All *unions* are in their essence a *reunion* in which two individuals share the same experience: I have never been here before, yet I feel I have returned. The reunion, even with that which never was, may include a need, a wish, an ancient yearning—one perhaps never fully allowed to emerge in full view for fear of disappointment, or even of shame for having it. And joy is perilous, as all unions threaten separation. By its satisfaction of reunion, joy acknowledges the precedent yearning.

As love remembered no longer inhabits yesterday, joy melds connection and unity. And joy may be never growing tired or even accustomed to simple pleasures: an amazing sunset, the wonder of new life in spring, new feelings along ancient trails of mind, the touch of true love. Joy is experienced in the help and development of personal growth of others. The joy of parenting often parallels the experience of the child's joy in mastery, satisfaction, and pleasure. Fear never lets us perform as joy does. Joy is a passion, an emotion that calmly energizes.

Joy's Creation

Joy is to enter into your own self. In the beginning it is difficult, arduous.
But the more you enter into it, the greater is the reward.
—Osho

Prerequisites of joy may include to let go of anger, to recognize what can't be determined, to avoid the unlucky, to accept what is already lost, and to release the impossible. The energy can then engage passion and embrace joy. Joy arises from our core, from returning home.

Joy seems to appear when obstacles are removed. From an internal perspective, joy emanates when obstacles are no longer created. Rather than overcoming, defeating, or circumventing an obstacle, consider that it is not there until it is constructed. The purpose of the obstacle may be to give fantasy free and safe release. The obstacle of unattainability (the desired person is married and unavailable, for example) may fuel the fantasy that is prohibited and taboo, yet also stimulating, for just a tiny chance that it can really be given exciting life. Yet if the obstacle were removed, and desire given free reign, another obstacle would most likely have to be created.

Just as fantasies inhabit the pretend mode, the creation of an obstacle may simultaneously allow one to proceed. Alternatively, the recognition of freedom may create paralysis, because the walls erected as obstacle are not there to restrain. Whatever we think, feel, and experience is what we create each moment. To not create the obstacle, initially anxiety-provoking in the uncertainty of new territory, is a step toward joy. Being unrestrained illuminates previous restriction, perhaps when a voice long silenced speaks. It feels like the burdens are lifting when you no longer create them.

Joy cannot be fantasized. Both fantasy and imagination have to evolve from present models. Is it possible that someone may know of happiness but find joy elusive? What is the piece of your life that is unlived? This link, if it is missing, may be as important as acceptance and letting go of what is beyond your determination.

Joy maintained recognizes that others make only self-statements, no matter how focused the content or intense the delivery, to not take personally what is said. We can never truly tell others what they feel or think, authoritatively assign motivation, or impugn intent. All we can ever do is offer our experience of someone else.

There are many things that postpone, even derail, joy: traumas, misfortunes, lost illusions, relinquishment of hope, settling for less. Perversions of acceptance include an ideal of suffering, of caregiving with denial of one's own needs, of masochistic surrender to a belief of predetermined destiny that incorporates suffering. Joy is precluded by subjugating any part of one's self. Putting an end to misery and unhappiness does not, in itself, bring joy, just as coming to the end of the past and an old story does not create a new one.

Resisting suffering intensifies suffering. We continue to engage what we run away from. Dread, resistance, and anticipation of the negative all enhance it. Steeling for pain insures its continued presence, a palpable agony. The focus on attempting to control a symptom enhances its adhesiveness. What we remember is an active construction of our present reality. And a lie does not change all other truths.

Trying to abolish a symptom, a doubt, or a fear leads to its intensification, to an alienation of one's self; acceptance, on the other hand, begins a process of hope by listening for the message contained. Joy occurs with acceptance, with the merger of what is and what can be. The essence of connectedness is about truly experiencing joy. And joy is never found, it is created.

Misery makes one special. People may feel friendlier, more sympathetic, and kinder to the sufferer. Extraordinary happiness may even evoke a silent jealousy, as others feel cheated that the sufferer has something not available to them. The more accustomed one is to misery, the more difficult it is to forgive, the more difficult to let go of hurts long since past, especially when suffering has become an identity.

To make someone else responsible for our unhappiness gives away our freedom. Responsibility and freedom are two sides of the same coin. When we accept our responsibility for any misery, hidden inside we find potential freedom, bliss, joy, enlightenment. And no savior is needed, as we become our own.

To be happy, to experience the bliss of joy, may require a new language of health, wholeness, happiness, and especially of joy itself.

While it should be the easiest thing in the world to drop suffering and anguish, yet for some it is departing from a fundamental identity. To be joyful evokes the discomfort of being in new territory, in a strange land far from home.

We have to have a new story to be in before we can give up the old story. Only by living fully in the present can we be able to forget and forgive the past. Awareness knows only the present, no past, no future. It has only one tense, the present.

Some problems cannot be solved, they have to simply be outlived. To dance more, to sing more, to engage passion in everyday life, energy will flow and problems give way to possibilities. Where we place our focus and energy determines what we experience. Whatever we have not lived remains as a need for completion in the mind. This can be relegated to dreams, or it can be recognized and experienced in waking life.

The Story of Joy

If you keep your mind on your destiny, then every moment in your life becomes an opportunity in moving closer to it.
—Arthur Golden, *Memories of a Geisha*

Joy is, for each of us, a unique story to write. The exciting recognition balances with the frightening truth that there is no destiny, no fate, no ghostwriter determining the story line. And to acknowledge that there never was embraces the sadness of unrequited hope while opening the door to an internal union with joy. Reunion with lost joy, we are told, allows death to lose its sting. We are never more aware of what was missed in childhood, such as true empathy or intimacy with another, than when we create it now for ourselves.

We have no way to describe joy. Yet we know its genuineness, just as we do of its sibling, contentment, or even its frequent companion, happiness. Both the inauthentic and the pretend search relentlessly for icons of the real thing, for symbols encoding experiences rather than the real experiences themselves. Examples of those stand-ins include sexual arousal by an object, picture, or piece of clothing, counterphobically recruiting a fetish as emblem of intimacy with the whole person, or attempting to chemically create an ersatz replica, or money as symbol of a continuum of meanings.

The full appreciation of this moment in time registers by our recognition of its ongoing dialectic of past repetition, current creation, and forward vision.

Like silence and time, joy is known by what inhabits it.

Manifesting Joy

Find a place inside where there is joy, and the joy will burn out the pain.
—Joseph Campbell

Many people don't have joy models—others in their lives who experience true joy—to really know what it means.

Perhaps one model of joy is in being with a small child, totally absorbed in the experience of the moment, knowing that you will remember it always.

At certain moments I knew, as they were happening, that they would be etched in my permanent memory. One of them was the day I showed my toddler son the stars. After a walk in the neighborhood, I perched him on a brick wall at the top of our front steps so we were eye to eye. The instant he really saw the stars was magical; his wide eyes actually reflected their gleam. We sat taking them in, he absorbing their wonder with his gaze, me absorbing his joy with mine. This perfectly clear view of the universe filled his soul and stretched his horizons, and for one brief, shining moment, we were part of those constellations of stars, inhabited by the souls of long-dead Greek gods and Indian warriors. His awareness was inscribed with the grandeur of the heavens. As he pointed to those stars, they were his.

On later walks, we would look up, affirming our discovery, our assurance that the universe would be faithful to its covenant of presence and predictability.

Joy is spiritual, distinct from pleasure and happiness. Joy has nothing to do with the outside, or the other, but is an inner phenomenon. Not dependent on circumstances, it is rather a state of peace and silence, a meditative state that is spiritual. Joy, like happiness, is a byproduct, an epiphenomenon, rather than the result of a direct pursuit.

The entertainments that are thought to bring joy do not. The antithesis of joy is not joylessness, but a driven nature to seek diversion and entertainment. Joy is freedom, not an escape from one's self. When we are in the experience of joy, there is no prison, no limitation.

And, we may say of joy, as of the one with whom true joy is first fully experienced: I never knew you to imagine that you would come, yet I never doubted you would be back.

Fairytales

The Work of Play

With Dr. Lauren Krueger Weeks[*]

And this I have learned: grownups do not know the language of shadows.
—Opal Whitley

Children remember what we have long forgotten. An illustrated children's book of talking animals must tell the truth, ring with emotion, and graphically depict concerns. As music and art bypass the conscious mind, animals in stories carry powerful emotion, resonate and evoke various elements of experience.

The images and animal characters give oxygen to the most basic building blocks of needs and longings, wishes and fears. Fairytales are stories about wishes, and wishes that come true. Often the predominant wish is to conquer a fear. On the surface, they are successful stories; the underlying content is of ancient wisdom, primal drives, and raw affect.

The animal characters offer the necessary veil so that the child does not too readily identify himself or herself. Fairytales are the fictional novels of childhood, and in each the protagonist resolves a conflictual situation. The child needs that necessary play space to not know unconscious motivations, to not question why such delight accompanies the unacceptable. The intangible crystallizes hopes and fears into vivid imagery and awareness.

---

[*]   Dr. Lauren Krueger Weeks is Founder and Director of the FUSE (Foundation for Understanding Social Engagement) School and Programs for special needs children in the Boston area.

Animals speaking intelligibly seem as natural to a child as plants talking, trees exchanging confidences, and objects becoming animated and alive. In the simple language of now, ducks and fire trucks speak at least as distinctively as parents. Children animate and vivify what we later analyze and dissect. In this way, children may not be lonely even when alone, for they surround themselves with countless companions, many of whom are in direct communication with them.

The wisdom of many fairytales portrays the richness of inner life, as well as the vividness of external life, such as birth and death, heroes and villains, mastery and defeat. The sensible and intelligent communication of animals may be more real than much communication from adults.

Fairytales show us that suffering can be transformed by words, that memory has many hiding places, that possibility is as limitless as imagination. And that the happiest stories are ones that end when they should. Eeyore, although pessimistic and gloomy (for whom the later adult Eeyore complex is named), and Winnie-the-Pooh even write poetry.

Fantasy and its menagerie go beyond realism. The intellectual surrender required of adults is neither necessary nor an obstacle for children. Reason does not limit nor logic restrain small children, for they have not yet learned those borders. Very young children, the recipients of illustrated books, have not yet evolved to abstract abilities, and operate at the level of instinct and feeling, closer to the unconscious than they will ever be again. They respond quite naturally to the animal archetypes, the deep primordial echoes of story, myth, and ritual.

The animal is ancestor of the unconscious, prototype of the old brain. These basic stirrings that are outside words and beyond language take animated shape and focus. The magic of the illustrated book is the child's experience of effectiveness, directly as reader, as well as by identification with a character. The reader will know, master, alter, rescue, or rescind, as well as set the stage by the page chosen. The animals and the stories leap out from those pages to dance with the child's imagination, unencumbered by the narrow path of intellect or the obstacle course of logic.

No two children hear exactly the same story or see exactly the same picture. Children bring their own uniqueness to refract each picture through a personal lens; each text bears the fingerprint of the listener's subjectivity. Animals are a Rorschach for a child's rich, unbounded internal life and emotion, free from the well-behaved reflections of parents' wishful thinking. The characters love, lie, yearn, hate, give, consume, scheme, and steal. They are kind-hearted, self-sacrificing, jealous, and selfish. They pursue goals relentlessly, triumph in the end. Their enemies die deliciously terrible deaths. Since some animals do all the things adults will not discuss, the stories have appeal to both child and adult.

The tales are told on at least two levels: literal for children and symbolic for adults. Nature dominates, as the primary process is its own animated free spirit.

The lives of children are intricately tied to the lives of others, especially to parents and siblings, as are many of the creatures whose story is entered. The plot often takes us back to the origin of all stories, the beginning of all relationships: to bond interpersonally and to grow individually.

But the animals are not solely a screen for projection of basic instincts and feelings, shaped by the type of animal. Even the big, bad wolf in *Little Red Riding Hood* is not just a remote and fabled beast; the scary castle and its ghosts are considerably more than metaphors for fear, danger, and abandonment. The wolf takes on a human personality, and becomes very real, with cleverness and his own brand of reason to depict the danger of a stranger. Significant knowledge and wisdom of human beings unpacks a familiar problem or conflict resolved in various ways to create a happy ending.

Timeless Themes

If we are lucky, a solitary fantasy can transform one million realities.
—Maya Angelou

These tales were passed on by word of mouth for centuries until the best ones were printed and illustrated. Identical fairytale themes are found in various countries and cultures throughout the world. Independent of time and geography, fairytales depict basic themes and universal situations of conflict. The stories lived by animals contain the most fundamental data of life and human relations.

Aesop, a Phrygian slave, lived about the sixth century before Christ. He understood that for fables, the people must be impersonal abstractions, and animals worked quite well. Fables end with a moral, a lesson, while fairytales only imply it. No good fables have human beings in them, while there can be no fairytale devoid of people-animals. The fable's immortality is that it talks of the simplest truths by using animals that do not talk. Everything is itself: The wolf is wolfish; the fox is foxy (thus he knew that the unreachable grapes were sour). These tales, both ancient and universal, are about all animals, including us. These large animal alphabets of humanity, symbols that speak for themselves, teach the strength of simplicity and the depth of truth. Fairytales, usually with animal characters and human heroes, present predicaments and obstacles, a fertile field of fantasies wonderful and horrible, each with a resolution.

Tales such as *The Parrott Tales* were told in folk recitals and date back to the 12th century. Many of these stories, told by a parrot to divert her mistress while her husband is away, are found in the medieval *Seven Wise Masters* circulated for centuries in Europe. Its popularity was second only to the Bible. Folk tales and fables are permissible lies, talking animals the necessary fiction. There has been no renaissance of animal stories in tales for children, for there has never been an absence.

The Work of Play

> *We don't stop playing because we grow old;*
> *we grow old because we stop playing.*
> —George Bernard Shaw

Fairytales, depicting internal states of mind by images and action, are not meant to be explained or interpreted any more than the child's play, dreams, or fantasies are to be deconstructed to have motivation imposed or to be interpreted by parents. Animal stories appeal simultaneously to the unconscious and the conscious, so that contradictions coexist, unlike in the *real* world where the child has to be only good, only loving. Animals unabashedly show fear, anger, jealousy, love, and a variety of other emotions essential in the building blocks of personality.

The animal characters narrate a transitional space between fantasy and reality in which animals freely roam with their menagerie of experiences and feelings. Through the play of art and words, the young child synthesizes the spatial and temporal, natural and cultural, inside and outside, self and other. The collaborative function of words and pictures maintains the difference between reality and fantasy without renouncing imagination.

In *Where the Wild Things Are* by Maurice Sendak, Max has a way of both containing and fostering his private fantasies. Max's disowned aggression takes form in the *wild things,* which he tames by transforming them into collaborators.

Some time ago I participated in a panel of authors responding to a question about their most moving moment in interacting with readers. Maurice Sendak talked about a young fan, not old enough to write, who asked his mother to pen a note stating the excitement and pleasure he had from *Where the Wild Things Are.* Sendak was so touched that he wrote a comment of thanks back to the boy on a postcard and sketched one of the animals on it.

Sendak reported that he received a letter from the mother of this child saying, *My son liked your card so much that he ate it.*

This young fan loved his hero so much that he wanted to totally incorporate him. Identification and imitation of our heroes sometimes is not enough, we have to *ingest* them.

Children create their own animal stories: imaginary companions as protector, a shadow receptacle of all that is reprehensible, or an actual pet as confidante. In *The Magic Years*, psychoanalyst Selma Fraiberg's niece's *Laughing Tiger* is such an example—the creation by a 2½-year-old of a tiger who never roars, never scares children, doesn't bite, just laughs, and occasionally has to learn to obey (as in not being able to go for an ice-cream cone). *Laughing Tiger*, according to Fraiberg, *was the direct descendant of the savage and ferocious beasts who disturbed the sleep of small children.*

Mirror and Container of the Psyche

> *Art is a lie that lets us see the truth.*
> —Picasso

The nameless and formless achieve finiteness in fairytales, often beginning with an existential dilemma in sharp focus and full illumination. Good and evil are each embodied and are crisply unambivalent—not good and bad at the same time, as people and reality tend to be. The simplicity and unidimensional polarization of good or bad allows a clear understanding of complex, ambivalent, often intangible feelings. The animal characters serve as projection figures for isolating and distinguishing an aspect of the child's otherwise unknown or chaotic experience.

In addition to mirror and container, actual pictures of animals in children's books delimit and circumscribe the range of possible meanings. In one study, children who heard the story in Sendak's *Where the Wild Things Are* without seeing the pictures said that they were too frightening; when they later read the story with the pictures, they changed their minds. Illustrations present conceptions of the animal; without these pictures the imagination may go beyond to the unknown and unthinkable. The pictures also have an inherent boundary: the white-bordered page to frame and contain.

The animals are human, reflecting the duality of the human animal. Anything less would be to deny both fantasy and truth. Beast is horrible and attractive, grotesque and appealing. Wild animals are essentially humane, perhaps quite comfortable inside enchanted castles, the antithesis of real toads and imaginary gardens. Without pictures, both the child and adult reader would be left to the Beast of their own making. The illustrations prevent that, keeping us to a predetermined story line with the containment of illustrations. When transformations occur, such as of Beast, illustrations show change over time, the evolution (mastery through transformation) of Beast (the animal within us) to refinement and reason of humanization.

Animals are personified by clothing them, by giving them human qualities such as human hands, thought, and words. The Beast whom Beauty could love is bestial from the waist up only; he also lives a refined life of leisure. Beauty, an attractive young woman, is shackled to an odious partner, not out of transgression, but out of virtue and love. Beast's essential humanity also allows identification with him. The illustrations verify Beast's transformation to a prince, validating our identity with Beauty's love for Beast.

Storytellers create illusions that may be the truest things we know. Animals may make sense of a world not especially noted for logic. In a good story, the words disappear, and the characters come alive at center stage. The animal story, a primer of the soul's picture-language, comes from a time before this remarkable menagerie of experience is tamed into adult conformity. Fairytales are equally for the parent, dealing with different, opposing feelings, of good, bad, and ambivalent.

Every good story is a voyage of discovery, and every animal a messenger through whom knowing and feeling are conveyed. Animal stories put us as adults in better touch with our own childhood, and help us to more fully understand the concerns of the child convoyed across the two-lap bridge of reading together. It is awe-full to confront the image of our own bestiality, the dark and exciting side of our psyche and unconscious. Both adult and child can imagine themselves as the animals that have human virtues and aesthetics, allowing a partial, temporary identification with exciting passions and frightful aggressions while both undergo transformation and refinement. This is the human mind in conflict, illustrated in story form.

Reading these stories with children allows us as adults the opportunity to open the doors, long ago closed by the logic and assumed sophistication of age, to the treasury of experiences of being lost in a story together with the child, to enter again,

Once upon a time. . . .

Death

When Words Aren't Important Enough

*There is the land of the living and the land of the dead and
the bridge is love, the only survival, the only meaning.*
—Thornton Wilder, *The Bridge of San Luis Rey*

In the last two years of my dad's twilight, I saw that his new memories would last only minutes, some even seconds. His immense love of his grandchildren, Ryan and Lauren, was a passion he no longer could grasp.

In recent time, his future and his past were fading equally. Old age became an assassin of his memory, sniper-like, selecting specific targets and leaving others intact. The most virulent attacks, a series of small strokes, introduced the need for a walker.

In his room at the nursing facility recently, here I was, a very old child, in the presence of a dying parent. Sitting in the nut-brown corduroy recliner I had given him for a past birthday, he drifted in and out of awareness, now mostly out. He was more content when asleep than at any waking moment. While he had never struggled against sentimentality or the expression of his passions, he was now in daily combat, a noisy struggle to grasp elusive, simple realities: the names of friends, of family, even at times including my own. In the last few months, time quickly stole his memory, rendering unavailable a lifelong nostalgic companion. He came to be in a state of total dependency, the common ghost of all childhoods. The helplessness we all run away from, and will all come back to, is lurking from before the beginning until after the end.

There are no longer footprints of my dad around the barn or implement shed of the old farm. It often seemed that his interests stopped at the boundaries of the fields and fence lines, certainly at least at the small town less than three miles away. Yet he taught me not to dream too little or too low.

When I was small, I heard stories from several people who knew my dad all his life. One was that he was the fastest runner in the area. When I got bigger, I challenged him to race me. He always declined. I pursued him for what seemed like years. Finally, weary of my constant cajoling, he agreed. Probably around thirteen years old, I was at least as tall as he, and he would have been fifty. We were to race from our yard fence to the barn, about a hundred yards, he in coveralls and work shoes, me in gym shorts and Converse basketball shoes. We started, and I was even with him, giving it all I had. Around the car shed, almost halfway, he asked me if I thought we had a fair start. I heaved, *Yeah.* He said, *Are you sure? No hurt feelings?* I said, even more annoyed, *Yes.* Then, like he was shot out of a cannon, his back became a blur in the dust to my astonished eyes. He got to the barn, and I think he sat down before I arrived. That was the last time I ever challenged him at anything.

Beginning when I was about three years old, he, my mom, and I had a family baseball game every Sunday morning before church, after he milked and fed the cows. Later he worked on my pitching; I'm sure he would rather have had me become a major-league baseball pitcher than anything else. Yet he encouraged me, incessantly, to be a doctor.

Experiences with my dad came back to me as I recreated them instinctively with my children. My dad's pitching an oversize softball to ensure triumph at my first at-bats reappeared two and a half decades later as my son and then my daughter, trailing in age by two years but never by more than a few minutes in attempts to join in her brother's activities, took their swings. Their actions, as mine before, had a common ancestor.

Later, to teach me tennis, Dad strung out binder twine between the corner fencepost and the car shed and restrung my mom's college racquet so he could play with me.

Dad would also reminisce about his childhood and the way it was *back then.* I listened with minimal interest and even less enthusiasm, but he kept talking. He described walking three miles to the one-room school—both ways always uphill and in the rain. I was amazed at how much flatter and drier it had become since he was a boy. As we fed and milked the cows in the early dawn and worked in the fields together, he kept telling stories. He taught me hard work and business.

When he started school, he had spoken no English, only German. He didn't quite make it through the eighth grade, because each year when his own dad kept him home from school for fall harvesting of cotton and grain sorghum, he got further and further behind each year. Finally, at age sixteen, he felt embarrassed to be much bigger and older than the other kids, so he quit. Much later, what he had needed would become known as ESL, or English as a second language, with special-education programs created. My dad's conclusion, however, was that he *was hard learning,* for his self-concept suffered when he couldn't pick up the lessons as quickly as schoolmates raised speaking English as a first language.

Because of his experiences, he wanted me to go as far as possible in school, and for nothing to stand in my way. Any school-related event took priority for him to let me off work at the farm. As you might guess, since it got me out of farm work, I was *very* extracurricular.

In the master bedroom at my weekend ranch I have a framed picture of the students of the country school my dad attended. All nine students in Grades 1–8 are standing in front of the one-room schoolhouse, in order of ascending height from left to right. My dad, at far right, in white shirt and tie, is the tallest of the nine, taller even than Miss Minnie, the teacher.

Dad's first affirmation of my emerging manhood was when he offered to drive me, before I legally could, to my girlfriend's house on a Sunday afternoon. I remembered that occasion most vividly when I heard the same words rolling from my tongue to my son at a similar age. Later, Dad listened to my expanding world visions while patiently waiting for me to become aware of the very ground beneath my feet. So, too, I listened patiently to my children.

Springtime, for Dad, was the anniversary of birth, of planting new seeds. It excited him to see things grow. Perhaps his excitement is the root of the joy and privilege I experience in my work in seeing people grow, earlier in psychotherapy and psychoanalysis, now in Mentor Coaching. He taught me passion for work by his love of farming.

A part of my dad's presence, of his just being there for me, helped me through many discussions with my own children. Even though as a boy I was often annoyed with his stories and showed it, my silence never seemed to send him back to lick his wounds, at least that I could see. Now I know. As parents, we try to listen. At other times, we try to keep talking, as my dad did. Not because it may make a difference now, but because someday it might. As professionals, we put our egos in a blind trust to not take things personally, in order to be of maximum help to patients and clients.

Living (and Dying) Out Loud

> *Dying is something you have no control over.*
> *Why waste your time being afraid of it?*
> —Guerney in the film *KPAX*

My dad always lived his life out loud, sharing successes and failures, doubts and fears. In his last two decades, he also aged out loud, often much more vividly than I would have wished. In dying, as in living, a parent teaches in the process of doing, sometimes by painful illustration how *not* to do something.

In the last years of my visits with him I reflected with Dad about his importance to me, of what really mattered, of many of our experiences together from my point of view while I was growing up. I loved him first for what he was; it took me far longer to admire him for the deprivation he assigned himself, even in good times, as he remembered and continued to live the Great Depression. His acts of abnegation, such as having only one beer a year, and that around Christmastime, may have even reminded him of his younger self when such pleasures were extravagant. Daily he followed the plotted line of his life as certainly as he did the ordered rows in his field.

He had seen me come around, full circle, to return to the farm, in a way, by having my own farm and ranch as a weekend retreat, the way I returned to my roots, to stay grounded and centered. To see permanently displayed on almost every wall and shelf the rustic memorabilia of farm items he saved from his own dad and granddad and passed to me while he was living so that he could witness the pleasure in my receipt. And to see how I displayed them, where they would be in place long after he was gone.

His character, like his body, became anorexic in its bony essence, and both had exaggerated edges. Easily provoked by the nursing-home staff where he spent his last five months, he became an enhanced version of what he always was. Old age does that, removing the filters and buffers of usual social graces, even the insulation around outbursts. Yet the pinkness and sweetness of this gentle farmer remained at the core as we both tried to reach into the grab-bag of memories one more time, to seize everything we could together put our hands on.

As the weeks unfolded and he got worse, eventually unable to speak, my dad went, unwillingly, back to his own beginning. His formless thoughts and unfocused perception seemed to be before a time when he had words and a language. On his way back, he would occasionally utter a German phrase.

He wanted to be alive when he died, to cross the finish line at full sprint. But that was not to be. He had given me plenty of time to be both sad and happy with him, to review and reflect our whole story together over the last two years of his dying, our whole history together, as many times throughout my life he had reviewed his life before I was born.

The intimacy between us shared, with him always first, the experiences of diapering each other, of loving and letting go of each other.

He had taught me, in his own simple way, the soul of the soil, the rhythm of the seasons, the circle of birth and death. He died out loud, as coherently as he could.

Every significant ending has thousands of little leavings that precede and follow: the quiet, soft letting-go when he is not there is answer to a question, the abrupt tripwire of a single object activating an entire memory scene, a phrase I recognize as plagiarized from him as soon as I speak it.

My own son and daughter see now, as many times before, that their dad is a son, too. To hear from me my final words of his eulogy: As a family, we share in continuing ways, whether we fully realize it or not, in one another's lives. Always. Time does not matter. Age does not matter. We have all experienced something true, something purposive, and those experiences unite us, just as it has shaped us. Most of it from now on may not be sharing the same space. We prepare, largely unknowingly, for the people and then for the parents we will become, and then for the people we will remain after being parents. We share ourselves and define each other as well as defining ourselves. We have gradually learned to accept satisfying conclusions rather than expect happy endings. And now, as in the future, we will come together from time to time as we continue to carry out the mission of the family. Family defines and reveals who we are. The ghosts of our ancestors come together and unite in our storehouse of gathered memories, their ancient spirits on the floor of our souls. All leavings are not endings. Sometimes we speak their names, our names, and sometimes not.

In that final moment of silence, each of us present, each of our younger and present selves, spoke an ancient voice, understanding at the same time everything, yet nothing.

We are all here, in this present moment.

And one of the saddest moments is when the person who shared some of the best memories becomes a memory.

Death ends a life, but it does not end a relationship.
Robert Woodruff Anderson

DAVID KRUEGER, M.D. is an Executive Mentor Coach and CEO of MentorPath®, an executive coaching, training, publishing, and wellness firm. His work integrates psychology and neuroscience with strategic coaching to help executives and professionals write the next chapter of their life or business stories.

Author of 23 trade and professional books on success, wellness, money, and self-development, and 75 scientific papers, his previous book, *The Secret Language of Money* (McGraw Hill), is a Business Bestseller translated into 10 languages.

He is Founder and Director of his own Licensed, Specialty-Certified *New Life Story® Wellness Coaching, and New Money Story® Mentor Training*. He has trained professionals worldwide, and develops internal mentor programs for corporations.

www.MentorPath.com
www.MentorPath.com/Corporate